RAISE THE FLAG!

RAISE THE FLAG!

THE 18TH WAFFEN SS PANZERGRENADIER DIVISION 'HORST WESSEL'

J. M. O'Brien

AMBERLEY

First published 2025

Amberley Publishing
The Hill, Stroud
Gloucestershire, GL5 4EP

www.amberley-books.com

ISBN 978 1 3981 1303 9 (hardback)
ISBN 978 1 3981 1304 6 (ebook)

British Library Cataloguing in Publication Data.
A catalogue record for this book is available from the British Library.

1 2 3 4 5 6 7 8 9 10

Typesetting by SJmagic DESIGN SERVICES, India.
Printed in the UK.

Appointed GPSR EU Representative:
Easy Access System Europe Oü, 16879218
Address: Mustamäe tee 50, 10621,
Tallinn, Estonia
Contact Details: gpsr.requests@easproject.com,
+358 40 500 3575

CONTENTS

NOTES ON UNIT DESIGNATIONS AND LIST OF MAPS

I appreciate that most people who are drawn to read a book about a specific Waffen-SS Division will have a good grounding in the broader history of the Second World War on the Eastern Front and will have encountered many German names and technical phrases associated with this conflict. However, I have tried to make the text as accessible as possible. In this spirit I have kept the use of foreign terms to a minimum and explained their meaning as far as possible the first time they appear.

I have included a rough conversion chart of Waffen-SS ranks to those used in the British Army during the Second World War in the appendix, but these ranks defy direct comparison as the Waffen-SS *Standarten* or Regiments largely retained the structure of the political units from which they were derived.

Place names have proved to be a particular stumbling block in some locations, particularly in western Ukraine and eastern Poland, potentially having a Russian, Ukrainian, Polish and German version or spelling of the same name. I have tried to use the local name that was in use at the time of the events that are being described. For example, I have used the Polish name of L'vov for that city rather than the German Lemberg or Russian / Ukrainian L'viv, with the most widely used alternative in brackets following the first use of that name in the text. I realise that this system is not perfect and tends to fall down if a place name appears in a quote, as German sources naturally use the German name for any place that they are describing, regardless of location.

I have followed the German Wehrmacht's nomenclature for unit designations. Companies are numbered using Arabic numerals (1, 2, 3 etc) while battalions are numbered in the Roman style (I. II. III. etc). Regiments, Brigades, Divisions and Armies have Arabic numbers, Corps have Roman. Army Groups tended to be named (Centre, South, North Ukraine etc) or be represented by a letter of the alphabet. However, I have chosen to use Arabic numerals only for all military units of other nationalities.

The maps have been reproduced from numerous written descriptions of the actions that they represent. All distances are in miles as they are in the text.

I hope that this explanation clears up any confusion that may arise. Some difficult decisions had to be made to produce a coherent narrative and any mistakes that have been made are entirely my own.

List of Maps

INTRODUCTION

In the history of warfare, the Waffen-SS carved out a name for itself both for its feats of arms and for the brutality that it inflicted upon its opposing combatants and innocent civilians alike, but even its most ardent detractors cannot deny that its units were a force to be reckoned with wherever they were encountered on the battlefields of the Second World War.

The SS or 'Schützstaffel', literally 'Protection Squad', had been established in 1933 as an elite armed bodyguard unit to protect the person of Adolf Hitler and had been a subordinate branch of the SA or 'Sturm Abteilung' which acted as the Nazi Party's paramilitary uniformed enforcers on the streets. In the years that followed, the SS evolved into two distinct branches: the Allgemeine (General) SS, which encompassed all of the internal security apparatus of the Third Reich and the Waffen-SS, its military arm. Hitler regarded the Waffen-SS as his own private army, honour-bound to serve him personally. For Himmler it was both a source of power within the ever-shifting hierarchy of the Third Reich and as an instrument for implementing his deranged racial policies abroad. The Waffen-SS was to showcase his 'Nordic' ideals for the German people, with an army of blond-haired, blue eyed 'supermen' bringing order to Europe and subduing those deemed to be 'sub-humans'.[1]

From humble beginnings, the Waffen-SS divisions quickly proved that they were competent and aggressive in battle, their effectiveness gained through a rigorous selection process and punishing training regime. At the height of its power in the first half of 1943, the original three divisions, grouped together as the SS-Panzer Corps, were more than a match for any unit of equivalent size then operating in any army in the world. The casual observer could be forgiven for thinking that all thirty-eight SS Divisions raised during the Second World War were of this calibre. The truth is very different.

The seven Germanic SS Panzer Divisions could be classed as a true elite, comparable with the finest Wehrmacht panzer units, but Himmler wanted more. He wanted the Waffen-SS to become the true defender of the German state and its people and went to ever greater lengths to recruit soldiers for his expanding empire. With the flow of German recruits jealously guarded and restricted by the army, he sought volunteers abroad, initially targeting the Nordic nations of northern Europe but as losses mounted and enthusiasm waned, he cast his net further afield.

Himmler and his henchmen concocted a web of lies and subterfuge to justify the relaxing of their own racial rules so that by 1944 virtually anyone capable of shouldering a rifle was eligible for enlistment, with French volunteers rubbing shoulders with ethnic Germans from Hungary and Romania, while whole divisions were created from disaffected and displaced peoples from within the Soviet Union. There were even a number of Moslem divisions complete with Imams to cater to the soldier's spiritual needs, although these proved to be wholly unreliable and one of these, 13.SS-Gebirgs Division 'Handschar', became the only Waffen-SS division to openly mutiny.

Analysing the resources used to supply these divisions also highlights the misapprehension that all Waffen-SS divisions were well-equipped with the best military hardware that German industry could produce. It is true that during 1943 the original three Waffen-SS divisions were re-equipped on a lavish scale, but for most units it was a case of making do with whatever was to hand. Throughout the war, armaments production never met demand and between the Wehrmacht, the Waffen-SS, and the Luftwaffe Field Divisions there was just too much competition to adequately outfit every division. While SS industrial concerns could churn out uniforms and to a certain extent small arms, many units had to utilise captured armoured and soft-skinned vehicles, which added pressure to an already strained logistical support system. Many period photographs show French trucks, Russian tanks, and even British vehicles captured during the retreat to Dunkirk sporting SS insignia in the depths of Russia.

This diversity in both men and materials multiplied throughout the war to the detriment of the German war effort until it became recognised that, generally speaking, the later in the war a division was created, the less reliably it performed in combat. This was a far cry from the small, close-knit, well-trained regiments fielded by the Waffen-SS in 1940.[2]

18.SS-Friewilligen-Panzergrenadier-Division 'Horst Wessel' was a product of this haphazard and paradoxical expansion of the Waffen-SS. It was raised as part of the 1944 expansion programme and was riddled with muddle and contradictions from the outset. Initially destined to be an infantry division of three regiments it was eventually upgraded, at Hitler's insistence, to be a *Panzergrenadier* or mechanised infantry division to bear the honour title of Horst Wessel, an SA junior officer and early martyr to the Nazi cause; the intention was that the whole division was to be manned by SA volunteers.

This must have been part of Hitler's deliberate policy of divide and rule that he practised amongst even his closest supporters, given that the SS had acted on his orders to suppress the SA and murder its leading lights a decade previously. Needless to say, virtually no SA volunteers came forward and the division was ultimately padded out with ethnic German conscripts from central Europe who had no ties whatsoever with either Horst Wessel or the SA. Himmler's reaction to having to name one of his precious divisions after a celebrated member of a rival organisation is not recorded, but he certainly accorded it no special favours.

18.SS-Panzergrenadier Division had a murky beginning, being formed from the *1.SS-Infanterie Brigade (mot)*, a unit comprised of men closely associated with the concentration camp system, an integral part of Hitler's war of extermination against Jews, Slavs and Communists in his 'Bolshevik Crusade'. Through casualties and sheer necessity, the brigade became a more conventional frontline fighting unit and was ultimately drawn upon to provide the core of the new division.

The murderous activities of 1.SS-Infantry Brigade (mot) are widely known and some of its more infamous actions are described in chapter 2, but a full list of every 'cleansing action' carried out by personnel under its control is beyond the scope of this work. A detailed account of the atrocities attributed to the brigade can be found amongst the original reports of *SS-Kommandostab RFSS*, collated and edited by Baade et al, while an English language précis has been produced by Pontolillo (see Bibliography). *18.SS-Panzergrenadier Division*, on the other hand, is largely overlooked in the English language histories of the war generally and the history of the SS in particular, and much that has been written is either too vague to be of much value or simply wrong. Generally speaking, the division is only included in the Order of Battle of Waffen-SS divisions, with some mention being made of the unique insignia that was designed for it.

Where historians have dug a little deeper, certain general assumptions have been made. The table of organisation for an average SS-Panzergrenadier division established in 1944 seems to have been applied to the division and usually there is no mention of the fact that it never existed or operated as a complete unit, which was one of the most important factors in its undistinguished performance on the battlefield. It also had a paucity of equipment that cannot be determined from a simple list of its component units: for example, SS-Artillery Regiment 18 was always missing at least one of its four battalion-sized *Abteilungen* at any one time, and those that it contained never had their full complement of guns.

The division also fought exclusively on secondary fronts during the war in the East, far away from the extensively researched great battles of movement and attrition that dominated the last years of the conflict. 18.SS-Panzergrenadier Division was heavily involved in suppressing the Slovak Uprising in September 1944 and this is perhaps the most well documented of its actions, although the Uprising itself has had very little attention in English language publications, especially when compared with similar events in Warsaw that occurred concurrently. The division's involvement in actions in central Galicia, in northern Hungary on the fringes of the Siege of Budapest and in Silesia in 1945 are practically unknown. Added to this lack of knowledge is an inherent bias within the remaining sources. First-hand accounts from surviving members of the division naturally tend to gloss over unappetising facts and avoid any hint of criminality in their unit's activities, portraying their comrades in the best possible light. There are also certain writers from the victorious nations who like to put a positive spin on the actions of both SS units and individuals. Others, particularly those German authors writing in the decades immediately following the end of the war, have been careful not to assign too many positive attributes to Waffen-SS units generally and tend to be either very critical of any contributions that they made to the fighting or ignore them completely, neither of which is particularly helpful in the search for facts.

This book aims to provide a full account of the 18.SS-Freiwilligen-Panzergrenadier Division 'Horst Wessel' from the inception of the SS paramilitary units, the *SS-Totenkopf-Standarten*, which would eventually evolve into its component parts, following the actions of 1.SS-Infantry-brigade (mot) and describing the creation and actions of this little known division until its virtual annihilation in May 1945.

1

HORST WESSEL AND THE SA

Germany after the First World War was a volatile mix of unemployment, poverty and soaring resentment at the treatment of the country by the victorious allies under the terms of the Treaty of Versailles, and its politics reflected that social unrest. The Weimar government had been formed as a direct consequence of the abdication of Kaiser Wilhelm II and Germany's formal surrender to the Allies on 11 November 1918. This was the first time in German history that it had been governed by a democratically elected government and it was faced with enormous difficulties from the outset.

The government was formed from a coalescence rather than a coalition of small political parties of almost every persuasion, from the far left to the ultra-right, with virtually no policies upon which they could all agree. In the years immediately following the end of the war, Germany suffered from a bankrupt economy which fuelled massive unemployment and hyperinflation, political violence that erupted into two separate coup attempts, one of which was launched by Hitler and his *Nationalsozialistische Deutsche Arbeiterpartei* (National Socialist German Workers Party) in 1923, and diplomatic isolation, from both the victorious powers and most of the rest of the world as well.

The centrist coalition, which held the balance of power in the Weimar Republic, was seen to be weak even amongst the more moderate elements of society, while they were utterly despised by the Nationalists. The right-wing hard-liners and a considerable number of the general population falsely believed that it was this group of politicians who were responsible for having sued for peace and had therefore 'stabbed the nation and the army in the back' leading directly to Germany's social problems at home and disgraced position internationally.

In this highly charged atmosphere, extremist political factions flourished and revolution was in the air. Violence and intimidation were an integral part of political rallies as each side tried to upstage the other. Hitler's fledgling NSDAP had many enemies but none more powerful than the German branch of the Communist Party, and it proved necessary to create a force to protect both the meetings and the party members themselves, not least their leader, and so the Sturmabteilung, or SA, was born.[1]

The SA could trace its origins back to the beginning of 1920 and in the following years its ranks were swelled by many embittered and under-employed ex-servicemen who were looking for an outlet for their frustrations, as were a large cross-section of German youth who, although having been too young to fight in the war, had nevertheless been influenced by wartime propaganda at home and were now desperate to prove their mettle.

Their main purposes were both defensive and offensive; to protect Nazi meetings, to create an aggressive atmosphere to dissuade opponents from challenging them openly and to gain both publicity and notoriety by breaking up opposition rallies, be they Communist, Socialist or Liberal. During the 1920s and early 1930s the SS formed a tiny adjunct of the SA with a specific mandate to protect Hitler and other key Nazi figures. It was very much a subordinate part of the larger organisation, although its members always considered it to be an elite unit and largely kept aloof from the general brawling.[2]

Media coverage of the political violence brought publicity to the Nazi cause and helped to solidify support amongst the more conservative and right-wing members of the capitalist hierarchy, terrified of a Communist insurrection which would likely lead to nationalisation of industry and redistribution of wealth. This threat seemed even more imminent following the Wall Street Crash of 1929 that sparked the 'Great Depression', heralding mass unemployment on an unprecedented scale and applying even more pressure to an already fractured German society.

The worst of the political violence in the late 1920s and early 1930s was predictably between the Nazi and the Communists, with widespread rioting claiming many lives on both sides. In 1931, the Nazi Party claimed that more than 4,000 of its members were wounded in political clashes all over Germany, while rioting in Altona in July 1932 cost the lives of eighteen men and the situation was only brought under control when the police brought in armoured vehicles to disperse the mob. The Berlin SA reported 82 dead and about 400 severely wounded in that year alone.[3]

It was against this backdrop of social and political upheaval that Horst Wessel lived and died. Horst Ludwig Georg Erich Wessel was born on 9 October 1907. His father, who was a protestant pastor, embodied many of the National Socialist virtues of nationalism, militarism, German racial superiority, and anti-Semitism, which clearly had a strong influence on the young Horst.[4]

His political 'education' started when he joined the Bismarck Youth, part of the German National People's Party, in 1922, but he became attracted to the more radical and violent Viking League at the age of 18 before finally joining the Nazi Party on 7 December 1926, becoming a full-fledged member of the SA. By the beginning of 1930 he had been made the leader of SA-Sturm 5 based in the working-class district of Frierichshain.[5]

Given the cult that grew up around him as a Nazi hero, it would be expected that his death should have resulted from some great deed, but the truth of Wessel's murder was much more mundane. It seems that Wessel died in an incident caused by a dispute over money with his landlady, Elisabeth Salm, who rented him a room in her apartment in the Friedrichshain district where Wessel ran with his SA buddies.

Wessel owed Salm back rent for his girlfriend using the accommodation and after repeated refusals to pay up Salm threatened that she would have him evicted, by force if necessary. On 14 January 1930, Salm went to the Baer tavern which was close by and a known haunt of communist activists to enlist the support of some of her deceased husband's political friends in evicting Wessel.

The Reds were not particularly interested in her plight until Wessel's name was dropped into the conversation, whereupon several members of the group, including one Albrecht Höhler, agreed to go and teach their SA adversary a lesson. Höhler took a loaded 9mm pistol with him as Wessel was assumed to be armed. The group approached the flat at around 9.30 in the evening and Salm led them into her third-floor flat, leaving several men acting as lookouts outside. Höhler and two other men marched up to the room occupied at the time by Wessel, his girlfriend, Erna Jaenichen and a mutual friend, Klara Rehfeld, and banged on the door. As the unsuspecting Wessel opened it Höhler shot him in the face at point blank range. Leaving the mortally wounded man on the floor in a pool of blood, the three intruders then searched the room, threatened the women with dire consequences if they did not remain silent and left. Wessel was taken to Friedrichshain Hospital where he died six weeks later, on 23 February.

The death of one relatively unknown SA leader would probably have gone largely unnoticed by history, even given the brutality of his murder, had not Doctor Joseph Goebbels, Nazi Party regional leader for Berlin and later Minister of Propaganda under the Nazi regime, orchestrated his state funeral. Goebbels portrayed Wessel as a martyr to the Nazi cause, a young man struck down in the prime of life in defence of Germany and the Party and an inspiration to all.

The anniversaries of his birth and death were celebrated after the Nazis' rise to power, each being marked by ever grander pomp and ceremony as the years passed. Wessel's posthumous elevation within the party also threw a spotlight upon a marching song that he had written for his comrades: 'Raise the Flag!' more commonly known as the 'Horst Wessel Song', which the Nazis took up as their official party anthem, further immortalising his name. Eventually, streets and squares across Germany bore his name, as did a *Kriegsmarine* training ship, launched in 1936, a Luftwaffe fighter squadron and eventually an *SS-Panzergrenadier Division*.[6]

Horst Wessel did not live to the see the triumph of the party that many believed he gave his life for. The National Socialist German Workers Party was democratically elected to govern on 30 January 1933, with Hitler being appointed Chancellor of President Paul von Hindenberg's government. Many took this as a sign of great things to come but, according to the official statistics at that date, there were 6,013,000 Germans unemployed and by mid-February the number had increased to peak at 6,047,000.

This lack of work was keenly felt amongst the unemployed elements of the SA, who felt that they had put their time, effort and often their blood into gaining the party its place in government and that now was the time that they should start reaping the rewards. Many believed that SA members should have priority when new jobs were being handed out, particularly over Marxist militants and 'non-Aryans'. With little to do now that their opposition had been officially crushed, SA men who felt that they had 'missed out' following the seizure of power began to whisper loudly of 'a second revolution' to overthrow the traditional, conservative ruling elite of German society; the industrialists, monarchists, and aristocracy.

The Nazi Party that had been elected was a far cry from the revolutionary rabble that had been formed more than a decade before. Despite the brown hordes of the SA, it was an essentially middle-class organisation with its membership consisting of small tenant farmers, teachers, small businessmen and office clerks and it was this class that had been hardest hit and seen their savings wiped out in the economic crash of the late 1920s. It was these very people who calmly and quietly paid their party subscriptions, attended the rallies, and turned out to vote. These people craved social, economic, and political stability, and the party recognised that it owed a debt to these unseen masses that gave the Nazi Party a veneer of respectability. However, this need for a stable society was what put them at odds with the working-class rank and file of the SA, which still saw itself as a revolutionary army. Admittedly, it had been the hard men from the coal mines of Silesia, the steel works of the Ruhr and shipyards of the Baltic coast that faced down Communist agitators in the battles that had raged in the streets of the major German towns for more than a decade, but following the election victory of 1933, the war was won, and now, as far as the party was concerned it was time for them to go back to work; except there were no jobs to return to.[7]

The time had come when the SA had outlived its usefulness. With the Nazis in power, they had to at least try to be seen to be representing a broader cross section of society and the hard-drinking, undisciplined, brawling image of the SA foot soldiers did not sit well with either the respectable middle-class establishment or, more importantly, the powerful right-wing industrialists who contributed literally millions of Reichsmarks to the coffers of the Party. It was the owners of the largest German steel-producing and heavy engineering companies such as Krupp and Messerschmitt, the chemical concerns like I.G. Farben, and the coal consortiums that powered these industries that looked to the Nazi Party to create a stable environment for rebuilding Germany's economy and promoting sales abroad while upholding the rule of law at home.[8] The Reichwehr, Weimar Germany's standing army, also viewed the Brownshirts as a potential threat to their position. Severely limited to just 100,000 men by the Articles of the Treaty of Versailles, the army was hard-pressed even to protect Germany's truncated borders and was therefore rightly intimidated by the three-million-strong membership which the SA had mustered by the end of 1933 and which it had been illegally arming with rifles and machine guns for several years, making them a force to be reckoned with in any armed struggle. To the horror of the conservative General Staff, Ernst Rőhm, the swaggering, outspoken Chief of Staff of the SA, talked openly of absorbing the Reichswehr into its ranks and it was this idea that set the army firmly against the SA.[9]

Rőhm had served as an officer during the First World War and had witnessed at first hand the vast slaughter wrought, as he saw it, by the professional career soldiers of the German General Staff for no real gain. His service with the paramilitary *Freikorps* amidst the postwar upheaval had convinced him that a people's army based on egalitarian principles of comradeship and nationalism would be far more effective.[10]

With this view firmly in mind Röhm's egotism would not allow him to sit quietly and wait for the Party that he helped bring to power to dilute his ideals when faced with the practicalities of running a country, and he was overheard to say: 'The SA is not going to allow the revolution to sleep or be betrayed halfway down the road... the brown army is the nation's last reserve.'[11]

Inwardly, Hitler was sympathetic with Röhm's idealistic proposals for a 'People's Army', but he knew that he needed the support of Germany's professional soldiers to carry forward his programme of national expansion and could not afford to let the SA provoke a conflict with them. He therefore brokered a truce between the two parties under which the SA agreed to conduct a training programme that would prepare up to 250,000 men a year for eventual entry into the army.[12]

Despite his acquiescence to this agreement while in Hitler's presence, Röhm clearly had no intention of honouring it and drunkenly declared to a roomful of SA officers; 'What that ridiculous corporal says means nothing to us... I have not the slightest intention of keeping this agreement. Hitler is a traitor and at the very least must go.'[13]

Unfortunately for the outspoken Röhm, one member of his audience was SA-Obergruppenführer Viktor Lutze. Whether Lutze saw an opportunity for his own advancement or whether he genuinely felt that treason was being plotted, he went straight to Hitler with a report of Röhm's words, also taking General von Reichenau of the Reichswehr general staff into his confidence. Hitler may have initially brushed off this warning, but von Reichenau was in secret negotiations with SS-Brigadeführer Reinhard Heydrich, head of the secret police, and Himmler's chief henchman.[14]

It was not just the Army that was threatened by his influential position. The SS was still nominally a subordinate branch of the SA, and its current leadership was a barrier to both its independence and further expansion. Additionally, the controlling apparatus within NSDAP itself felt that they had effectively lost control of the SA, which still represented the party's uniformed presence on the streets. The large number of senior SA officers holding key posts within the new government and the police also represented a potential adversary to Hermann Göring, who was carving out his own power base in Prussia. This ultimately led him into an alliance with Heinrich Himmler.[15]

As Himmler was in the process of gathering all aspects of policing within Germany under the SS umbrella, Göring was able to trade the Gestapo, which he himself had established in 1933, for SS support in getting rid of Röhm and diminishing the power of the SA as a whole, while gaining SS support for his bid to seize control of the fledgling Luftwaffe.[16]

Amongst all these backroom tradeoffs, the Nazis' hold on power in the days and weeks following their election seemed to be tenuous and there was a real fear in Hitler's mind that he could be ousted, either by external forces or by elements within his own circle – with the most likely source of this insurrection being Röhm and the SA. Aside from the potential disloyalty of his subordinates, in a practical sense Hitler did not wish to see his governmental work ruined by the hare-brained ambitions of a few hard-headed underlings. Two weeks before Hitler and the SS moved against the SA leadership, he made a speech at Tempelhof airport following his return from a visit to Mussolini where he stated: 'By all this talk of a "second revolution", the SA is separating itself from me in all reasonable elements... I am not a Lenin. What I want is order.'[17]

With the whole German hierarchy seemingly arrayed against Röhm it was only Hitler's personal sense of loyalty to his old comrade that stayed his hand. However, Hitler was also a pragmatist, and he didn't need to be an astute politician to recognise the danger of Rőhm having control over a private army exceeding three million members that no longer had an enemy to fight and was also feeling unjustly treated in victory. Senior Nazi figures were also offended by the morally corrupt conduct of the SA leadership as they saw it. Rőhm and several of his inner circle were openly homosexual.[18]

These factors were beginning to tip the balance against the continued existence of the SA and whether Rőhm intended to challenge Hitler for leadership of both the party and the country or not, it took little convincing to plant that seed of doubt in Hitler's mind. Himmler went to considerable lengths to fan the flames of Hitler's paranoia, endorsing Reinhard Heydrich's production of a dossier of spurious evidence that 'proved' that the SA was planning a coup, which he fed to selected army generals, leading them to deliver an ultimatum that effectively sealed the fate of the Brownshirts.[19]

Hitler met General von Blomberg, the Minister of Defence, on 21 June 1934, where the minister demanded that Hitler would have to eliminate the army's SA opponents if he wanted to gain the full support of the army in his bid to become president of Germany following Hindenburg's death, which by this date was imminent. Hitler now knew that the time to act had arrived and he ordered Himmler to make the appropriate preparations.[20]

It was decided that SS men from Sepp Dietrich's newly formed Leibstandarte 'Adolf Hitler' Regiment and staff from Theodor Eicke's concentration camp at Dachau would make the initial moves against a long list of presumed 'enemies of the state' and these same troops would deal with the prisoners afterwards. Army headquarters was under strict instructions to supply the SS with whatever weapons, vehicles, and facilities that they might require. In order to gather as many of those considered to be conspirators in one place as possible, Hitler issued an order on 28 June for Rőhm to muster all SA senior group leaders, group leaders and inspectors for a conference at the Hanselbauer Hotel in Bad Wiessee on 30 June. An unconcerned Rőhm did as he was ordered, only to be awoken in the early hours of 30 June by Hitler, revolver in hand, flanked by a squad of his bodyguards banging on his door and informing him that he was under arrest for high treason. Hitler was accompanied by a strong escort who quickly rounded up the other SA leaders who were promptly locked in a cellar while transport was organised to take them to Munich.

In simultaneous actions, Heydrich's plainclothes SD officers and Gestapo officials made a host of arrests of SA chiefs and took the opportunity to detain a number of political opponents of the regime. Most of these men met their ends before firing squads at the Lichterfelde Barracks in Berlin and Stadelheim Prison in Munich, where Dietrich had quietly moved two companies of his men to carry out the executions, although others fell victim to more ad hoc arrangements, having officially been 'killed while resisting arrest'. Conservative estimates put the number of dead between 85 and 200 victims, of whom the majority were members of the SA, although some sources offer much higher totals.[21]

Theodor Eiche was sent to Stadelheim Prison, where Rőhm had spent the whole day awaiting his fate, to deal with him personally. Eiche presented Rőhm with the latest edition of the *Völkischer Beobachter* newspaper, which carried the headline: 'Rohm arrested and dismissed – far-reaching purge in the SA'. Eicke placed a loaded pistol on the table and gave the prisoner ten minutes in which to kill himself. When the time had elapsed and Rőhm had not taken matters into his own hands, Eicke and his adjutant, SS-Sturmbannführer Michael Lippert, both drew their pistols and shot him at point blank range. He died at 6 pm on 1 July.[22]

Himmler's role and that of the men under his command in what became known as the 'Night of the Long Knives' were fully rewarded, as he had anticipated. On 20 July 1934, the SS freed itself from the control of the SA and became an independent organisation. The army also kept to its side of the bargain and when Hindenberg died on 2 August it supported Hitler's scheme to combine the offices of Chancellor and President, which was ratified by the overwhelming majority of the German people in a vote just two weeks later.[23]

Viktor Lutze was appointed to be the new Chief of Staff of the SA a few days after Rőhm's death and Hitler charged him with creating a new, more modest and 'decent' organisation. The unassuming Lutze was no political animal or extrovert leader of men as Rőhm had been, which made him Hitler's ideal choice for a leadership role. His first directive to the SA's new chief was that in future, 'SA men should be leaders, not ludicrous apes.' This was only the start of the degradation of the organisation, which lost much of the hardware, vehicles, aircraft, and weapons that it had meticulously hoarded over the years. It did, however, retain its distinctive brown shirt uniform, which remained prominent at Nazi Party rallies and marches and was still an intimidating force on the streets to any would-be opponents of the regime.[24]

The 'Night of the Long Knives' may have broken the back of any potential internal threat to Hitler's rule, but although the organisation never again reached the heights of power or numbers that it had enjoyed in 1933 the SA retained a great deal of influence within the Nazi Party and the events of 30 June–2 July 1934 had earned the SS the undying hatred of many of the remaining SA members. Hitler was always capricious with his favours and willing to sow discord amongst even his closest supporters and as the power of the SS increased, he seemed more inclined to re-introduce SA men into influential roles as a counterweight, from which positions they endeavoured to cause as much annoyance and inconvenience to the SS as possible, regardless of the wider effects to Germany and its war efforts.[25]

2

1.SS-INFANTRY BRIGADE (MOT)

1939–1941

In September 1939 the German army stunned the world with a blisteringly fast campaign which overran the western half of Poland in just six weeks, a feat that was repeated across Western Europe the following summer and added a new term to military phraseology: 'Blitzkrieg' or 'Lightning War'. Several Waffen-SS units had shared the laurels of these victories and with his prestige rising, Himmler was keen to expand the armed forces under his control for the great ideological battle to come: the invasion of Soviet Russia.

Recruitment for the Waffen-SS was in the hands of the energetic and resourceful head of the *SS-Hauptamt* (Main Office), SS-Obergruppenführer Gottlob Berger who shared Himmler's vision of turning the Waffen-SS into a force to rival the power of the Wehrmacht. However, the Wehrmacht saw this as a direct challenge to their sole right to be the bearer of arms in defence of the Third Reich[1] and, with Hitler's consent, imposed severe restrictions upon the number of German men that the Waffen-SS could recruit into its ranks.[2]

Forced to resort to other sources of manpower, Berger exploited three categories of men that were exempt from conscription into the Wehrmacht and who already belonged to formations within Himmler's empire; the *Totenkopfverbände* composed of concentration camp guards, the reinforced *SS-Totenkopf Standarten* who were to act as police reinforcement in times of war, and sections of the *Ordnungspolizei*, the ordinary uniformed police who kept order on the streets.[3]

It was the second of these groups, which were eventually expanded into sixteen regimental-sized *SS-Totenkopf-Standarten* that Himmler had built up from the police reserves granted to him by the Wehrmacht, that provided many of the future mass murderers in the three SS Brigades and the Einsatzgruppen.[4]

The four Einsatzgruppen deployed on the Eastern Front were each composed of around 1,000 men and were essentially mobile killing units which followed closely behind the German army's frontline units to exterminate any and all of the long list of social, political and religious groups that the Nazis deemed unworthy of life in their 'new order'.[5] The SS Brigades were created to be distinct from the Einsatzgruppen but came to play an increasingly supportive role in their activities throughout 1941–42 until it became difficult to distinguish between the two types of unit.

After the occupation of Poland, the existing *SS-Totenkopf-Standarten* were expanded for use in a pseudo-police role with the *Standarten* being bulked out with personnel from across many departments of the General SS. As is often the case in both military and civil organisations, those in charge took the opportunity to get rid of their troublemakers, incompetents and riffraff into these new units, which were hastily equipped with trucks and small arms for which the recruits had little training. They were largely led by inexperienced officers and NCOs from the General SS men who had virtually no preparation for leading large bodies of men beyond crude ideological training programmes provided by Party organs.[6]

In the aftermath of invasion, 900,000 Poles were forced to leave their homes in the western provinces of the country, which were absorbed into the 'Greater Reich' and resettled by ethnic Germans from the former Soviet territories in the Baltic States and Eastern Poland. With Soviet Russia occupying the eastern portion of the country, this large body of displaced people, which contained a large section of the Polish Jewish population, were forced into the central area of the country around Warsaw and Krakow. The Germans dubbed this the 'General Government' (*Generalgouvernement*). This area eventually played host to almost all Nazi extermination camps.[7]

The *SS-Totenkopf-Standarten* were used extensively to carry out the expulsions and to police the General Government area, earning themselves a reputation for brutality and slaughter of innocent people in the process.[8]

Amongst these units were *SS-Totenkopf-Standarten* 8 and 10, which were to form the basis of 1.SS-Brigade (mot) and ultimately 18.SS-Panzergrenadier Division 'Horst Wessel'. The two *Standarten* were established in the first half of 1940 and spent the second half in various garrison posts in Poland. In an attempt at uniformity with other units of the Waffen-SS prior to the invasion of Russia, the SS Leadership Main Office issued an order on 12 November 1940 that redesignated them as *SS-Infanterie Regiment (mot)* (hereafter referred to as SS-Infantry Regiments) and they began the process of re-training and equipping to bring them up to an equivalent strength of their Wehrmacht counterparts.[9]

In recognition of their new status as infantry units and as a shift away from their roots in the *Totenkopfverbande*, SS-Infantry Regiments 8 and 10 were ordered to discard their Death's Head collar patches on 25 February 1941 in favour of the SS Sigrune insignia as used by the Waffen-SS.[10] The standards of discipline and efficiency within the newly designated SS-Infantry Regiments remained way below that of the well-established Waffen-SS regiments due to a shortage of skilled manpower.

As the Waffen-SS expanded, the most experienced personnel from the *SS-Totenkopf-Standarten* were skimmed off to create the Totenkopf Division, which in turn created a serious lack of trained men to flesh out the remaining units, further reducing their efficiency. Some of the replacement officers were provided through the pool of concentration camp staff but most of the recruits were completely new, and many had not even previously been members of the SS. A statistical sample of former members of the 1.SS-Brigade (mot) showed that they primarily came from the German lower and lower middle classes of society and that the proportion of ill-educated manual labourers such as farmers, artisans and factory workers was well above the average. A post-war survey of 409 members of the 1.SS-Brigade (mot) indicated that 83 per cent of its members had volunteered to serve in the Waffen-SS, although it cannot be known whether this was for ideological reasons or in the hope of a less dangerous form of military service.[11]

On 1 May 1941, SS-Infantry Regiments 8 and 10 were used to form the core units of 1.SS-Brigade (mot) which was to be based in Cracow awaiting its full complement of men and materials. The brigade was finally brought up to strength at the Waffen-SS training facility at Debica in eastern Poland in the months leading up to *Barbarossa* and units were issued with the infantry weapons required to bring them up to the equipment standards of Wehrmacht Regiments. They were also intended to be fully motorised. However, it is unlikely given the procurement difficulties that Waffen-SS units experienced during this period that these regiments possessed a full range of specialist support equipment.

According to George Nafziger in his series of books on the order of battle of the German military during the Second World War, in its original composition the Brigade's primary units, SS-Infantry Regiments 8 and 10, both consisted of three rifle battalions of four companies. Each regiment possessed an additional 13 and 14 Company, which in Wehrmacht regiments represented the supporting Infantry Gun and Flak companies respectively. There was also a Light Infantry Column of unspecified composition within each regiment. Additional Brigade units were made up from a Medical Company, a Signals Company, and Transport and Maintenance Platoons.[12]

However, despite their reorganisation the personnel of the brigade were still more used to guard duty and riot control and remained almost wholly unprepared for combat conditions.[13] Such training that was undertaken included conventional military tactics but also had a heavy emphasis on police tactics for operating against an elusive foe in urban areas, which was thought would aid in the pacification of the larger towns and cities of western Russia and the Ukraine.[14]

As the invasion of Russia got underway 1.SS-Brigade (mot) was moved up to the Polish-Russian border. While in Poland the two regiments had been under the orders of the *Befehlshaber der Waffen-SS Ost* (the commander of the Waffen-SS East), but following in the wake of Operation *Barbarossa*, the new brigade was to be directly subordinated to the *Kommandostab Reichsführer-SS*.[15]

Kommandostab RFSS was directed by Himmler personally, with SS-Brigadeführer Kurt Knoblauch acting as Chief of Staff, and it had been expressly raised to co-ordinate security measures in the civilian-administered occupied areas of the Eastern Front and reinforce the security forces in anti-partisan operations, as distinct from safeguarding the Wehrmacht's rear areas of the combat zone proper. For this purpose, three SS Brigades had been formed: two motorised infantry brigades and one cavalry brigade. However, the command role of *Kommandostab RFSS* was almost immediately circumvented by both the Higher SS and Police leaders responsible for pacifying the occupied zones and SS-Obergruppenführer Reinhard Heydrich's retention of personal control over the Einsatzgruppen.[16]

Himmler had created the role of Higher SS and Police Leader (*Höhrere SS und Polizeiführer or HSSPF*) in November 1937 to co-ordinate police and SS activities and to provide political direction in various parts of Germany. After the start of the war the HSSPF's assumed responsibility for all police activities within the area of their jurisdiction in the occupied territories and to carry out assignments of a 'political nature' as directed by Himmler personally. In the east these men became the driving force behind the Holocaust.[17]

The HSSPF's jealously guarded their authority in their new fiefdoms, which left the *Kommandostab RFSS* with the severely truncated role of training and administering the three SS-Brigades. But, while the command staff remained adrift with no specific mandate, the *Reichsführer-SS* still retained direct control over these three large, highly mobile units with a total strength of 18,500 men.[18] According to SS personnel records, SS-Infantry Brigades 1 and 2 totalled between 7,200-7,300 men each, while the SS-Cavalry Brigade mustered around 4,000 men. *Kommandostab RFSS* also had under orders the Begleit (Escort) Battalion '*Reichsfuhrer-SS*', the SS-Hamburg Regiment, the *SS-Flak Zug* (anti-aircraft platoon), and a number of service units with a total strength in excess of 25,000 men.[19]

Kommandostab RFSS took direct control of the SS-Brigades on 21 June 1941 and its 'cleansing actions' began along the Polish-Russian border just four days later.[20] As they moved up to their jumping-off positions near the border, they immediately acquired an unsavoury reputation by conducting brutal food acquisitions from the local population. Any Polish peasants who resisted were shot out of hand.[21]

However, the 1.SS-Brigade (mot) had not even settled into its envisioned role when the Führer personally ordered that it should be assigned to the XLII.Army Corps as an operational reserve, to screen gaps in the frontline left in the wake of 9.Army's advance on the northern flank of Army Group Centre, more than 250 miles north of its envisoned operational area. Between 23 and 25 June, the Brigade committed war crimes against civilians in the eastern Polish cities of Grajevo and Augustinovo, where members of both SS-Infantry Regiment 8 and 10 shot Jews and alleged partisans and burned down a number of houses. The Commander-in-Chief of the 9.Army, Colonel-General Adolf Strauss, strongly approved of this action carried out by the SS troops subordinate to him and had SS-Brigadefuhrer Knoblauch convey his 'fullest appreciation' to the Reichsführer-SS for their aggressive nature.[22]

The success of the opening stages of Operation *Barbarossa* meant that vast territories fell under German control with relatively few military resources available to control them. The disintegration of whole Soviet Armies ensured that mixed in with the civilian population were thousands of military personnel, police, and Communist Party functionaries. Already fearful of a Fifth Column existing in the rear of his armies, Hitler was exultant to learn of Stalin's call for a partisan movement to be established in the summer of 1941, exclaiming 'That's only good, it gives us a possibility to exterminate everyone who challenges our rule.'[23]

1.SS-Brigade (mot) received the order to march to Lemberg on 22 July 1941, where it was to be subordinated to the HSSPF for Southern Russia, SS-Obergruppenführer Friedrich Jeckeln, and committed to action on the following day. Publicly, its main function was to fight partisans, mop up Red Army stragglers and conduct security operations in the occupied territories behind the frontline of Army Group South in western Ukraine.[24] [25] However, the SS, SD (*Sicherheitsdienst*, the in-house intelligence service of the SS tasked with searching out enemies of the Reich) and Gestapo had long since learned to use their own jargon to disguise mass-murder and 'the terms "security operations" and "anti-partisan operations" were often synonymous with murderous "cleansing" operations; any such designations cast suspicion on an operation.'[26]

Under Jeckeln' s command the Brigade was to operate in the role of 'second police security wave' in the areas which the Einsatzgruppen were unable to cover due to their lack of manpower. These initial actions were referred to in official documents as '*Befriedungsaktion*' (pacification) or '*Sauberungsaktion*' (purification) actions.[27] 1.SS-Brigade (mot) was to participate in many such actions and its subordinate units were associated with over sixty separate atrocities committed against Jews, Gypsies, alleged partisans, and Soviet POWs.[28]

The Brigade's commander, SS-Brigadeführer Richard Herrmann, was ordered to comb through the wooded area south of the Rovno to the Zhitomir road with his two regiments and round up scattered units of the Soviet 124.Rifle Division. Elements of the Russian division were thought to have dispersed over an area of thirty square miles, with some trying to fight their way back to their own front line while others were content to slip away from the action.[29]

In a report from the brigade to the *Reichsführer-SS*, it appeared that this action produced very modest results; by the end of July Herrmann's people had only managed to track down forty Ukrainian Red Army soldiers who had returned to their own homes and who were handed over to the Wehrmacht for processing. Meanwhile, a dozen Russian soldiers and alleged party officials were shot. It was only in the report's conclusion that the true purpose of the mission was revealed. SS-Brigade (mot) 1 had also shot 800 Jews of both sexes aged sixteen and over in various unspecified locations 'for favouring Bolshevism and Bolshevik militants'.[30]

Amongst the murder and mayhem, the SS bureaucracy continued to concentrate on the minutiae within its expanding empire. Absurdly, on 1 August 1941 the SS-Brigade (mot) 1 was officially renamed as *1.SS-Infanterie-Brigade (mot),* (hereafter referred to as 1.SS-Infantry Brigade (mot)) although some official documentation continued to refer to it by its former title.[31]

Himmler, ever a pedantic numbers man, wanted to be kept constantly updated on the 'security actions' carried out by the brigade and demanded accurate facts and figures regarding the number of Jews, Communists and other 'undesirables' who had been liquidated. SS-Sturmbannführer Fritz Freitag served as Ia (Operations Officer) on the staff of 1.SS-Infantry Brigade (mot). As Operations Officer, Freitag was responsible for compiling daily reports sent directly to Himmler, regarding the units' action in pacifying the rear areas of the advancing German Army. The contents of these reports make it clear that the 1.SS-Infantry Brigade (mot) acted both separately and alongside *Einsatzgruppen* units in the ruthless subjugation of the conquered areas in which it operated.[32]

Meanwhile, the massacre of Jews continued throughout the first half of August. In Starokonstantinov, west of Berditschew, two battalions from SS-Regiment 8 murdered almost 500 Jews of both sexes, which was witnessed by HSSPF Jeckeln, and other units assisted a police battalion by providing firing squads for the execution of around 2,000 Jews in the nearby town of Ostrog. Only the intervention of Wehrmacht officers from the local command, who wanted to prevent the senseless slaughter of 'valuable workers', led to an abandonment of the massacre.[33]

The preserved text of the War Diary of *Kommandostab RFSS* provides a detailed description of each action carried out by the three SS-Brigade during the summer and autumn of 1941, including when, where and how many people were executed. The pace of these operations was frenetic, averaging one action every two to three days and slaughter on this scale took a toll on the men who carried it out. To acclimatise their men to the work that was to come, the officers of 1.SS-Infantry Brigade (mot) had organized a mass shooting of several hundred Jews, followed by a speech from Jeckeln himself where he told the assembled men: 'It is necessary to annihilate the Jews: Because of the Jews, the world is at war. They, the Jews, are plotting to destroy our people.'[34]

Some of the soldiers had nervous breakdowns and a small minority committed suicide. The records of *Kommandostab RFSS* noted that the new commander of SS-Infantry Regiment 10, SS-Obersturmbannführer Karl Sattler, arrived in Debica on 14 July 1941 in preparation for taking up his new duties but failed to report that he was dismissed

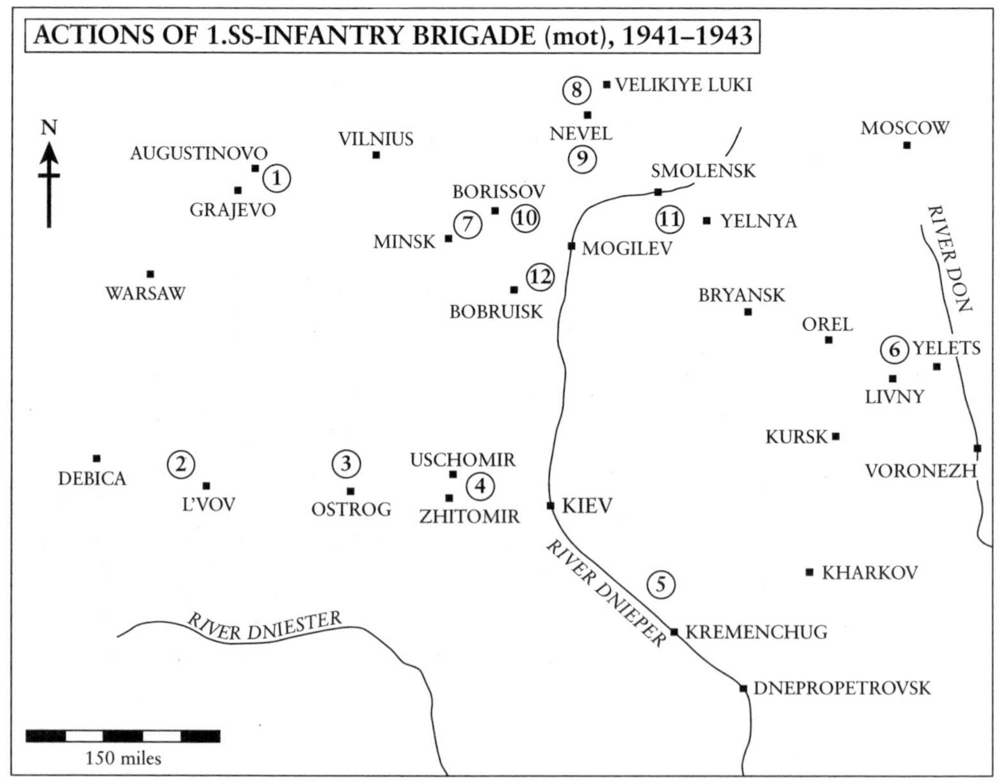

Actions of 1.SS-Infantry Brigade (mot), 1941-43 Map Notes

1 Following the commencement of Operation Barbarossa, 1.SS-Brigade (mot) was assigned to XLII Army Corps to screen the rear areas of 9.Army. Between 23 and 25 June, the Brigade committed serious war crimes against civilians in the eastern Polish cities of Grajevo and Augustinovo.

2 1.SS-Brigade (mot) marched to L'vov on 22 July 1941 where it was to be subordinated to the HSSPF for Southern Russia, SS-Obergruppenführer Friedrich Jeckeln.

3 Back under the command of HSSPF Southern Russia, the brigade was ordered to comb through the wooded area around Rovno and the road to Zhitomir, rounding up Soviet troops while also carrying out ethnic cleansing operations around Ostrog.

4 In early August 1.SS-Infantry Brigade (mot) was screening the northern flank of 6. Army north of Zhitomir and carried out an action near Uschomir to disperse a Soviet regiment that had been cut off on the wrong side of the frontline during the fighting.

5 The brigade spent much of the rest of the year following in the wake of XVII Army Corps as it crossed the Dnieper River and fought its way deeper into Ukraine. It was now actively supporting Einsatzgruppe C in conducting the Holocaust, which included large-scale operations around the cities of Zhitomir, Berdiczew, Biala-Cirkew, Nowgorod-Wolinski, Nikopol, Uman and Dnepropetrovsk.

6 In early December the Soviet winter offensive threatened to overwhelm the German eastern Front. The Brigade was diverted to the east of Orel to strengthen 2.Army front and fought in support of the shattered XXXIV Army Corps between Yelets and Livny. It remained under the command of LV.Army Corps, which was sent in as reinforcement, for almost eight months,

7 At the beginning of August 1942, 1.SS-Infantry Brigade (mot) was ordered to Borissov in Belarus to counter the growing partisan threat in the countryside surrounding Minsk. The brigade was involved in Operation *Swamp Fever* at the end of August, followed by Operation *Karlsbad* in mid-October, Operation *Frieda* at the beginning of November and by Operation *Nurnberg* 22–26 November 1942.

8 The second Soviet Winter Offensive threatened the northern flank of Army Group Centre and 1.SS-Infantry Brigade (mot) was involved in the battle for the relief of Velikiye Luki, where it was attached to LIX Corps from December 1942–February 1943.

9 From 21 February 1943 the brigade took part in the two week-long anti-partisan operation Operation *Ball Lightning* to the south of Nevel, which was closely followed by Operation *Thunderbolt* in a neighbouring area between 31 March and 2 April.

10 By mid-summer 1.SS-Infantry Brigade (mot) had returned to Borissov to participate in another anti-partisan action, Operation *Herrmann*, on 7 July.

11 The Soviet Western Front initiated Operation *Suvorov* on 7 August 1943 to crack open the German 4.Army's defences and liberate Smolensk. 1.SS-Infantry Brigade (mot) was assigned to this front on 2 September and spent the next three weeks defending the city. On 24 September Smolensk was abandoned and 1.SS-Infantry Brigade (mot) was pulled across the Dniepr River.

12 On 10 November, the Soviet 1.Belorussian Front began its major offensive to break out of its Dniepr bridgehead. 1.SS-Infantry Brigade (mot) formed a Kampfgruppe which was redeployed to the area east of Bobruisk. It remained under the command of LV Army Corps within 9.Army until early December when it was withdrawn from the front to be converted into 18.SS-Panzergrenadier Division 'Horst Wessel'.

from this post in October for repeated drunkenness on duty.[35] There were also men who simply could not face the strain of mass murder and refused to play their part, but these were quickly weeded out and posted elsewhere as being bad for the morale of those who remained. The objectors might have been abused by their officers as cowards, but they were generally not punished for such refusal. In fact, there was little need for compulsion as there were always volunteers to replace the very few who chose to leave. Most men simply accepted their orders and soon got used to the work.

The SS men also received special inducements in the form of better and more generous rations, including extra schnapps, cigarettes, and sausage as a reward for the work. There were also those who preferred this kind of work as being less hazardous than standard military service.[36]

Even at this early stage in its operations, it was clear that the units of 1.SS-Infantry Brigade (mot) would be spread very thinly while carrying out their assigned tasks in the Russian interior. Outside of its assigned role the brigade carried out roving missions wherever the Wehrmacht could not spare troops for a mopping-up action and it was usual for the two infantry regiments to operate many miles apart from one another, either at the end of long and fragile communications system back to brigade command or temporarily assigned to another larger unit.

The following action around the village of Uschomir, near the town of Korsten in north-western Ukraine, gives an indication of the isolation in which these units sometimes operated. It also gives an idea of how ill-equipped the unit was for conventional warfare in almost every sense of the term.

On the morning of 9 August, the 1.SS-Infantry Brigade (mot) moved into a bivouac area approximately 20 miles north of the city of Zhitomir in order to screen the northern flank of 6.Army. As part of this role the Brigade was ordered to carry out a clean-up operation in the southern area of the Prypet Marshes where a Soviet infantry regiment had been passed over and, finding itself on the wrong side of the frontline, was attacking supply vehicles of the Army's rear echelons.

The brigade dispatched SS-Infantry Regiment 10, at this date around 3,000 men strong, to deal with the cut-off Russian regiment and their mission order was curt: 'To annihilate the Russian troops, equivalent to more than one strong battalion [around 1,000 armed men], who disturb the rear of the 6.German Army'. The search area consisted of roughly 850 square miles of dense forest and treacherous swampy patches interspersed with tiny, isolated villages of about twenty houses, each within its own cleared area of arable land.

Information was scant but it was assumed that the Russian force would try to retreat to the north into the densest area of marshland before attempting to penetrate back through the frontline to return to their own forces. With this in mind, the regimental commander placed I./SS-Regiment 10 (SS-Obersturmbannführer Kistler) in a defensive position around the village of Uschomir at the northern end of the search area facing south as a covering force. II./SS-Regiment 10 (SS-Sturmbannführer Strathmann) and III./SS-Regiment 10 (SS-Sturmbannführer Kummer) would then advance northwards, acting like beaters, to drive the Russian force onto the guns of I.Battalion.

Given the nature of the terrain, the motorised aspect of the unit was no advantage and the mission was undertaken on foot. Supply of any kind was also exceedingly difficult in the forest and the troops were forced to leave behind both their heavy machine guns and their field kitchens. Therefore, armed only with light infantry weapons they started their sweep at first light on 10 August. The battalions were obliged to search every village and clearing within the search area, and as the units became dispersed their officers quickly displayed their inexperience in forest fighting.[37]

Red Army units were generally much better trained in forest fighting than their German counterparts, simply because the vast wooded areas throughout the country had no equal in Germany. No allowance had been made for the fact that German armed forces would have to fight under such conditions.[38]

The riflemen of SS-Infantry Regiment 10 were at an even greater disadvantage as they had largely been trained as glorified policemen. The companies advanced in close order, shouting orders, hacking at the undergrowth to clear their way, and congregating in open spaces that quickly drew the attention of Russian snipers. Officers and non-commissioned officers suffered particularly heavily until they learned to disguise their ranks.[39]

The rate of advance was less than a mile an hour and although several deserters had been gathered up, III.Battalion only came upon the first entrenched Russians around nightfall. The point company,

12.(Heavy Weapons) Company minus its heavy weapons, consisted of around 120 men. Suspecting that they may be opposed by a much stronger force, they were reluctant to become involved in a firefight in the dark without substantial reinforcement. However, all attempts at communication with battalion command failed. 12.Company did manage to link up with 9.Company on its left, but even with this increase in manpower they had little choice but to fall back half a kilometre and wait for daylight.

Dawn revealed that the Russian force had withdrawn to the north during the night, but deserters provided the vital information that there were still between 700 and 900 soldiers well-armed with heavy machine guns and anti-tank guns, although their morale was low and it was only the presence and threats of a handful of political commissars and fanatical communists that held the unit together.

As II. and III.Battalion followed the trail of the retreating Russians it became clear that they were more practised than the Germans at forest fighting generally, were familiar with the area that they were operating in, and had horses and mules to move their heavy equipment, which put them at a huge tactical advantage. In the middle of the afternoon III.Battalion was suddenly attacked by four Russian fighter bombers that ranged in on the clearings where the German troops habitually congregated. As they only possessed small arms, there was little the Germans could do to retaliate as they endured the lethal rain of steel fragments and splinters from trees. When it was possible to resume the march, it was found that eight men had been killed and it had to be assumed from the accuracy of the bombardment that the Russian force was in radio contact with their superiors on the other side of the front line.

The search continued until midnight when extreme fatigue caused a halt, by which point III.Battalion's companies were spread out over a five-mile-long front. The tension of the hide and seek nature of the fighting combined with the heat, clinging vegetation and swarms of mosquitos were taking their toll on the men's morale and although mosquito nets and mepacrine tablets were distributed, malaria was a real threat.

Both battalions advanced more energetically on 12 August, however, and by mid-afternoon the point units were taking heavy fire from the heart of the forest, indicating that they had caught up with a substantial portion of the pursued enemy. The weight of fire persuaded the III.Battalion commander to hold off from a direct assault until the Russian positions had been softened up by two 10.5cm artillery pieces provided by 6.Army. One hundred shells were fired in quick succession, which broke up the Russian defences and as darkness fell the infantry moved in to mop up. Dead and dying men and pack animals littered the forest floor and during the night 200-300 deserters surrendered to the SS forces.[40]

III.Battalion did not wait until dawn but continued to pursue 400 Russian soldiers who had broken away and continued to retreat to the north. By the afternoon of 13 August, the trap was almost set. III.Battalion was advancing from the south while II.Battalion was moving in from the west. I.Battalion in its positions around Uschomir had utilised all available truck drivers, clerks, and motorcyclists to patrol into the forest and provide warning of the Russian approach. All night the troops waited tense and alert, with flares at the ready to illuminate their enemy, but it wasn't until the afternoon of 14 August that the outposts of I.Battalion encountered the foremost Russian soldiers.

As I.Battalion attempted to slow the Russian advance, III.Battalion closed in from the rear at around 17:00. In desperation the Russians had laid an ambush for III.Battalion placing their antitank guns, mortars, and heavy machine guns across their line of advance, covered by snipers in the treetops. In a three-hour running battle, the German attack was beaten back and with thirty-six dead and forty wounded III.Battalion was forced to retreat. II.Battalion failed to arrive in time to force the issue.

However, the action of III.Battalion had fragmented the Russian battalion into several smaller groups, which streamed away to the north and east, their cohesion gone, to be rounded up by combat units of I.Battalion. The following morning II.Battalion took possession of the main Russian position where the bodies of the Commissar and three political officers were identified amongst the dead. Most of the rest of 15 August was taken up with scouring the surrounding forest for individual Russian soldiers who had escaped the carnage and were trying to make their way to safety in the north. The next day the regiment was pulled back to rest.[41]

SS-Infantry Regiment 10 had been lucky. Given the Russian troops' generally superior training in forest fighting and the weight of fire support that they could count upon, the lightly armed, poorly led SS troops could have suffered far high casualties than the ninety or so dead and wounded that they did sustain. They had blundered into a situation of which they had no real knowledge and the two pursuit battalions had failed to carry out even the most basic of reconnaissance. Fortunately for them, the Russian's spirit of resistance was crushed when their most effective leaders were killed.

Generalfeldmarschall Walter von Reichenau, commander in chief of 6.Army, was very satisfied with actions carried out by 1.SS-Infantry Brigade (mot) while under his command, and for services rendered during the Uschomir operation he rewarded twenty-one SS men with the Iron Cross 2nd Class. Himmler, however, was less than impressed with SS-Oberführer Herrmann's brigade regarding the figures for executions, which were 'lean when compared to Fegelein's cavalrymen' who had already killed more than 25,000 Jews and many 'others', and he felt the need to re-affirm that the Führer had ordered the murder of all Jews. The efficiency of 1.SS-Infantry Brigade (mot) was not improved when in September 1941 SS-Standartenführer Heino Hierthes was transferred from his commanding role at SS-Cavalry Regiment 2 to lead SS-Infantry Regiment 8 as he was deemed to be 'not aggressive enough' by Hermann Fegelein.[42]

The brigade spent the rest of the month following in the wake of XVII Army Corps as it crossed the Dnieper River and fought its way deeper into Ukraine. By now, the brigade was actively supporting Einsatzgruppe C in conducting the Holocaust, which included large-scale operations around the cities of Zhitomir, Berdiczew, Biala-Cirkew, Nowgorod-Wolinski, Nikopol, Uman and Dnepropetrovsk. There is also anecdotal evidence that the 1.SS-Infantry Brigade (mot) participated in the murder of 23,000 Hungarian and Ukrainian Jews at Kamenets-Podolsk, but this is not borne out by the disturbingly frank reports the brigade itself submitted to higher authorities. 1.SS-Infantry Brigade (mot) was the largest force under Jeckeln's command during this period and his personal mandate from Himmler was to murder Jews first and foremost, to 'impose peace' on the occupied territories. During August alone, Jeckeln's forces killed over 44,000 Jews in the Ukraine.[43]

The records show that Jews were not the only targets of this campaign of terror, as amongst those listed are 'bolshevist plunderers,' 'asiatics,' 'vagabond Mongols' and 'partisans', basically anyone that they did not like the look of. Reports reveal that prisoners of war were also murdered. By the end of 1941, 1.SS-Infantry Brigade (mot) had been responsible for the murder of tens of thousands of people, primarily civilians,[44] with conservative estimates indicating that troops under *Kommandostab RFSS* control had killed at least 100,000 Jews in less than five months,[45] but with the onset of winter and the downturn in Germany's military fortunes the brigade was needed for actual frontline service.

By the beginning of December, the headlong German advance had ground to a halt in the mud and snows of the Russian winter. The III. Panzer Corps, which contained the elite SS-Leibstandarte 'Adolf Hitler' Regiment, was battling at the end of its strength to take the southern city of Rostov before the onset of severe winter weather put an end to German mobile operations. Having been involved in relatively little actual combat, the brigade was still a powerful fighting force, mustering around 6,000 men and fully motorised with over 1,600 vehicles. Himmler planned to use this strength to bolster the battered units of the Leibstandarte, but before the transfer could take place Stalin's winter offensive broke over the whole Eastern Front.[46]

Soviet Marshal Timoshenko's Southwest Front smashed into the right wing of Army Group Centre on 6 December and in just three days General Kostenko's 5.Cavalry Corps supported by the Soviet 13.Army had surrounded XXXIV. Army Corps in the area of Yelets, in the centre of 2.Army's front, while its neighbouring XXXV.Army Corps was pushed backwards to the north-west, creating a massive hole in the frontline. Fortunately for 2.Army, the three trapped German divisions, namely 45. 95. and 134.Infantry Divisions, managed to maintain some cohesion and fought their way back to the west, but all sustained heavy casualties and lost most of their vehicles and artillery in the process.[47]

In the face of this impending disaster, 1.SS-Infantry Brigade (mot) was diverted to the east of Orel to strengthen 2.Army front. At this stage of the war, the Brigade was significantly below divisional strength with only limited artillery assets and was considered to have little value as an independent tactical unit. It was therefore frequently broken up, its regiments subordinated to army divisions. On 14 December, SS-Infantry Regiment 8 was placed under the command of 56.Infantry Division where they set up a covering position for the battered units of XXXIV.Corps, allowing them a breathing space to form a new line of defence. Over the next few days, the SS-Infantry Regiment 8 defended the area around the town of Russki-Brod, 15 miles to the north-west of Livny where it threw back Red Army infantry attacks in company and battalion strength with the aid of an army assault gun battery.[48]

As XXXIV.Corps had lost much of its heavy equipment, small units of artillery from the brigade were parcelled out to add much needed firepower to the infantry divisions. A member of the 14.(Flak)/SS-Infantry Regiment 8 remembers:

> I joined the 1.SS-Inf.Brig (mot.) with the two 2cm anti-aircraft companies in the winter of 41/42 in Malo Arkhangelsk. Our company was spread all over the place. My platoon was assigned to the Inf.Rgt.278 (95.I.D.) and took part in defensive fighting at the Belaya River. It was not until June 42 that my platoon returned to the company and thus to the brigade.[49]

However, shortages of vital supplies were endemic, and the SS troopers were just as unprepared for the trauma of winter warfare in Russia as the Wehrmacht. There was a near total absence of any kind of cold weather clothing to protect even against the more temperate climate of central Europe. But in the extremely cold temperatures of the worst Russian winter for over 100 years the troops were total debilitated. There were no felt boots to save frost-bitten toes, no fur-lined coats to prevent sentries from freezing to death on duty and no reliable anti-freeze to ensure that the weapons fired when the enemy appeared.[50]

Added to this was the fact that 1.SS-Infantry Brigade (mot) had a general paucity of effective weapons for fighting in the front line. While its two newly arrived companies possessed 20mm Flak guns and other elements were equipped with 37mm anti-tank guns, which were of little use against the packs of heavily armoured T-34 tanks that were thrown against their lines. The brigade did contain a battery of French 150mm howitzers towed by Czech artillery tractors but, as their Wehrmacht compatriots had also discovered, none of this equipment was built to withstand the rigours of a Russian winter.[51] The cold was so intense that the engine blocks of the vehicles burst. All movement relied upon horsepower. Heavy weapons were practically immobilised while lighter guns had to be taken apart and transported on locally procured 'panje' sledges.[52]

Bitter fighting took place in killing temperatures as low as -50 degrees Celsius. SS-Rottenführer Richard Lunkenheimer, a member of 14.(Flak)/SS-Infantry Regiment 10, participated in several savage defensive actions:

> We soon occupied a new defensive position in the Trudy sector. We were involved in murderous fighting on the first day of Christmas. The Russians attacked in five waves and our 2cm Flak mowed them down, but our ammunition was nearly all used up. Then came the sixth wave; riders who rode toward us in tight formations, swinging their sabres. It degenerated into bloody hand-to-hand fighting once all of our ammunition had been used up and many of my comrades were killed by sabre blows. The situation was confused. We had no contact to the sides. Were we already bypassed, surrounded? To the west, that seemed the only way out. In very low temperatures, I struggled through high snow and across rutted, iced-up roads with my towing vehicle; fully loaded with wounded and a saved 2cm Flak in tow. We reached the Brigade command post on 27 December.[53]

Lunkenheimer lost two toes to frostbite during the winter fighting.[54]

Eight guns had been lost and a ninth was badly damaged. One gun crew had been ridden over and cut down while defending their weapon at close quarters and the company suffered over one hundred casualties killed and wounded. IV.Platoon had remained relatively unscathed and was able to cover the retreat of their comrades and the survivors were re-assigned to the infantry battalions.[55]

As the fighting raged, the brigade commander SS-Brigadeführer Richard Herrmann was killed by shell splinters outside his command post. With a dislocated command structure and inadequate means of defending themselves, SS-Infantry Regiment 10 was unable to hold its position at the Trudy Bend, a feature of the Trudy River which in the frigid conditions was little more than a line on the map, and on 27 December the Russians broke through.[56] The Chief of Staff of 2.Army, Major General Gustav Hartenek, was quick to blame the SS-Infantry Regiment 10 for the collapse of the line in their sector that exposed the important road junction at Yelets.[57]

On 28 December, the brigade, minus I./SS-Infantry Regiment 8 which was still reinforcing 95.Infantry Division, was assigned to 'Gruppe Moser'. This mixed force was under the command of General Moser of 299.Infantry Division and also contained II. and

III./ Infantry Regiment 529 (299.Infantry Division) and III./Infantry Regiment 278 (95.Infantry Division) which were under the direction of LV.Army Corps. 'Gruppe Moser' managed to create a solid defensive line and after SS-Oberführer Wilhelm Hartenstein had temporarily assumed command, 1.SS-Infantry Brigade (mot) helped to stabilise this sector of the front over the next few months.[58] However, certain elements within the Wehrmacht nevertheless remained unimpressed, as the High Command of the 2nd Army commented: 'The SS had to replace a lack of training with combat experience and now seem to be able to cope with simple circumstances.'[59]

1942

Following the stabilisation of the front, the brigade remained with LV.Army Corps for almost eight months, returning to its 'security duties' as the Soviet partisan movement slowly gained momentum. During this relative hiatus the Brigade was re-organised and large scale exchanges of personnel took place.[60]

As Hitler's ideological crusade against the Slavic countries of the Soviet Union had ground to a halt during the autumn and winter of 1941, the more perceptive minds amongst the German military establishment had begun to suspect that a swift victory was no longer within their grasp. By the end of 1941, as casualties amongst the fighting units had mounted at an alarming rate, the German administration in Galicia implemented a local initiative to recruit racially suitable volunteers of German descent as replacements for frontline Waffen-SS formations.

In a cynical ploy, the SS played upon the Ukrainians' desire for independence by spreading the rumour that they were recruiting to form a Ukrainian National Army, and from the many thousands who volunteered 2,000 of the most promising men, both physically and racially, were selected.[61]

One of those selected was told to report to L'vov in mid-January 1942 along with ten others. They were informed that they had been selected

> ... as a sample; that we would be observed closely and should behave properly because we would eventually become officers of the Ukrainian Army. Recruit training for my group of eleven men took place at Heidelager. We were then sent to the city of

> Zhytomyr and from there I was despatched to the 1st SS-Motor Brigade for three months' front experience before I was to have been sent to officers' school.[62]

As the acceptance of non-German personnel into the Waffen-SS became more accepted practice, 1.SS-Infantry Brigade (mot) would become a testing ground for large numbers of ethnic Germans from all over Europe. Throughout 1942, ethnic Germans from Hungary and Romania in particular formed the bulk of the replacements sent to the two SS-Brigades, as well as being used to expand the SS-Cavalry Brigade into the 8.SS-Cavalry Division 'Florian Geyer'.[63]

It is recorded that over 2,000 Reich German personnel were transferred out of the brigade in late 1942 and were replaced by a draft of 2,300 ethnic German, or Volksdeutsche recruits, and it is presumably this movement of men that Robert Koehl refers to in his book *The Black Corps* when he states that the 10.SS-Panzer Division 'Frundsberg' 'was formed from the remnants of the First SS Brigade', although this fact is not supported by other sources.[64]

The new recruits to 1.SS-Infantry Brigade (mot) were immediately thrown into the dirty war being fought in the Russian hinterland, far behind the frontlines. By the summer of 1942 it was becoming increasingly evident that the unmitigated slaughter meted out by German forces on the Russian and Ukrainian civilian populations was having a detrimental effect on security in the occupied territories as able-bodied men and women flocked to join the partisans in the swamps and forests for fear of worse to come. The Wehrmacht's Army Group Centre rear area command reported that by March 1942 they had killed 63,257 partisans, for the loss of less than 2,000 casualties of their own, which strongly suggests that many of these so called 'partisans' were in fact unarmed civilians.[65]

The partisans were also inspired by hope as well as terror. The success of the Red Army's winter offensive had destroyed the myth of German military invincibility and had tied down many of the security troops who were tasked with hunting down the partisans. By August the number of partisans operating in the German rear areas had ballooned from 30,000 in the previous winter to 150,000.[66] Large partisan units had emerged and were beginning to threaten the major road networks and Wehrmacht supply bases in central Russia. There was an alarming increase in the murder of German-installed mayors and auxiliary policemen around the city of Minsk, and in these areas the Stavka (Soviet high command) controlled guerrilla bands were re-establishing Soviet control.[67]

This situation led to 1.SS-Infantry Brigade (mot) being ordered to Belarus at the beginning of August, where it again came under the command of the *HSSPF 'Ostland'* SS-Obergruppenführer Jeckeln, who had moved from his previous posting as HSSPF Southern Russian, and was employed in a succession of operations against partisan groups in the densely wooded and swampy countryside surrounding Minsk.[68] At this time the brigade was based in Borissov, to the north of Minsk, where there was ample evidence of the rapidly expanding activities of the partisan forces. When SS-Oberjunker Erich Heller was assigned to SS-Infantry Regiment 10 it took him over a week to travel the 450 miles from the brigade's old area of operations near Kursk via Kiev to the unit's new base at Borissov. He was delivering a motorcycle combination to the brigade and was forced to travel on a circuitous route by both train and in organised armed convoys, as lone and lightly armed road traffic was liable to be ambushed by partisans in many areas.

Heller found the assembly point for the brigade in a village near Borissov and was ordered to report to SS-Infantry Regiment 10, but travelling alone, even in the heart of the brigade's area of operations, was a risky business and while driving on a road through dense forest between the two positions he was shot at by partisans and wounded in the arm, which put him out of action for a considerable period.[69]

It was clear to the German High Command that the partisan problem was getting out of hand and 'Operation Sumpffieber' (Swamp Fever) was launched on 25 August against the groups in the Borissov area, for which Himmler himself authorised the use of nerve gas and stun grenades. 6,500 German troops were assigned to the task, but the partisans avoided a pitched battle and slipped away through terrain believed to be impassable by large bodies of men. The frustrated Germans again lashed out at the civilian population and official records cite the shooting of 389 'bandits', 1,274 'suspects' and the burning down of 12 villages. More than 10,000 Jews and suspected partisan sympathisers were also interned in labour camps.[70]

Following this action, the brigade moved 100 miles north-east to the area around the city of Orsha to participate in Operation *Karlsbad*, which was aimed at eliminating an estimated 6,000 well-equipped and trained partisans led by Soviet officers who were thought to be operating in this region alone. The partisans disrupted German supply lines and targeted the Borissov-Tolochin railway line on an almost daily basis.

The operation began on 11 October and the force sent in to deal with the partisans was an incredibly mixed one even by the standards of German rear-area operations. 1.SS-Infantry Brigade (mot) formed the main body of the force with about fifty men of the *SS-Sonderkommando 'Dirlewanger'* attached. These were reinforced by parts of Police Regiments 13 and 14, the Lithuanian Schützmannschaft Battalion 255, the I./Infantry Regiment 638 (French) and the Cossack Detachment 102, which all came under the command of HSSPF 'Mitte', SS-Gruppenführer Erich von dem Bach Zelewski. Operation *Karlsbad* ended on October 23 in failure, the partisans again having slipped the net; but for a total loss of 24 dead and 65 wounded the German forces managed to kill 1,051 civilians and partisan suspects. The ratio of losses between the German and partisan forces highlights the fact that almost no actual fighting took place and that this mission was nothing more than the systematic slaughter of people that the Third Reich deemed undesirable.[71]

On 23 October, Himmler introduced further measures to escalate the war against the partisans. He appointed SS-Gruppenführer Bach-Zelewski as 'Commissioner for anti-partisan warfare', effectively making him overlord of all security operations conducted on the Eastern Front, and he transferred SS-Brigadeführer Carl von Gottberg to Belorussia with a remit to create a unit for waging war against the partisans on a permanent basis.[72]

Zelewski wasted no time in exercising his authority launching Operation *Frieda* on November 5, which consisted of a five-day long security sweep through the forests and swampland south of Borissov. This was a relatively small affair when compared with Operation *Karlsbad* with only *SS-Sonderkommando 'Dirlewanger'* being subordinated to 1.SS Infantry Brigade (mot). The operation supposedly searched for a group of 500-600 partisans, but thick forests and swamps hindered their efforts. Annoyed by the lack of progress, the commander of 1.SS Infantry Brigade (mot), SS-Brigadeführer Karl Herrmann, examined the conditions for himself, noting rather acidly: 'On November 7, 1942, after a several-hour march, I personally convinced myself that the swamps can be walked through from willow stump to willow stump. What the bandits can do, the Waffen-SS can do too.'[73]

300 'partisan' bodies were counted for the loss of two dead and two wounded Germans. Again, these figures speak for themselves.

The next mission that the brigade took part in was Operation *Nurnberg*, 22-26 November 1942, under the auspices of *Kampfgruppe Gottberg*. The pretext for the operation was the presence of three large partisan camps in dense swampy forest near Poetawy to the north of Minsk. The camps were thought to contain up to 3,000 well-armed men with trained leaders who had a direct radio link with Moscow, as well as large numbers of Jews and Gypsies who had congregated in this area under the protection afforded to them by the partisans. The operational plan was for the force to surround the hostile area and compress the partisan forces into a small killing zone. 1.SS-Infantry Brigade (mot) was to advance from east to west with SS-Infantry Regiment 10 on the right wing and SS-Infantry Regiment 8 on the left, while other forces approached from the north and south, driving the surrounded partisans onto the guns of security forces provided by the Lithuanian Regional Commissioner who were manning the easily defended line formed by the Dryswiata River and Lake Bohin.

Special *SD-Einsatzkommandos* were assigned to the regiments to ensure that gang suspects, Jews and Gypsies were treated with the upmost ruthlessness while other specialist officers were responsible for organising the collection and transport of captured agricultural produce and livestock. Unfortunately for the Germans, the operation was robbed of much of its tactical advantage by a lack of fuel for the SS-Infantry Regiments, which massively reduced their mobility and forced them rely on their motorcycle company to rush from point to point plugging gaps that inevitably appeared in the encirclement. The troops slogged through the wild countryside finding several abandoned partisan camps but little else. Occasional sniping caused minimal casualties, but the envisioned battlefield was no more than a morgue for the hapless civilians.[74]

According to the official report, the operation resulted in the death of '60 bandits, 10 Jews, 7 gypsies, 638 specially treated people [against our] own loss [of] 4 dead, 1 slightly wounded. The enemy losses on 24 November could not be fully ascertained because the enemy succeeded in recovering the wounded and dead in the dense forest area.'

Captured loot amounted to two heavy machine guns, 10 rifles, 2 machine pistols, one flare gun, ammunition, hand grenades, one radio receiver and one transmitter. In addition, large quantities of food, grain and cattle were seized, and several captured Wehrmacht soldiers were released. However, in the face of such a large and unwieldy force, the bulk of the fighting men were able to separate into small groups and slipped away.[75]

Battle for Velikiye Luki

Operation *Nurnberg* was to be the last large security operation that the 1.SS-Infantry Brigade (mot) would participate in that year. Far away to the south-east the unfolding German disaster at Stalingrad was drawing in all available resources from all over the Reich, leaving German forces stretched to the point of disintegration at many points along the central and southern sectors of the Eastern Front. Recognising their numerical advantage and again capitalizing on their superior training and equipment in winter warfare, the Russian high command launched a series of massive offensives along the entire length of the Eastern Front.

In Army Group Centre's area of operations, the Russian Kalinin Front began its winter offensive on 25 November with the 3. and 4.Shock Armies aiming to break through a weak spot in the front and capture the town of Vitbsk from the north-east. The German corps-sized 'Gruppe Chevallerie', based around General Kurt von der Chevallerie's LIX.Army Corps, held a line of strongpoints along the 'Toropets Bulge' in 3.Panzer Army's defensive zone at the vulnerable junction between Army Groups Centre and North.[76]

The Kalinin Front attacked through tangled, snow-encrusted forests, lakes, and swamps, initially by-passing Velikiye Luki, a vital communications centre, but as the 3.Shock Army thrust towards Vitbsk it first had to take the town to secure its flank. Russian reconnaissance quickly established that there was no continuous German frontline around Velikiye Luki, just a string of strongpoints – and those on the northern flank were in fact not strong. The town itself contained around 7,500 German troops with the garrison comprised of a mixture of frontline troops and construction and service personnel centred on parts of 83.Infantry Division.[77]

Infantry elements of the 3.Shock Army were ordered to invest the town while its motorised units continued the advance. By

27 November, the Russian spearheads were fifteen miles west of the town, which by this date was effectively surrounded, and Von der Chevallerie was demanding that if the garrison was to be saved it should break out immediately. Hitler ordered that the town should hold until relieved, although German high command could not afford to spare any units to make up a relieving force.[78] Woefully short of resources, Von der Chevallerie resolved to hold the line as best he could with his LIX.Corps while General of Infantry Otto Wöhler, the newly appointed Chief of Staff of Army Group Centre, used every trick to free up troops to form a combat group for the relief of the city.[79]

Army Group Centre wasn't in much of a position to help as it was facing multiple Red Army incursions along its entire front, but it did release 1.SS-Infantry Brigade (mot) from its reserve, which was subordinated to 'Gruppe Chevallerie' on 6 December. The brigade was transferred from its previous position to the north of Minsk to Nevel, approximately 30 miles south-west of Velikiye Luki to bolster the southern flank of the penetration area. Here it had the newly arrived 6.Luftwaffe Field Division on its southern flank, which, although superbly equipped, was dismally trained for infantry fighting and significantly under-strength when compared with an army infantry division.[80]

1.SS-Infantry Brigade (mot) took over the Komshanskaya Rudnya-Balabolkino sector of the defensive line previously manned by 291. Infantry Division and parts of 20.Infantry Division (mot), which enabled the freeing up of three infantry battalions and six batteries of artillery from these units for the relief effort.[81] The attack began on 9 December, but it lacked a powerful armoured punch and the motorized element of the relieving force were severely hampered by the absence of roads and difficult terrain. Quickly losing momentum, the attack had ground to a halt by 12 December.[82]

On 15 December, General Wöhler launched a second assault using the strongest elements of 'Gruppe Chevallerie', 83. and 291.Infantry Divisions reinforced by 20.Infantry Division (mot), with weaker units including 1.SS-Infantry Brigade providing flank cover. I./Panzer Regiment 15, acting as an independent command, was brought up to spearhead the assault, but again the attack quickly ran into trouble, literally bogged down in the marshy ground while the relief corridor was hammered by Russian artillery on three sides. Rain and fog during the day prevented Luftwaffe air support and freezing temperatures at night ravaged the frostbitten troops.[83]

Meanwhile, the Russians inserted the fresh 19.Guards Rifle Division into the line ahead of the relieving German column, while 21.Guards Rifle Division made spoiling attacks to the south-west of Velikiye Luki to pin the German defenders in their positions. A battalion of this division attacked Hill 190 to the south-east of Chernosem on 21 December which was defended by 1.SS-Infantry Brigade (mot). The attack was repulsed but such tactics ensured that the relief attempt was starved of local reinforcements.[84] Russian attacks had more success in breaking into the defences of 6.Luftwaffe Field Division. A battalion of 1.SS-Infantry Brigade (mot) managed to clear up the penetration and recover three 2cm *Flak Vierling* anti-aircraft guns that the Luftwaffe troops had abandoned in their retreat, but these short sharp attacks kept the flank units pinned to their fortifications.[85]

By 22 December, both 291.Infantry Division and 20.Infantry Division (mot) had been reduced to fewer than 1,000 combat-effective troops. The end of the relief effort allowed the Russians to redouble their attacks against the besieged town while keeping up pressure on the German defences to its north and south.[86] 1.SS-Infantry Brigade (mot) held its positions throughout the latter half of December and its radio company supplied technical personnel to maintain the radio link between 'Gruppe Chevallerie' and the besieged garrison. One of its radio stations was positioned at the easternmost end of the relief corridor at Poretschje, where they were so close to the Russian trenches that they could hear their troops talking in their bunkers.[87]

The brigade's fighting strength was augmented at this time by the arrival of the 1,100-man strong *SS-Freikorps Danmark,* which arrived in Nevel on 5 December and was placed under the command of the brigade. The companies took over positions in a relatively quiet part of the line, enabling the brigade to create a small but viable reserve. The Danes were deployed to the north of Bobrikowo along the railway line between Velikiye Luki and Nevel and were expected to man a frontline almost three miles long, which was only possible by creating strongpoints and conducting aggressive patrolling in the intervening spaces to keep the Russians off balance.[88]

The final attempt to relieve Velikiye Luki was dubbed Operation *Totila* and began on 4 January. It initially used the remnants of 291. Infantry Division and parts of 20.Infantry Division (mot) to make the breakthrough with the main weight of the attack being provided by 331. and 205.Infantry Divisions, which had been squeezed out of the line for this effort.[89]

By 9 January, with the situation in the besieged town deteriorating by the hour, a group of riflemen from 5.Jäger Battalion mounted in armoured personnel carriers and supported by nine tanks from I./Panzer Regiment 15 volunteered to smash through the Soviet

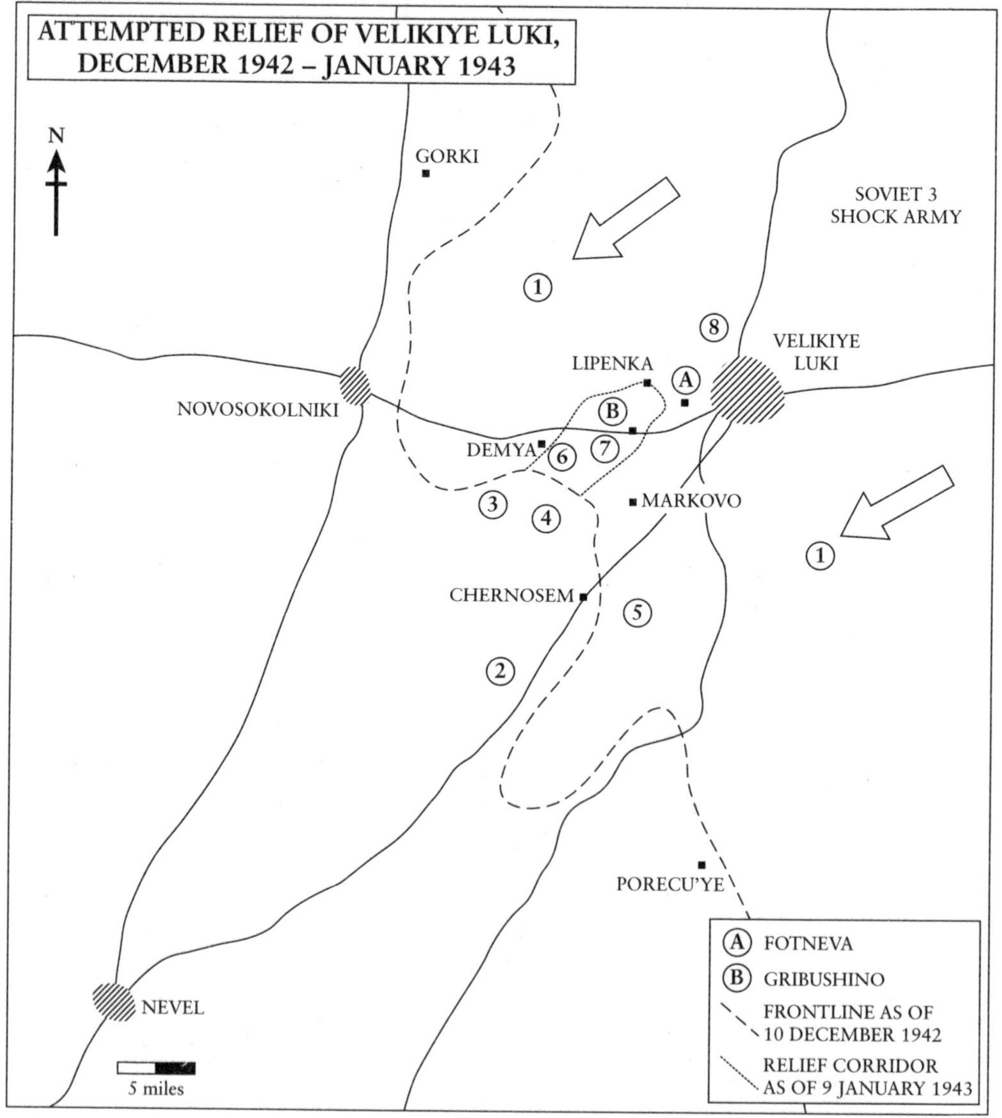

Velikiye Luki Map notes

1 As part of the Soviet Winter Offensive of 1942–43, the Kalinin Front tasked 3. and 4.Shock Armies to break through the weak northern flank of German Army Group Centre and capture the town of Vitbsk from the northeast. In the path of this advance was the town of Velikiye Luki, defended by a mixed garrison of 7,500 troops including parts of 83.Infantry Division. The attack began on 25 November 1942 and within two days the Russian spearheads were fifteen miles west of the town. The defence of this front fell to 'Gruppe Chevallerie', based around General Kurt von der Chevallerie's LIX Army Corps, but with few reinforcements available was unable to prevent Velikiye Luki being surrounded by the end of November.

2 Army Group Centre dispatched 1.SS-Infantry Brigade (mot) to 'Gruppe Chevallerie' on 6 December to bolster the southern flank of the penetration area, alongside 6.Luftwaffe Field Division. These two units were able to free up elements of 291. Infantry Division and 20.Infantry Division (mot) for a relief attack organized by General Otto Wöhler.

3 The relief attack began on 9 December and attempted to force a corridor on the most direct route to the town from west to east. However, it lacked an armoured punch while the motorized element of the relieving force were severely hampered by difficult terrain. Quickly losing momentum, the attack had ground to a halt by 12 December.

4 A second relief attempt began on 15 December, but although the force included 83. and 291. Infantry Divisions reinforced by 20.Infantry Division (mot) and I./ Panzer Regiment 15 brought up to spearhead the assault, it was carried out over the same ground using the same tactics. Marshy ground constricted the advance, which was hammered on three sides by Russian artillery and quickly ground to a halt. The Germans now held a narrow corridor to within a few miles of Velikiye Luki but could not make the final breakthrough.

5 Meanwhile, the Russian 21.Guards Rifle Division made spoiling attacks to the south-west of Velikiye Luki to pin the German defenders to their positions. A battalion of this division attacked Hill 190 to the south-east of Chernosem against 1.SS-Infantry Brigade (mot) on 21 December. The attack was repulsed but such tactics ensured that the relief attempt was starved of local reinforcements.

6 With time running out to rescue the defenders of Velikiye Luki, Operation *Totila* was launched on 4 January. It employed the remnants of 291.Infantry Division and parts of 20.Infantry Division (mot) to make the breakthrough, the main weight of the attack being provided by 331. and 205.Infantry Divisions. After several days of hard slogging the attack disintegrated and on 9 January an armoured Kampfgruppe, led by Major Günther Tribukait from I./Panzer Regiment 15, fought their way into the citadel in the afternoon of 9 January but once inside its vehicles were destroyed by artillery fire and Tribukait and his men were trapped inside the fortress.

7 A final relief attempt was made by 'Kampfgruppe Ramdohr', largely comprised of units from 205.Infantry Division and a reinforced company from 1.SS-Infantry Brigade (mot) utilizing the brigade's tracked vehicles based and around its *Kradschützen* (motorcycle) Company. Kampfgruppe Ramdohr struck out from the eastern end of the German-held corridor at Lakhny towards the village of Fotneva but this was essentially a carbon copy of the previous attempts and also ended in failure, with Hauptmann Ramdohr being killed in action.

8 The starving and exhausted defenders of Velikyi Luki surrendered on 16 January with only 150 men able to stumble back to the German lines.

defences in a lightning thrust to enable the breakout of the trapped garrison. The Kampfgruppe led by Major Günther Tribukait fought their way into the Citadel in the afternoon of 9 January, but once inside his vehicles were destroyed by concentrated artillery fire and he was forced to break out with his men and the few remaining defenders on the night of 15-16 January.[90]

With the failure of Major Tribukait's mission, 'Gruppe Chevallerie' was almost out of options. Although several other small-scale advances were attempted, none could muster the strength to save the situation. The last, best hope, carried out on 11 January, was a forlorn hope in the military sense of the phrase conducted by 'Kampfgruppe Ramdohr', largely comprised of units from 205. Infantry Division. This unit was an ad hoc collection of troops mounted in whatever armoured vehicles could be scraped together and included a reinforced company from 1.SS-Infantry Brigade (mot) commanded by SS-Hauptsturmführer Bildstein, utilizing the brigade's tracked vehicles based around its *Kradschützen* (motorcycle) Company.[91] Photographs show that the brigade possessed captured French Renault UE light armoured tractors that were used as prime movers for their anti-tank guns and were proof against small arms fire. It is also probable that the motorcycle company had a platoon of light armoured cars, although the movement of these would have been severely restricted by the weather and terrain.

Kampfgruppe Ramdohr's mission was a copy of those that had failed previously; to strike from the eastern end of the German-held corridor at Lakhny towards the village of Fotneva and from there to the besieged perimeter, but powerful Russian artillery barrages were able to smash the columns of vehicles and struggling infantry before they had advanced more than half a mile. Hauptmann Ramdohr was killed during this debacle.[92]

The starving and exhausted defenders of Velikyi Luki surrendered on 16 January with only 150 men able to stumble back to the German lines. However, the battle for the town had drawn in reinforcements on both sides and a sort of stalemate ensued, both sides settling down to bolster their defences and regain their strength.

1943

1.SS-Infantry Brigade (mot), with SS-Friekorps Danmark still attached, remained at the front as part of LIX.Corps until 21 February

1943 when it was temporarily placed under the command of 201. Sicherungs (Security) Division, where it took part in the two-week-long anti-partisan Operation *Kugelblitz* (Ball Lightning), in the swampy woodland to the north of Vitebsk. This operation was closely followed by Operation *Donnerkeil* (Thunderbolt) in the area between Vitebsk and Gorodok carried out between 31 March and 2 April.

In between these operations the Brigade returned to the frontline where it was essentially employed in trench warfare, interspersed with patrolling. During this period, it reported that its infantry was 70 per cent mobile, but its heavy artillery consisted of just four 15.5cm guns of French origin for which they only possessed one towing vehicle. In the opinion of the 3.Panzer Army under whose overall command the brigade now came, it had a Combat Value of III, making it 'fully suitable for defence' but unsuitable for offensive action.[93]

Himmler was desperate to wrest back control of one of his precious brigades from the control of the army and in May 1943 he planned a conversion of 1.SS-Infantry Brigade (mot) into a European formation by the addition of a large influx of Estonian volunteers. However, after much vacillating it was decided to create the 3.Estonian SS Volunteer Brigade as a wholly Estonian unit and only a cadre of 300 men were transferred to help with the set up and training, and so for the time being the bulk of the brigade languished in their bunkers amongst the forests and swamps to the east of Vitbsk.[94]

By mid-summer the partisan pressure on the German communications network in central Russia and Belarus was again reaching alarming proportions and Army Group Centre finally pulled 1.SS-Infantry Brigade (mot) out of the frontline and returned it to Borissov for the commencement of Operation *Herrmann* on 7 July. This action was again under the command of SS-Gruppenführer von dem Bach Zelewski in his role as Higher SS and Police Leader Russia Centre and was initiated to tackle several partisan units, each of approximately 200 men, which were operating in the Mir-Rakow-Kholchlo Kozdanov area.

Another large and motley collection of security units was gathered for this operation, with almost every branch of the German armed forces involved in some capacity: 1.SS Infantry Brigade (mot), Einsatzgruppe 'Körner', SS-Police Regiment 2, SS-Sonderkommando 'Dirlewanger', Special Purposes Police Commando 'Kreikenbon',

Police Rifle Regiment 31, Schützmannschaft Battalion 57, Police Panzer Company 12, 4 battalions of infantry and 1 artillery battery from Oberfeld Command 392, and sundry security personnel provided by the Luftwaffe.

The area of operations was thought to be extensively mined, so to avoid losses the German troops drove Russians civilians ahead of their advance. Again, the partisans were not brought to battle, but the operation carried out the secondary task of deporting all able-bodied civilians for employment as slave labour in Germany. Most of the villages were then burned down to deny shelter to the partisans.[95]

Defence of Smolensk

Operation *Herrmann* was the final large-scale anti-partisan action that 1.SS-Infantry Brigade (mot) was to be involved in as a complete unit. While the brigade had been chasing 'bandits' around Belarus the German army had suffered a huge defeat at Kursk and the entire German front in the east was slowly but surely edging westwards. With significant numbers of irreplaceable panzers left wrecked upon the battlefield, the Red Army was ready to take the initiative.

As the German armies fell back there was one spot where the front remained solid. In the middle of Generalfeldmarschall von Kluge's Army Group Centre's sector, 4.Army had enjoyed a relatively peaceful period throughout the late spring and early summer of 1943. Its divisions were grouped in four Corps; XXVII.Corps, XXXIX.Panzer Corps, IX.Corps, XII.Corps, arrayed from north to south in that order.[96] These Corps covered the direct approach to the strategically important cities of Smolensk and Bryansk and under the command of an expert in defensive fighting, Generaloberst Gotthard Heinrici, had been given ample opportunity to prepare defences in depth against a disaster, as had occurred around Kursk. However, 4.Army was primarily an infantry force with very few mobile reserves, which would limit its strategic options in the face of a strong armoured attack.[97]

The Red Army planned to crack open 4.Army's front with a massive blow mounted by their Western Front, commanded by General Sokolovsky, with General Eremenko's Kalinin Front providing support from the north, under the codename Operation *Suvorov*. Initial probing of the German positions began on 6 August with major assaults being launched all along the Army's front the following day.

For three days the Russian forces battered the German lines, and while a shortage of artillery ammunition and ineffectual support from the Red Air Force slowed progress to a crawl, they finally managed a comprehensive breakthrough on 11 August. Heinrici countered these moves by juggling his extremely limited mobile resources from one hot spot to another and by cannibalising units in less threatened sectors to keep up the fighting strength of others he managed to maintain a coherent defence against the first phase of the Russian offensive. Although 4.Army had suffered over 28,000 casualties and had lost many irreplaceable artillery pieces, it had brought the Russian offensive to a halt by 20 August. Once again, it was a case of scraping together every viable unit to strengthen the line and, almost as a last resort, 1.SS-Infantry Brigade (mot) was assigned to 4.Army just as the Red Army geared up to renew its onslaught.[98]

The Soviet Western Front rapidly regrouped its forces for the next assault that would herald the second phase of the operation with the capture of the city of Yelnya, rather than Smolensk itself, as a more realistic objective.[99] Four Armies would concentrate their attack against the weakened XII Corps to make the breakthrough with strong mobile forces ready to exploit the penetration, while other forces tied down the XXXIX.Panzer Corps and IX.Corps to the north to prevent them from reinforcing XII.Corps. XII.Corps held a frontline to the east of Yelnya, approximately 50 miles to the south-east of Smolensk, which consisted of nothing but a few shallow trenches, having been driven out of its prepared defensive positions during the first phase of *Suvurov*. To add to XII.Corps problems, the Corps command staff was removed and transferred to 9.Army, leaving its depleted divisions to be directed by IX.Corps. General Schmidt, commanding IX Corps, now inherited the responsibility for directing and supplying three extra infantry divisions as well supervising the vulnerable boundary between 4. and 9.Armies, which did not bode well for the coming battle.

The Russian artillery and aerial bombardment began on the morning of 28 August, closely followed by infantry and armoured attacks by units from 10.Guards Army and 21.Army, aimed at the IX.Corps' southern sector.[100] By nightfall, Russian advanced units were up to five miles behind the German front and bearing down on Yelnya, which played host to several large German army supply dumps but was virtually undefended, and a sizeable gap now separated 4. and 9.Armies. By the evening of 29 August, IX.Corps' right flank was on the point of disintegrating completely as the Russians pumped fresh forces into the breach and the next morning 10.Guards Army was making good progress against fragmentary German resistance and was advancing directly on Yelnya. By 13:30hrs, General Schmidt realized that Yelnya could not be held and received permission to evacuate the city. Meanwhile, 9.Army pulled back south-westwards towards Roslavl, which only served to widen the gap in the front line.[101]

As the leading units of 1.SS-Infantry Brigade (mot) arrived at 4.Army, Heinrici positioned them on the direct route from Yelnya to Smolensk to buy time while General Schmidt gathered together the remnants of IX.Army Corps' units into something resembling a coherent frontline. On 1 September I./SS-Infantry Regiment 10, commanded by SS-Sturmbannführer Hörnicke, was acting as point unit for the Brigade's move to reinforce the front at Yelnya when a surprise Russian breakthrough forced the battalion to be diverted to an area north of the Yelnya-Baltukino road.

Hörnicke's men quickly dug in and were able to fend off several Russian attacks carried out by troops of the Soviet 68.Army while covering the retreat of the 35.Infantry Division. On their left flank, elements of 342.Infantry Division were also falling back under strong Soviet pressure and this withdrawal was quickly degenerating into a rout. Hörnicke now took decisive action, rounding up and reorganising the panic-stricken troops into a fighting force that threw back the Russian infantry and restored the old frontline.[102]

SS-Brigadeführer Karl Herrmann established his headquarters in Ehki on 2 September,[103] while his command joined forces with parts of 330.Infantry Division which had also been sent to reinforce this sector. Both units were grouped together into the ad hoc 'Division Fiebig' commanded by Oberst Heinz Fiebig, commandant of 4. Army's weapons-training school. An improvised new front line had been established by 3 September, based upon the XXXIX.Panzer Corps to the northeast of Smolensk and 'Division Fiebig' in IX.Corps' defensive zone to the south-east. These new defences were soon to be tested.[104]

On 5 September, after an hour-long artillery and mortar barrage, the defensive positions of 1.SS-Infantry Brigade (mot) to the south of the Yelnya-Baltutina road were attacked by strong infantry forces supported by tanks. T-34 tanks rolled over the German foxholes, crushing their occupants while assault troops followed closely behind to mop up any survivors. Two companies were almost totally wiped out and a gaping hole was torn in the brigade's line.

I./SS-Regiment 40, acting as the Brigade's reserve, was thrown into the counterattack to restore the situation and in bitter hand-to-hand fighting, in which SS-Sturmbannführer Hörnicke fought at the head of his men, the battalion was able to evict the Russian forces and regained the brigade's old defensive line, which they subsequently held against every new attack until the brigade was relieved.[105]

That relieving force came in the form of the battle-hardened 78.Sturm-Division which was despatched by 9.Army to join 330. Infantry Division in bolstering the IX.Army Corps' southern flank and to try and patch up the gap between the two armies.[106] These reinforcements freed up the bulk of 1.SS-Infantry Brigade (mot) for re-deployment and, largely due to its mobility as one of 4.Army's only fully motorised units, was switched to a position in the Yartzevo area, approximately 25 miles northeast of Smolensk, where it was attached to the 25.Panzergrenadier Division in General Paul Völckers XXVII.Army Corps.[107]

As it departed, General Schmidt officially recognised the contribution made by the brigade to the defence of Smolensk, in an order of the day dated 5 September 1943:

> The 1. SS-Infanterie-Brigade (mot) fought magnificently during the time from 1 September to 5 September 1943 while it was attached to IX. Armeekorps. I express my thanks and unreserved appreciation to the officers and men of the Brigade.[108]

By 9 September, Heinrici's three remaining corps were arrayed in a semi-circle to the east of Smolensk, covering a little over 100 miles of front with fewer than 30,000 troops. Völckers' XXVll Army Corps held the northern corner post of the defensive line, anchored on the key town of Dukhovshchina, and he anticipated that the main threat would be against his positions to the east of Dukhovshchina. It was here that he deployed his strongest forces; 25.Panzergrenadier Division and 1.SS-lnfantry Brigade (mot) with the much depleted 18.Panzer Division held in readiness as a tactical reserve. 1.SS-lnfantry Brigade (mot) took up its position to the east of Dukhovshchina, with

SS-Infantry Regiment 8 on the left of the brigade front, butting up to Panzergrenadier Regiment 35 while SS- Infantry Regiment 10 was on the right in the vicinity of the Baranovo.

Eremenko's Kalinin Front spearheaded the next phase of Operation *Suvurov*, attacking in a south westerly direction against XXVII. Corps as Völckers had anticipated. Intensive reconnaissance had identified the increased strength of XXVII.Corps' newly reinforced right flank and in response Eremenko shifted the main weight of his attack further to the west where his forces attacked 256.Infantry Division on the morning of 13 September. Hoping that this move would draw off some of Völckers reserves, Eremenko also attacked 197.Infantry Division and 52.Infantry Division which held the centre of the Corps' position, covering the town of Spas-Ugly. Following a short, intense artillery barrage, four divisions of the Soviet 39.Army attacked the weakened German units and quickly penetrated the frontline, smashing Grenadier-Regiment 163. As Russian tanks drove into the breach left by the shattered regiment, 52.Infantry Division was routed, losing virtually all of its horse-drawn divisional artillery in the process.

At the same time, 83.Rifle Corps attacked 25.Panzergrenadier Division and 1.SS-Infantry Brigade (mot) and, while all assaults were beaten off with heavy losses, this action prevented even small elements of these units from being transferred to the west for use against the breach in the front.[109]

The remnants of 18.Panzer Division were ordered to counterattack to relieve the pressure on 52.Infantry Division, but given its severely depleted state was given the Kradschützen (Motorcycle) Company from 1.SS-Infantry Brigade (mot) to cover their left flank in the area to the north of Dukhovshchina. The motorcyclists took up defensive positions north-west of Podsselje and their commander, SS-Obersturmführer Sonne, sent out several reconnaissance patrols to examine the lie of the land and observe Russian activity.

At dawn on 15 September, the Russians attacked down the main road with tanks in support but with the aid of a battery of Sturmgeschütze assault guns, probably from Sturmgeschütz-Abteilung 190, the position was held. Boggy ground prevented the assault guns being used to their full advantage and the Russian infantry had to be thrown back in hand-to-hand fighting, which involved every man including Sonne himself and his headquarters troop.

As this attack unfolded, a new Soviet thrust rolled westwards along Maloje-Klisslokvo road. A company of Russian infantry infiltrated behind the Motorcycle Company's position and the situation was only saved when Sonne took some of his men from his defensive line and hit the advancing Russian infantry in a flanking attack, forcing them to retreat and regaining contact with 18.Panzer Division. Despite losing almost two-thirds of their combat strength, the Motorcycle Company held its positions against vastly superior odds for 12 hours, delaying the Soviet's capture of Duchowtschina and preventing the encirclement of the 18.Panzer Division. SS-Obersturmführer Sonne received the Knight's Cross for this action on 10 December 1943.[110]

Although the Soviets failed to follow up very aggressively it was clear that XXVII.Corps' position was untenable and, with 197. Infantry Division threatened with encirclement, Völckers ordered his corps to break contact and retreat southwards on the afternoon of 15 September, giving up Yartsevo in the process. On the following day the much-reduced German rear-guard units were unable to prevent the 2.Guards Rifle Corps from pushing on towards Dukhovshchina, which fell that night.

The German front was clearly tottering, but the Russian Armies had suffered massive losses in both men and materials and their logistical services were no longer keeping up with the demands of the fighting units, but despite their battle-weary state the Soviets launched a concerted effort to push the Germans back to the west and liberate Smolensk. In this they were aided by the German command itself as Feldmarschall Von Kluge was intent on retreating to the Panther Stellung, the German fortified line along the Dnieper River which at this date was little more than a line on a map, to save his armies rather than squandering them in trying to defend Smolensk. Under the circumstances it was imperative that the defensive line held to gain a breathing space to allow the retreat to be conducted in an orderly manner and prevent the German Corps from being split up and destroyed piecemeal. However, the loss of Dukhovshchina and Yartsevo, which were essentially the cornerstones of the defence of Smolensk, was not the only crisis facing 4.Army's front.[111]

The Red Army's reconnaissance units had identified another weak point in the defences and their 5.Army attacked 337.Infantry

Division on the south-eastern approaches to the city. As the situation deteriorated, 1.SS-Infantry Brigade (mot) was pulled out of the Dukhovshchina front and was again ordered to move with all speed to the southeast of Smolensk to the area of Dolgomostje on the evening of 21 September, where it was temporarily attached to 337.Infantry Division in an attempt to prop up the most exposed part of the sagging front.[112] The precise mission given to the brigade was to plug a gap in the line between XI.Army Corps and XXXIX.Panzer Corps where, again, the much depleted 35.Infantry Division was in danger of disintegrating in the face of attacks by the Soviet 68.Army.[113] At this time the brigade was without SS-Infantry Regiment 10 which had initially been placed in 4.Army's reserve after the shift from Dukhovshschina, but subsequently came directly under the command of 35.Infantry Division.[114]

This hurried redeployment occurred just as a change of commander within 1.SS-Infantry Brigade (mot) was taking place. As the senior regimental commander, SS-Obersturmbannführer Trabandt stepped into the role to replace the sick SS-Brigadeführer Herrmann. August-Wilhelm Trabandt had joined the SS on 7 May 1936 and quickly rose through its ranks to command III.Sturmbann of the elite SS-Leibstandarte 'Adolf Hitler' Regiment, Hitler's personal bodyguard unit. His unit was redesignated III./SS-Regiment 'Liebstandarte' during its work-up to a proper military unit prior to the outbreak of war, and while leading it in battle he won both classes of the Iron Cross during the Polish campaign.

He was promoted to SS-Standartenführer in May 1940 in recognition of the role that he played during the campaign in France but fell into disgrace with Himmler after he was caught by customs officials trying to smuggle a large quantity of wine back to Germany. He was relieved of his command and held a post without rank or authority at the Waffen-SS Main Replacement Office until he was expelled from the SS in May 1942.

After languishing in obscurity for over two years, Sepp Dietrich, Trabandt's old comrade and commander of the 'Leibstandarte Adolf Hitler' Division, petitioned Himmler directly on his behalf for his reinstatement and the Reichsführer relented, although at a cost. Trabandt was given the provisional rank of SS-Hauptsturmführer and command of a Ukrainian Schutzmannschaft Battalion fighting the dirty war against the partisans in central Russia, a post that he took up in October 1942. These roles, far from the glory of the battlefield, were seen as a punishment for many men and a place where those who had displeased the Reichsführer were sent to languish.

However, within a year Trabandt had either sufficiently rehabilitated himself through his own actions or the need for experienced officers was such that he was promoted to SS-Sturmbannführer and transferred to 1.SS-Infantry Brigade (mot) where he replaced SS-Obersturmbannführer Paul Massell in command of SS-Infantry Regiment 8. Slated to command a regiment in the Estonian Brigade, Trabandt was promoted again, but when this fell through he took control of 1.SS-Infantry Brigade (mot) following the illness of Karl Herrmann.[115]

Trabandt was briefed at the command post of the 35.Infantry Division to the south-east of Smolensk where he learnt that strong Russian forces had advanced westwards on both sides of Cholm and encircled Grenadier Regiment 11, which was holding the town itself. The Russians had occupied the villages of Lichatschewo and Rossnowo and were continuing their attack in order to reach the Roslavl-Smolensk road. With their positions penetrated in multiple places 35.Infantry Division was no longer holding a coherent frontline.

As the situation was deteriorating rapidly, Trabandt took the initiative and in the early morning of 22 September, without waiting for orders, advanced southwards from the brigade's forming up area near Panskoje on the Roslavl-Smolensk road, southeast of Smolensk itself. The troops fanned out to either side of the railway line that passed through Cholm with the aim of relieving Grenadier Regiment 11 and establishing a defensive line to both sides of Cholm. As the brigade approached, Grenadier Regiment 11 broke out of the town and linked up with the attacking SS battalions.[116]

During the attack on Cholm, I./SS-Infantry Regiment 39 received orders from a higher authority for it to go onto the defensive, which directly conflicted with those instructions issued by brigade. Unable to resolve the paradoxical situation on the spot, the battalion commander, believed to have been SS-Hauptsturmführer Otto Ertl, returned to regimental headquarters for clarification. During his absence the battalion adjutant, SS-Obersturmführer Karl Rubatscher, took temporary charge and on his own authority sent out scouts to warn against a surprise attack. These scouts indicated that strong

Russian forces were converging on the battalion's position from several directions.

The battalion was deployed with its heavy weapons, a platoon each of anti-tank, anti-aircraft, and infantry guns, and knocked out two Russian armoured cars that were probing the battalion's position. The Russians quickly followed up with an infantry attack supported by tanks which was also held off, but Rubatscher was becoming concerned that if they remained where they were the battalion risked being cut off and destroyed.

With Russian forces present on all major roads heading north and west, the Battalion was left with little choice but to move its vehicles and guns across country, a feat that seemed to offer little chance of success due to the soft ground. Rubatscher arranged the battalion in such a way that there were two companies of riflemen in the lead, with the heavy weapons in the middle of the column and a further infantry company providing security to the rear. The companies were already exhausted after the hard fighting around Yelnya and Dukhovshchina and they only had a combat-strength of around 25-30 men each. Additionally, due to the constant movement of the battalion between different commands their logistical support had failed to keep up and they had already gone two days without any food supplies.

The retreating battalion struggled on with Russian infantry and cavalry repeatedly attacking their column head on and from both sides. Following a five-hour march, the battalion approached the village of Belorushje, which was occupied by the Russians and blocked their way back to the German lines. Rubatscher positioned his heavy weapons to lay down a withering fire on the village while he himself led the infantry in a bayonet charge that threw the Russians out, carrying on the attack to tackle a column of Russian reinforcements arriving on his western flank. Although he was wounded in the initial fighting, Rubatscher succeeded in leading the battalion breakthrough back to his own lines complete with vehicles and heavy equipment, for which he was awarded the Knight's Cross on 27 December 1943.[117]

Meanwhile, as strong Russian forces with tank support followed up the retreat of Grenadier Regiment 11, the rest of 1.SS-Infantry Brigade (mot) established a blocking position across their line of advance two miles to the northwest of Cholm and halted their attack with heavy losses. The brigade held their positions for several days preventing 68.Army from capturing the Smolensk-Roslavl road, which would have cut off those units of XI Corps still fighting to the south.[118]

By the time Grenadier Regiment 11 returned to it on 22 September, the much-reduced battalions of 35.Infantry Division had been forced back to the line of the Smolensk-Roslavl railway line. With SS-Infantry Regiment 10 still temporarily under its command, 35.Infantry Division patched up its front line by parcelling out the SS battalions to various hotspots with III.Battalion being employed in front of the village of Kraspoff to cover the left flank of the division.

As SS-Sturmbannführer Schäfer, commander of III./SS-Infantry Regiment 10, came forward to orientate himself to his new position he observed strong Russian mobile forces advancing past his right flank. Schäfer divided his forces in order to occupy two areas of high ground where he and his men fought off determined attacks by infantry and cavalry supported by artillery, mortars, and aerial bombardment. Two tanks attacked the position, but the defenders held their nerve and let them roll over them, before engaging the accompanying infantry with machine gun fire and grenades. The two tanks were destroyed by artillery fire.

From this position Schäfer's battalion covered the northern flank of 35.Infantry Division and also maintained the tenuous link between IX.Army Corps and XXXIX.Panzer Corps. For the decisive defensive action fought by his battalion, SS-Sturmbannführer Ernst Schäfer was awarded the Knight's Cross on 14 October 1943, becoming the first member of 1.SS-Infantry Brigade (mot) to officially receive it.[119]

Concurrently, having been dispatched to 4.Army's reserve after the loss of Dukhovshchina, I./SS-Regiment 10 had been released to rejoin its parent regiment on 22 September and was assembling in the village of Nemykari, southwest of Arefino, to support the defence of the Smolensk-Roslavl road when the adjutant of an infantry regiment belonging to 35.Infantry Division reported to the battalion commander, SS-Sturmbannführer Hörnicke, that a broad gap had opened in the German frontline which his men could not fill.

Hörnicke confirmed that the Russians were occupying Hill 257.1, to the south of Arefino, which dominated the local area and threatened to cut off 35.Infantry Division as it prepared to retreat. Without waiting for orders, he launched an immediate assault on the high ground with his entire battalion supported by their integral infantry-gun and anti-tank elements.

In close combat, the SS riflemen ejected the Russian forces from the hill, but the Soviets were reluctant to give up the commanding position and counterattacked with waves of infantry strongly supported by tanks. The battle see-sawed for more than five hours with both sides gaining and then losing ground until, having had both of its flanks turned, the SS battalion was forced to withdraw or risk being overrun. Its actions did, however, successfully cover the withdrawal of 35.Infantry Division into its new position. For his leadership of his battalion both in the breakthrough battle west of Yelnya and for securing the Roslavl-Smolensk road, SS-Sturmbannführer Hörnicke was awarded the Knight's Cross on 1 December 1943.[120]

Despite the best efforts of all of the German units involved, by 23 September, the last defensive positions before Smolensk were being outflanked and Schmidt's IX.Army Corps in particular was on the point of collapse. That evening Heinrici ordered the evacuation of Smolensk. XXXIX.Panzer Corps was assigned to conduct the rear-guard before Smolensk, while the rest of 4.Army withdrew westwards and German engineers demolished key facilities in the city. Under XXXIX.Panzer Corps command, a Kampfgruppe from 18.Panzer Division and the remnants of 113.Infantry Division were positioned on the north-east approaches to the city, covering the direct line into the city along the Minsk-Moscow Highway, while 337.Infantry Division with 1.SS-Infantry Brigade (mot) defended the southern approaches. These two units supported by the last two operational Tiger tanks from schwere Panzer-Abteilung 505 mounted a delaying action around Smolensk's southern airfield in the face of attacks by General Zhuralev's Soviet 68.Army.[121]

However, as the brigade relocated to the assigned sector, it discovered that the Red Army had got there first. Trabandt ordered his men to attack, and they drove the Russian infantry eastwards before establishing their own defensive line. The Soviets lost many men, both casualties and prisoners, and left behind large quantities of weapons, ammunition and equipment.[122]

On 24 September, 1.SS-Infantry Brigade (mot) finally pulled back through the city and across the Dnieper bridges which were already rigged for demolition and that night the Soviet Western Front mounted an all-out attack to finally capture the city.

By 4 October, 4.Army was dug in on the western bank of the Dnieper where 1.SS-Infantry Brigade (mot.) was again subordinated to 25.Panzer Grenadier Division, within XXXIX.Panzer Corps. In acting as fire Brigade for 4.Army the brigade had had its fighting strength halved in less than four weeks of fighting, with forty one of its 109 front line officers becoming casualties.[123] However, despite its losses, the brigade remained on a defensive footing in the front line and more than held its own, as a Wehrmacht communiqué dated 15 October indicated:

> Yesterday vigorous breakthrough attempts by the Soviets again failed west of Krichev, and especially west of Smolensk. Forty-six Soviet tanks were destroyed in the combat zone southwest of Smolensk. In the last three days the enemy lost a total of 354 tanks and 233 aircraft in his vain attacks... The 1st SS Motorized Volunteer Grenadier Brigade distinguished itself in the fierce defensive struggle in the central sector of the front.[124]

Near constant attacks by Russian ground attack aircraft continued to take its toll of casualties, but the brigade was not entirely defenceless in the face of this bombardment and on 15 October the quadruple flak gun assigned to the regimental headquarters of SS-Infantry Regiment 10 succeeded in shooting down an Il-2 fighter bomber.[125]

In mid-October, while the fighting continued to rage, the units of the 1.SS-Infantry Brigade (mot) were officially re-numbered in order to fit into the numerical sequence for existing Waffen-SS regiments. This was the first official confirmation that the brigade was to be converted from what was essentially a security unit to a frontline fighting force and was a prelude to it being built up to divisional strength. SS-Infantry Regiment 8 became SS-Grenadier Regiment 39 while SS-Infantry Regiment 10 received the title of SS-Grenadier Regiment 40. The artillery battalion and motorcycle, anti-tank, flak, signals, and field replacement companies were numbered '51'.

There was also the intention of raising a new SS-Grenadier Regiment 41 to turn the brigade into the equivalent of an army infantry division, but this idea was dropped in favour of a two-regiment Panzergrenadier divisional structure. After the creation of 18-SS-Freiwilligen-Panzergrenadier Division 'Horst Wessel', SS-Grenadier Regiment 41 was never created and the senior regiment of 19.SS-Grenadier Division was numbered 42, leaving a curious gap in the sequencing.[126]

At around the same time, an excerpt from XXXIX.Panzer Corps order of the day dated 23 October 1943 was full of praise for the actions fought by 1.SS-Infantry Brigade (mot) throughout September: 'In particular, the Brigade prevented a breakthrough by far superior hostile forces against Smolensk whilst engaged in heavy combat SE of the city. In doing so it enabled the city to be evacuated without major difficulty.'[127]

Amidst administrative rearrangements and congratulatory proclamations, the fighting went on unabated. The brigade was ground down in the war of attrition as a signaller from the newly designated SS-Nachrichten-Kompanie 51 remembered: 'Such a determined defence did require a price: The rear areas (for us in Dubrowno) were constantly "combed out". Whoever could be spared from the office, to the unemployed radio operator, were sent to the infantry regiments.'[128]

On 10 November, the Soviet 1.Belorussian Front began its major offensive to break out of its Dnieper bridgehead and advance to the Gomel-Bobruisk area. The attack was led by 48. 61. and 65.Armies which battered their way through the positions of the weakened German divisions and reached Retschitza (thirty-five miles to the west of Gomel) in just over one week.

As the German formations were forced back westwards 1.SS-Infantry Brigade (mot) was ordered to form a Kampfgruppe from its operational remnants under the command of SS-Obersturmbannführer Trabandt, which was to be immediately redeployed to the area east of Bobruisk between the Dniepr and Beresina Rivers, right in the path of the advancing Soviet armies. The combat group was placed under LV.Army Corps control, within 9.Army, in mid-November and was immediately thrown into heavy and costly defensive fighting south of Klitschev. Even while this fighting was going on and the infantry battalions were sustaining heavy casualties, the brigade was further weakened on 2 December by the detachment of SS-Kampfgruppe 'Wiedemann', a battalion-size force drawn from SS-Grenadier Regiment 39 (formerly SS-Infantry Regiment 8) under the command of SS-Sturmbannführer Harry Wiedemann. This battle group was pulled out of the fighting and sent south to screen the bridgehead that the Soviets had established on the west bank of the Beresina River near Parichi. While the bridgehead remained quiet for the most part as the Russians marshalled their strength, the battle group fought several pitched battles against Soviet partisans who were intent on cutting the German force's rearward communications.

In the meantime, a shortening of the frontline in LV.Corps' sector had allowed the remainder of the Brigade to be withdrawn from action in the first few days of December and these elements were sent to SS-Training Camp Stablack (Stablawki) near Königsberg in East Prussia to rest and reequip. SS-Kampfgruppe 'Wiedemann' remained in action until the end of December when it was able to re-join the bulk of the brigade that had already left.[129]

3

EXPANSION TO DIVISIONAL STRENGTH

On 25 January 1944, the SS-Hauptamt (SS Main Leadership Office) issued order *SS-FHA Tgb.Nr. 179/44 g.Kdos.* specifying the expansion of the 1.SS-Infantry Brigade (mot) into the 18.SS-Freiwilligen-Panzergrenadier Division. On January 30, 1944, Hitler gave the division the honour title 'Horst Wessel' after the murdered SA-Sturmführer and ordered that the division should be 'predominantly composed of SA volunteers'.[1]

The expansion of 1.SS-Infantry Brigade (mot) to divisional strength was a symptom of a wider problem across all of the German armed forces; namely that Hitler and his immediate circle revered quantity, usually at the expense of quality.

The way in which the SS-FHA chose to expand the Waffen-SS was to use cadres of experienced men of all ranks from established divisions and form the new divisions around them using levies of raw recruits. Under these circumstances the older divisions tended to select the men for transfer that they felt that they could do without; the troublemakers, the lazy or those who were judged to lack sufficient aggression or initiative.[2]

However, many of these soldiers possessed significant frontline experience and their loss naturally led to a dilution in the quality of the older elite Waffen-SS divisions. Problems with unit cohesion were further exacerbated by a refusal to guarantee that any wounded soldiers would be returned to their original units once they had recuperated. This procedure was in total contrast to the Red Army's policy of reconstituting its old elite divisions rather than creating new ones, bringing them back up to strength with drafts of new recruits and therefore preserving their unity, traditions and fighting spirit.

As a result, the newly formed German divisions never reached the same levels of combat effectiveness as the original divisions, but Hitler believed that the political ideology of the Waffen-SS division significantly added to their combat performance, which partly explains their proliferation in the last year of the war.[3]

At the beginning of February 1944, the surviving elements of 1.SS-Infantry Brigade (mot) were concentrated in the Agram (Zagreb)-Cilli (Celje) areas of Croatia and Slovenia with the newly promoted SS-Standartenführer Trabandt assigned to lead the new division.[4]

The division was to consist of the full complement of units possessed by an SS-Panzergrenadier Division with two fully mechanised infantry regiments, ideally with a battalion from each mounted in half-tracked armoured personnel carriers, a self-propelled artillery regiment and a Panzer *Abteilung* combining to form the main striking force. The term Abteilung, literally meaning 'Detachment', was usually applied to non-infantry units with the equivalent strength of about a battalion.

Command and control of the division was provided by the divisional commander and his headquarters staff which usually contained at least 160 personnel for planning, communications and administrative purposes and was complete with motorcycle messengers, a mapping section, and an escort company for local defence.

The quality of Waffen-SS unit leadership had improved exponentially with its accumulated combat experience. They were no longer derided as 'troop killers' by their Wehrmacht counterparts as they had been in 1940, but the quality of staff work at divisional level and higher was still less than satisfactory even by 1944. It has been suggested that this was in large part due to the aggressive nature of the Waffen-SS and its established nature as an elite fighting force, where its leadership put more emphasis upon combat commands and had little time for the much less glamourous administrative side of soldiering. Additionally, the Waffen-SS was essentially still a young organisation and did not have the long tradition or esprit de corps that the Wehrmacht General Staff had developed over decades.

These factors had resulted in several large-scale administrative debacles that lead to the loss of much needed food, ammunition and medical supplies to the enemy and ultimately weakened the combat troop's ability to fight. One of the most prominent of these staffing errors was committed by IX.SS-Mountain Corps after it had been designated to defend the city of Budapest. This staff positioned the Corps' supply dumps too far to the west of the city and failed to ensure sufficient transport should the supplies need to be moved at short notice. The result was that on Christmas Eve 1944 the Red Army encircled Budapest and captured 450 tonnes of ammunition and 300,000 units of rations sorely needed by the besieged defenders.[5]

To mitigate against the inexperience of Waffen-SS trained staff officers, the most important staff roles were often filled by Army officers with relevant training who were transferred to Waffen-SS units as the need arose, regardless of whether they wished to go or not. For example, as early as 1943, Colonel-Leutnant Rüdiger Pipkorn was transferred into the Waffen-SS and served as Chief of Staff with II.SS-Panzer Corps before being raised to the command of 35.SS-Police Division with the rank of SS-Standartenführer. He was killed at the head of his division in the last days of the war. According to Pipkorn himself, he was given no choice in the matter and was simply transferred to the Waffen-SS, regardless of his wishes.[6] As the war turned against Germany, it is likely that most Wehrmacht officers would have preferred to distance themselves from the Waffen-SS and their methods.

The divisional staff was directed by the First General Staff Officer (la), which was essentially the role of Chief of Staff that only existed in Corps level commands and above in the German military. The First General Staff Officer was responsible for the operational and tactical leadership of the division and as a rule was one of only two specially trained staff officers within a division. In Wehrmacht units the abbreviation 'i.G.' for 'in the General Staff' followed the officer's rank and denoted that he had graduated from the prestigious General Staff course. An officer carried this with him when seconded to the Waffen-SS.

Within the 18.SS-Panzergrenadier Division, the original First General Staff Officer was Major Erich Wulff who was transferred from the army (period photographs show him in SS uniform with the rank of SS-Sturmbannführer) followed by SS-Sturmbannführer Emil Stürzbecher and finally another army man, Major i.G. Gunther Wind, who joined the division in the autumn of 1944 and remained in this role for the rest of the war.[7]

The Second General Staff Officer (Ib) was usually the only other trained staff officer and was primarily the quartermaster who led a staff of roughly fifty officers and men who coordinated the delivery of supplies to the division and their distribution to sub-units. In the wake of Operation *Barbarossa* the German High Command envisaged its troops 'living off the land' with the aim of feeding their troops entirely from the occupied territories, which inevitably made the supply staffs of many divisions complicit in plundering conquered territory. Department (Ib) was also responsible for implementing occupation policy in the divisional area when the division was in a fixed defensive position or pulled out of the line to a rear area for refitting. However, in practice this duty usually devolved to higher commands.

The Third General Staff Officer (Ic) acted as intelligence officer and worked closely with the reconnaissance unit, where he was largely involved with gaining an accurate picture of the type and strength of any opponent that the division faced. This officer also had responsibility for questions of morale within the division, propaganda, and any dealings with the press. The Third General Staff Officer also assisted the Ia in his everyday duties and was directly subordinate to him. Each of the three primary staff officers was also assisted by an orderly officer. The Ic for 18.SS-Panzergrenadier Division was SS-Hauptsturmführer Stüber who held this post from the division's creation until the disintegration of the division in the last days of the war.[8]

While the above-mentioned staff officers and their departments essentially dealt with the operational aspects of running the division and keeping it supplied, Adjutant's Departments IIa and IIb were responsible for matters of human resources; pay, promotions, training etc. Department III was in charge of legal matters including court martials within the division. Medical, veterinary and administrative services belonged to Department IV. Technically, the division was fully motorised, but in practice horse-drawn transport was used on an ad hoc basis as and when circumstances demanded.[9]

The fighting arm of the division was centred on two Panzergrenadier regiments and an artillery regiment. The newly titled SS-Panzergrenadier Regiment 39 had three battalions plus flak, infantry gun and pioneer companies. Each regiment also had an integral anti-tank gun element. SS-Panzergrenadier Regiment 40 possessed the same composition as Regiment 39. SS-Artillery Regiment 18 theoretically had four battalion-sized Abteilung, each with one heavy and two light batteries.

The three main fighting units of the division were supported by ancillary units of roughly battalion strength, each trained and equipped for a specialised task. SS-Panzer Abteilung 18 was to be equipped with three batteries of ten Sturmgeschütz III assault guns plus a headquarters unit with two more assault guns. The Panzer unit had a maintenance section that probably assisted with repairs throughout the division. SS-Panzer Aufklärungs (reconnaissance) Abteilung 18 (hereafter abbreviated to SS.Pz.Aufkl.Abt.18) was planned to have one armoured car company, two mechanised companies in half-tracked vehicles and a heavy support company. SS.Pz.Aufkl.Abt.18 contained three batteries of ten tank destroyers or assault guns plus a headquarters unit with two more guns. SS-Pioneer Battalion 18 contained three pioneer companies and a light bridging column. SS-Flak Abteilung 18 was to be armed with one heavy and three light batteries of anti-aircraft guns.

The frontline support units of the division consisted of SS-Sanitäts (medical) Abteilung 18 possessing one ambulance and one medical company and SS-Nachrichten (signals) Abteilung 18, which had one radio and one telephone company plus a headquarters element. There were also the usual rear echelon elements of the division including a Feld Ersatz (Field replacement) Battalion for training and integrating new recruits, a supply troop and truck park, butcher and bakery units, field post office and military police.[10]

However, from the start there several serious deficiencies within the new division. The Panzerjäger-Abteilung and the Pioneer Battalion, as well as the pioneer companies of the two Panzergrenadier Regiments and the pioneer platoon from the reconnaissance unit, were created at the same time as the rest of the divisional units, but due to lack of equipment and length of training time they did not join the division until a year after its inception in February 1945. The reconnaissance unit never possessed a 1.Company, receiving armoured cars only in the very last weeks of the war, while the division remained deficient in every type of artillery piece, with the Artillery Regiment always missing at least one Abteilung, or a quarter of its strength, at any one time.

As the 1.SS-Infantry Brigade (mot) moved from East Prussia to the division's formation area at the beginning of February 1944, the various units found that their billets straddled two command zones. Those on the Croatian side of the border came under the nominal command of LXIX.Army Corps z.b.V of 2.Panzer Army, the acronym z.b.V. stood 'for special purposes' and usually denoted an ad hoc unit temporarily created for a specific task, which in this case was a combat command to control the expanding partisan movement in Croatia, while those on the Slovenian side of the border in the Untersteiermark region came under XVII Army Corps, a reserve army organisation based in Vienna.[11]

For those troops located in Croatia, there was disproportion between their military pay, the official exchange rate and high prices which were not experienced by those units fortunate enough to be stationed on Reich territory. There were also frequent delays in the delivery of food supplies to the troops in Croatia, which could not be made good locally for lack of both money and resources. This did little to enhance morale of the men just returned from the fierce battles around Smolensk.

Recruiting for the new division foundered from the start as the vast majority of SA members were already serving in the Wehrmacht or staffing administrative posts across the Reich. Additionally, given the history of animosity between the SA and SS no self-respecting SA man would have willingly served with an SS division, regardless of its honour title. Two months after its official formation, the division was still short of almost 10,000 men and lacked 3,500 vehicles. The provision of even basic necessities was so poor that only enough equipment was available to outfit 4,000 men in any case. Specialist troops of every type were lacking, even down to clerks to staff the various headquarters. There was also a chronic shortage of drivers.

Between 5–7 March, the parts of the division which were billeted in the LXIX.Army Corp z.b.V. zone of operations were obliged to take part in Operation *Schneeschmelze* (Melting Snow) against partisan forces in the immediate vicinity of Agram and areas to the north. Infantry elements of the division supported by three companies of the Landesschützen Battalion 649 were used to form a barrier to cordon off the Reich border from potential infiltration, although no action was reported by these troops.[12]

Less than two months after instructions were issued to raise the division, with no new recruits having been mustered and during the reorganisation of its unit, SS-Oberführer Tranbandt received the order to prepare a combat-worthy unit to participate in Operation *Margarethe*, the German occupation of Hungary.

Operation Margarethe

In the autumn of 1943 Germany's military position in southern and Eastern Europe was critically undermined by the swift and largely unexpected defection of Italy to the Allied cause. The so-called 'soft underbelly of Europe' was now exposed to the onslaught of the Anglo-American armies currently campaigning in Italy, who were looking to exploit any opportunity to expand their activities into the Balkans. Germany was now seriously concerned by the wavering commitment of its other allies – primarily Hungary and Romania – as the Eastern Front crept closer to their borders.

With insufficient resources to occupy both countries, OKW decided to concentrate its planning efforts on Hungary, which appeared to be the most eager to escape the war following the utter destruction of its 2.Army on the north flank of Stalingrad. Therefore, the Wehrmacht's Operations Staff devised Operation *Margarethe*, which envisioned partial German military occupation, prioritising the capture of the critical Hungarian oilfields and associated infrastructure, and other key strategic targets.[13]

By the spring of 1944, the German intelligence services had uncovered ample evidence that the Hungarian Prime Minister, Miklós Kállay, had been negotiating an armistice with the Allies with the approval of Hungary's Regent, Admiral Miklós Horthy, which prompted Hitler to initiate Operation *Margarethe*. However, this move coincided with the launch of the Soviet's spring offensive, which forced the Germans to divert several battle-hardened divisions that had been earmarked for the operation back to the frontline. With the plan faltering from the outset, Hitler had to employ a ruse to mitigate against his lack of experienced troops. He invited Horthy to the Schloss Klessheim, near Salzburg in Austria on 18 March, ostensibly to discuss Hungarian-German co-operation, to keep Horthy out of the country and deny their army its commander in chief as German forces quietly moved in.[14]

Generalfeldmarschall von Weichs, who in his role as Oberbefehlshaber Südost was the overall commander of the southeast front, bore the responsibility for carrying out the occupation. Operational command was in the hands of Generalleutnant Foertsch, the Chief of Staff of Army Group F.[15] The forces under Foertsch's control were clearly insufficient to gain effective control of the entire country and the plan called for the seizure of all key installations west of the Tisza River, which would cut off the eastern quarter of the country and become a bulwark against those Hungarian troops still in action against the Russians.

The occupation force approached from four directions, and each was composed of fully motorised troops to aid with the element of surprise. D-Day was scheduled for 19 March with the operation planned to commence at 04.00. As any reaction to the occupation would come from either the Hungarian government or Armed Forces Headquarters it was essential to gain control of Budapest at the earliest stage of the operation. This was to be carried out by troops supposedly transiting through Hungary on the eve of the operation. They would be ideally placed to overwhelm any resistance in the city. The capture of Budapest was carried out by troops of the highly experienced Brandenburg Panzergrenadier Division supported by the Panzer Lehr Division. Once these troops were in position, the operation began in earnest.[16]

LVIIl.Reserve Panzer Corps was charged with the invasion of Hungary from Austria, advancing southeast towards the capital in two columns with Panzer Lehr Division aiming to take the northern cities of Györ (Raab) and Komaron en route to Budapest. 16.SS-Panzergrenadier Division 'Reichsführer-SS' was directed towards Stuhlweissenburg and Budapest by way of Sopron, Sarvar and Veszprem.

A second force crossed the border from Slovakia to secure the industrial area around the city of Miscolc and take control of the Tisza bridges between the Slovak border and Szolnok to the southeast of Budapest. This task fell to LXXVIII.Army Corps z.b.V. and for this mission it controlled three replacement regiments from the elite Grossdeutschland, Feldherrnhalle and Brandenburg divisions with attached supporting units.

A southern force, commanded by XXIl.Gebirgs (Mountain) Corps, was sub-divided into three battle groups built around Grenadier Regiment (mot) 92, 42.Jäger Division and 8.SS-Cavalry Division 'Florian Geyer'. Each unit advanced north out of Serbia and up the west bank of the Tisza, neutralising garrisons and seizing bridges and airfields as they moved north to screen the Budapest operation from interference from the east.

Finally, the southwestern prong of the takeover was under the auspices of LXIX.Army Corps z.b.V. with several divisional sized Kampfgruppe under command. The first was built around 1.Gebirgs

(Mountain) Division and was tasked with seizing bridges over the Drava river marking the border between Hungary and the former Kingdom of Yugoslavia, before seizing the important railway junction and industrial facilities at Fünfkirchen.

The second divisional group, designated Kampfgruppe Zwade after Generalmajor Zwade of the 367.Infantry Division who commanded it, consisted of the entirety of that division with as strong a unit as could possibly be provided from 18.SS-Panzergrenadier Division attached alongside bridging unit Brüko (mot) B 815.[17]

The embryonic 18.SS-Panzergrenadier Division was in a parlous state when it received the order to form a battle group for inclusion in *Margarethe*, possessing little more than the burnt-out remnants of 1.SS-Infantry Brigade (mot) that had been withdrawn from Russia the previous winter. Under the circumstances, the division was only able to man and equip a battalion-sized unit commanded by SS-Sturmbannführer Hörnicke of Ill./SS-Panzer-Grenadier Regiment 40. The battle group was very mixed indeed and contained personnel from virtually every service within the division, built around an ad hoc rifle battalion drawn from both grenadier regiments, a heavy company and single battery of light howitzers, supported by medical and supply troops.[18]

Kampfgruppe Hörnicke moved out of its staging areas to the northeast of Agram and joined Kampfgruppe Zwade as it crossed the Drava River at Varazdin and moved eastwards along both shores of Lake Balaton to capture another vital communications and industrial centre at Stuhlweissenburg. Next, the whole force moved on to their primary task of securing the oilfields at Lispe and the industrial complexes around Aika and Urkut.[19]

Upon his return to Budapest after a fruitless and frustrating meeting, Admiral Horthy was greeted by a German honour guard as he descended from his train to find that his country had been effectively garrisoned. The German Foreign Ministry informed Horthy that Hungary could only retain sovereign by removing Kállay and instating a pro-German Prime Minister. On 23 March they issued a six-hour ultimatum for Horthy to accede to their demands, which he reluctantly did, appointing Döme Sztójay who had formerly been Hungarian ambassador in Berlin.[20]

By the end of March Nagykanizsa had been captured and Kampfguppe Hörnicke was employed in security duties in the oil-producing region of Lispe, while also covering bridges over the Mur River and Tapolca airfield. During the planning phase for *Margarethe* it had been decided that several of the divisions involved in the operation should remain in Hungary on occupation duty while they either completed their training or refitted. 18.SS-Panzergrenadier Division was one unit chosen for relocation. On 16 March 1944 the division's formation area was transferred to the Verbas (Brvas) area in the Batschka and it was to this region that Kampfguppe Hörnicke went at the beginning of May following the peacefully ending of its deployment.[21]

Waffen-SS recruitment in Hungary

At the time of the invasion of Russia the Waffen-SS had a combat strength of 95,868 men of whom ninety per cent were Germans from within the borders of the German Reich.[22] As early as the winter of 1941 even the most credulous of Nazis could see that the war in the east was going to be a much bloodier and more protracted affair than most had appreciated six months previously. Despite the decimation of entire Russian armies, the Wehrmacht and Waffen-SS had both incurred huge losses.[23] By 1943 severe manpower shortages were beginning to affect both the combat efficiency of the frontline Waffen-SS Divisions and the SS-Hauptamt's ability to raise new ones. It is estimated that even before the battle of Kursk, more than one third of the fighting soldiers of the original Waffen-SS Divisions had fallen in Russia, and Himmler was forced to consider recruits who would never have passed inspection in the early years. With Waffen-SS recruitment all but dried up in Germany and the flow of Germanic volunteers from the northern European countries reduced to a trickle, it was the turn of the central European Volksdeutsche to play their part.[24]

Volksdeutsche were essentially 'persons of German origin who did not belong to the German state as residents or citizens', while Reichsdeutsche were nationals of the German Reich.[25] In the early 1940s there were an estimated 10 million Volksdeutsche living in Europe, largely scattered through the central and eastern European states,[26] and these were a resource that the Waffen-SS were forced to make use of at an early point in the war in the east. The result was that in 1943, twenty-five per cent of new recruits were Volksdeutsche, foreigners by birth but of German descent. Added to this were large drafts of redundant Luftwaffe ground crew and Kriegsmarine personnel who, although largely German by birth, did not possess the ideological zeal of the early volunteers.[27] By the end of 1944 the Waffen-SS consisted of approximately 400,000 German citizens, 310,000 Volksdeutsche and 200,000 foreign volunteers.[28]

Stymied by the total lack of SA volunteers for the new 18.SS-Panzergrenadier Division during the first half of 1944 the majority of the recruits that were provided to expand the 1.SS-Infantry Brigade (mot) to divisional strength came from the Batschka and Banat regions of central Europe. The Batschka was a strip of land straddling the border between southern Hungary and the then Kingdom of Yugoslavia. The Banat, principally the western part, or Serbian Banat, was a large tract of land to the northeast of Belgrade. The German minority in these areas had migrated during the eighteenth century but regarded themselves as Swabians, essentially more German than Hungarian or Yugoslav and some still used German as their first language.[29]

The Banat was home to many different nationalities and ethnic groups, largely due to shifting land borders following the collapse of the Habsburg Empire, with the Volksdeutsche making up a significant minority. In the Serbian Banat there were somewhere in the region of 120,000 Volksdeutsche representing approximately one fifth of the population. After the fall of Yugoslavia in 1941 the Banat region came under the direct control of Berlin and the Banat Volksdeutsche were given preferential treatment by the Nazi regime over the natives of their homeland under a deliberate policy of divide and rule. Many Volksdeutsche farmers were given grants of land taken from dispossessed Jews and Slavs. The middle classes provided bureaucrats to administer their local regions, again at the expense of the native population. The antagonism fostered by this policy meant that the Volksdeutsche communities became reliant upon the military might of the Wehrmacht to support their new prominence, which in turn had to be paid for in both goods and services, food for the Reich and conscription into the armed forces.

Being of German origin the Volksdeutsche ranked highly in the Nazis' racial hierarchy and were therefore seen as a useful and suitable source of manpower for the Waffen-SS. While some recruits saw it as their duty to serve their ancestral homeland, many more were coerced by the threat of what would happen to their families if the Germans withdrew their support for their communities.[30]

For his part, Himmler was convinced that all members of the German race, whatever their formal citizenship status, shared its fate and must therefore fulfil their obligations, which included military service, ideally in the Waffen-SS.[31] Himmler's vision was largely enacted through the Volksdeutsche Mittelstelle (VoMi) or Ethnic German Liaison Office, which co-ordinated central government activities concerning Volksdeutsche communities living abroad. Although never formally part of the SS, VoMi fell into its sphere of influence and acted as a rallying point for Volksdeutsche enrolment into the Waffen-SS and other security organisations.[32]

Recruitment reached staggering proportions and a report indicated that 'a chronic labour shortage [was] exacerbated in 1942 by the conscription of virtually all able-bodied Banat Volksdeutsche into the Waffen-SS.'[33] By the end of 1943, more than 22,000 Germans from the Serbian Banat had served in the armed forces of the Third Reich, most of them having passed through the ranks of 7.SS-Gebirgsjäger Division 'Prinz Eugen', although a large number were also sent to 1.SS-Infantry Brigade (mot),[34] and subsequently served in 18.SS-Panzergrenadier Division 'Horst Wessel'.

Despite being adjacent tracts of land, there were significant differences between the recruitment procedures in the Batschka to those in the Banat. While the Serbian Banat, as already mentioned, was under direct German control with a Serbian Volksdeutsche administration directly implementing Berlin's conscription policy, the Batschka was part of Hungary, the Volksdeutsche community being eligible for conscription into the Honvéd, the Royal Hungarian Army.

After the Axis conquest of Yugoslavia, the Germans allowed the Hungarians to occupy the Yugoslav Batschka, the Baranya and a small part of Northern Slovenia known as Prekomurje. These areas collectively were home to an estimated 175,000 Volksdeutsche bringing the total number living under Hungarian rule to around 700,000. This was the largest German minority group concentration in Europe and would provide fertile ground for the Waffen-SS recruiters in the following years.[35]

Initially, the various ministries of government of the Third Reich were reluctant to antagonise Hungary over the utilisation of the Hungarian Volksdeutsche for service within the German forces. The Germans needed to preserve the good will of the Budapest government to keep the Hungarian Army fighting in the meat grinder of the Russian Front. However, these practical considerations did not prevent the SS from employing underhand tactics to attract 'volunteers'.

Young Volksdeutsche men were lured to the Reich by Waffen-SS recruiters with a promise of generous work placements or sporting scholarships, only to be subjected to propaganda, military training, and pressure from their home communities to enlist, although these tactics met with limited success.[36]

It was in the Balkans, in the states that were allied to Germany but essentially still independent, that the head of recruitment for the Waffen-SS, SS-Obergruppenführer Gottlob Berger, encountered the upmost difficulty in recruiting ethnic Germans, which was in no small part due to his personal history. Berger had been a very early convert to National Socialism and had been an enthusiastic member of the SA until he was expelled from that organisation over a fracas with a subordinate. Following the 'Night of the Long Knives' and with the SA leadership still reeling, Berger had spied an opportunity to ingratiate himself back into its ranks, but after swearing undying loyalty to the SA leadership he entered into an alliance with SA-Obergruppenführer Friedrich-Wilhelm Krüger who was regarded as a traitor within the SA for aiding the SS in Röhm's downfall and in fact left to join the SS soon afterwards. Berger's association with Krüger led to Berger being ordered before a court of arbitration, which again sought to expel him, but he 'jumped ship' before a verdict could be reached and also joined the SS. The whole episode caused a festering resentment between all parties involved. Unfortunately for the SS Volksdeutsche recruitment policy, three of the judges on the arbitration panel were SA-Obergruppenführers Hanns Ludin, Dietrich von Jagow and Adolf-Heinz Beckerle.[37]

These men were three of a group of five SA Generals that headed important German legations from 1940 onwards. Siegrfried Kasch was appointed as ambassador to Croatia in 1940, Manfred von Killinger was sent to Romania, Ludin represented German interests in Slovakia from December 1940, Beckerle managed diplomatic interests in Bulgaria and most importantly of all, von Jagow was placed in Hungary.

All five of these men were 'Old Fighters' for the Nazi cause and Ludin, Beckerle, von Killinger and Kasch had only survived the 'Night of the Long Knives' by swearing personal allegiance to the Führer. It was Hitler himself who appointed these SA men to their foreign postings as insurance against opposition from the old guard of professionally trained diplomats and as a counterweight to SS influence in foreign affairs.[38] All entreaties from Himmler to governments allied to Germany for recruiting rights amongst their ethnic German populations had to be presented through the offices of the German embassy in each country, putting the SA Generals in a perfect position to hinder efforts to enlarge the Waffen-SS.

As the military crisis deepened, at the beginning of 1942 Himmler made increasingly frantic appeals to the Reich Foreign Office to intercede with Budapest to allow Waffen-SS recruitment offices to open on their territory. In February, the Hungarians agreed to the voluntary enlistment of 20,000 Volksdeutsche, although stipulating that the volunteers would be stripped of their Hungarian citizenship and that Germans already serving in the Hungarian armed forces were exempt. 18,000 new recruits were enlisted, much to the chagrin of the Hungarian military authorities who did everything in their power to both hinder recruitment at a local level and withhold payments made to the dependents of fallen SS men by the Reich, which resulted in falling morale and recruitment.

Following the disaster at Stalingrad in March 1943, Himmler sought a further 30-50,000 recruits from Hungary and this time the Hungarian government, haunted by its own military debacle in Russia, removed the constraints previously imposed, making Germans serving in the Honvéd eligible for call-up to the Waffen-SS. By the end of 1943, 22,125 Hungarian Volksdeutsche were serving in the ranks of the Waffen-SS, but this recruitment success was vastly outstripped by the catastrophic losses suffered as the military fortunes of the Third Reich plummeted.[39]

These relatively ineffective recruitment efforts persisted until the completion of Operation *Margarethe* and the German occupation of Hungary, which led the Hungarian authorities to look upon SS recruiting practices in a more favourable light. Immediately following the German intervention, a delegation led by SS-Obergruppenführer Georg Keppler visited the Honvéd (Hungarian Armed Forces) Minister, Lajos Csatay, on 25 March 1944 and demanded a new agreement regarding drafting recruits into the SS. The Germans complained that only five per cent of the men residing in Hungary who were eligible for recruitment into the Waffen-SS had joined up while the figure was closer to twenty five percent for Volksdeutsche populations in neighbouring countries. To remedy this shortfall the SS-Hauptamt wanted to scrap all previous agreements and carry out compulsory screening for everyone the Volksbund, the association that represented Germans living in foreign countries, declared to be German.[40]

The Hungarian government naturally disputed this and there was a great deal of disagreement between the German and Hungarian authorities over the question of whom amongst the Volksdeutsche communities should be classed as being German. The Volksbund considered anyone with three German grandparents to be of German descent, while the Hungarians insisted that only those who considered themselves to be German and had indicated this in the 1941 census could be classed as such.[41] Eventually, a new agreement was hammered out and signed by Prime Minister Sztöjay on 14 April 1944:

> The members of the German nationality, persons with Hungarian citizenship, without citizenship and with foreign citizenship are placed at the disposal of the German Wehrmacht (Waffen-SS) by mutual agreement for the duration of the war.[42]

This document rendered all Germans between the ages of 17 to 62 subject to compulsory military service and examining commissions were set up throughout the country to decide an individual's 'Germanness' on a case-by-case basis. An amendment to the agreement on 30 May made it legal for ethnic German women to be allowed to be recruited into SS auxiliary units, primarily in medical and signals units.[43]

Understandably, there were significant numbers of Hungarian Germans who did not want to enlist in the Waffen-SS and many of these had to be escorted before the commissions for examination by gendarmes. There was much bitterness amongst large sections of the German-speaking population who, if they had to fulfil their military obligations at all, would have preferred to serve out their time in the Hungarian Army. This was highlighted in a letter to the Minister of the Interior Andor Jaross from the Volksdeutsche community in Dorog, which stated that they had been drafted into the Waffen-SS against their will: 'We have always felt and known ourselves as Hungarians, even with a German name... We have only one fatherland: Hungary.'[44]

SS-Obergruppenführer Berger blamed the Hungarian authorities in early July for the fact that only one division could be formed from a list of 202,000 names drawn up by the Volksbund commissioners, as the Hungarian military authorities had immediately crossed out 70,000 names citing concerns over their ethnicity. Another large group was also prevented from serving due to Hungarian claims that they were employed in vital economic or war work. Finally, by the end of August, the thirty active commissions had managed to agree upon 42,000 men who they deemed eligible for German military service and were allowed to sign on for the Waffen-SS.[45] Waffen-SS records showed that of these, 35,000 men 36-45 years old were inducted into its ranks while all older men were sent to the Order Police.[46]

These were the men that were used to flesh out the newly formed 18.SS-Panzergrenadier Division 'Horst Wessel' and 22.SS-Cavalry Division 'Maria Theresa'. In the Batschka, most recruits entered service in September and October 1944. By this stage of the war it was clear that Germany had no hope of winning and many Volksdeutsche men, especially the older ones, had no illusions about what fighting for the Waffen-SS would mean. Even at this late date there were a number of ethnic Germans who still attempted to enrol in the Honvéd to avoid service in the Waffen-SS, but the Hungarian authorities were prohibited from accepting them.[47]

It was obvious that numbers alone were not enough to win battles. After the great slaughter of the first winter of the war on the Eastern Front a large percentage of the idealistic volunteers who had filled out the pre-war ranks of the Waffen-SS had fallen, including a catastrophically high proportion of NCOs and junior officers who provided the backbone and the fighting spirit of the frontline regiments. Rumours of harsh discipline within the Waffen-SS combined with high casualty rates circulated amongst the recruits and it quickly became apparent that pressganged soldiers would only fight with great reluctance, while their indifference to the cause adversely affected the morale of their comrades. This was compounded by a woeful lack of training received by many recruits, as the charnel house of the Eastern Front did not allow for prolonged acclimatisation before they were thrust into action, significantly heightening the attrition rate and creating a vicious circle.[48]

A report from the headquarters of the 8.SS-Cavalry Division 'Florian Geyer' concluded that it was 'perfectly possible that many of the racial German volunteers do not regard this war as their own nor consider service in the Waffen-SS as their duty to the German people.'[49]

A further problem was frequently the language barrier. Many racial Germans could neither read nor write German and often had a poor grasp of the more technical vocabulary. In the heat of battle, it was found that orders relayed by telephone or radio were often misunderstood, with dire consequences. By mid-1944 the calibre of recruits had hit such a low point that it was recognised that the higher percentage of racial Germans a Waffen-SS Division possessed, the worse it performed.[50]

SS-Hauptscharführer Doctor Röhrs was assigned to SS-Pz.Aufkl. Abt.18 as the detachment's medical officer, and one of his first official duties was to stand in for the former Romanian Army doctor who was undertaking the physical inspections of the new draft of recruits for one of the division's Panzergrenadier regiments but who had fallen ill.

A special order was issued by the SS-Hauptamt that the medical screening could only be carried out by authorised groups of specialists formed for this purpose, rather than leaving the judgement of who was fit to serve to the regiments themselves; but under the circumstances the inspection had to be completed by an appointed date and Röhrs was drafted into the role.

Röhrs travelled from village to village in a motorbike and sidecar combination as the individual companies were spread out over a large area, with one unit sometimes being billeted across several villages. Eventually, he managed to classify more than a thousand men into the three distinct groups: fit, conditionally fit, and unfit. From the start Röhrs found himself under pressure to pass men who were clearly medically unfit for active service but could not do so in good conscience, and he declared a full third of those examined unfit. This decision caused a storm of protest from SS Command in Budapest, who berated the regimental commander for the shortfall in recruits.

However, when the regimental commander – who would have to lead these men in battle – made his own inspections he concurred fully with results of Röhrs' examinations and travelled directly to Budapest to complain about the standard of recruits being supplied to the division. A second medical commission was sent from Budapest to carry out a trial investigation, which arrived at the same conclusion, but this did not avail anything; the men stayed regardless of their health. It was an unpromising start for the division.[51]

The problems only multiplied when training began. The instructors were primarily Germans, used to dealing with German boys who had received pre-military training in the Hitler Youth. Only a tiny number of ethnic German youths had entered the Hungarian 'Levente' youth organisation and therefore had at least a notion of parade ground discipline, but most had to be taught everything from scratch. The older men posed a different problem. Many had been reservists in either the Hungarian or former Yugoslav armies and they often resented having to go through basic training again.[52]

Although some of the younger recruits treated their role in the Waffen-SS as a great adventure, at least until they were committed to action, there was a general attitude of war weariness, which became especially marked with the evacuation of the Volksdeutsche communities from the Batschka to Silesia and its subsequent occupation by the Red Army during October 1944. Many of the conscripted recruits took the first opportunity simply to run away and rejoin their families, while those who stayed suffered under harsh discipline compounded by severe shortages of weapons, uniforms, and rations. Apathy and belligerency were widespread and morale plummeted.[53]

In stark contrast to the Panzergrenadier regiments, many of the specialist sub-units within the division had a higher percentage of Reich German recruits and although many of these youths were as raw as their Volksdeutsche counterparts they tended to have better morale and unit cohesion. *SS-Panzer-Aufklärungs-Abteilung 18* proved to be one of the more reliable elements of the division, but its inception provides a good example of the rather haphazard way in which the divisional units were put together.

Elements of two companies of recruits were transferred from the II.SS-Aufklärungs-Ersatz-Abteilung (II.SS-Reconnaissance Replacement Detachment), at that time based in Latvia, to the small spa town of Rohitsch-Sauerbrunn in Lower Styria in Austria, where they were combined with sections of 51.SS-Motorcycle Company from 1-SS Infantry Brigade (mot). Wilhelm Tieke was assigned to the new 2./SS-Pz.Aufkl.Abt.18.

Only enough recruits arrived in the first draft to form one company, but from its creation it was assumed that the reconnaissance battalion would be committed to action sooner rather than later. Following the allotment of the men to their sub-units, priority was given to making the Abteilung combat ready.

One of its first tasks was to unload 200 *Schwimmwagen* light amphibious cars that arrive by rail in Cilli and had to be transferred to Rohitsch-Sauerbrunn. As none of the recruits had been taught to drive, any members of the company who dared were given the opportunity to partake in 'on the job training'. Almost unbelievably, the movement of the new *Schwimmwagen* was made without serious incident, but the lack of relevant training amongst recruits across the division was to be a recurring problem that was never fully addressed.

After three weeks in Rohitsch-Sauerbrunn the company was moved by train to Batsch-Topyla in the Batschka, but this proved to be just a short stopover with no time to settle into a steady training routine before they were moved again. In June 1944, the expanding companies of the reconnaissance battalion were finally brought together for the first time in the small Batschka town of Obecze where they began to be integrated into a single unit. It was here that SS-Sturmbannführer Sonne, former commander of the 51.SS-Motorcycle Company, was introduced as the Abteilung commander.[54]

Tieke, having previous frontline experience was promoted to SS-Unterscharführer and put in charge of a heavy machine gun troop, but most of his comrades were seventeen- and eighteen-year-olds and only three other men in his platoon had seen action before. There was a lack of experienced officers and NCOs and a general unfamiliarity with the weapons that they were issued.[55]

The lack of equipment and training time was compounded by the need to keep veteran divisions supplied at the front. Unhappily for Tieke and his colleagues in the reconnaissance battalion, the fledgling division was forced to give up the 200 schwimmwagen and also 300 trucks at the end of April to the 3.SS-Panzer Division 'Totenkopf' which was being refitted after another mauling in the east. This left 18.SS-Panzergrenadier Division almost totally immobile, which both incapacitated it tactically and of course had a detrimental effect on driver training.[56]

Equipping the new division

While the manpower problems involved in creating new divisions in the summer of 1944 were largely qualitative, the opposite was the case when it came to arming and equipping them. By this stage of the war German military hardware was certainly equal to, and in many cases better than, that fielded by the Allies, but German industry could not keep up with demand. In 1943 the Wehrmacht developed the concept of the Panzergrenadier division: powerfully armoured mechanised infantry units capable of surviving on the battlefield side by side with the Panzer divisions. The Wehrmacht's experiences on the Eastern Front, particularly at the battle of Kursk, had shown how vulnerable their tanks were to enemy infantry tank hunting teams when they were separated from their own accompanying infantry screen.

This idea was to expand the already existing motorised infantry divisions and mount their infantry in armoured personnel carriers that could keep pace with the Panzers wherever the ebb and flow of an armoured battle would take them. By the end of 1943, over 200 Panzergrenadier battalions were in existence, spread between the Army and Waffen-SS divisions, but only around 10 per cent of these were equipped with half-tracked armoured vehicles while the rest were truck-borne at best. Even the army's elite Groβdeutschland Panzergrenadier Division could only be outfitted with one half-track battalion per Panzergrenadier regiment[57] and it is unlikely that 18.SS-Panzergrenadier Division received any, aside from a few of the radio-equipped command versions used by divisional headquarters.

In the first few months of 1944 there were three new SS-Panzergrenadier Divisions being raised, numbered 16. 17. and 18. alongside a host of expanding SS Brigades and Legions of foreign volunteers, all of which had to be equipped to a standard where they could be used on a modern battlefield. However, by this date, the seven Waffen-SS Panzer divisions were soaking up the bulk of available armoured and soft-skinned vehicles, and those units further down the list of priorities just did not get their equipment needs met. The following example was typical of the paucity of materials for new divisions: '...in February 1944, 17.SS-PzGR Division Götz von Berlichingen had only 245 trucks out of the 1,686 it should have had and an almost complete absence of prime movers for the artillery!'[58]

The 1.SS-Infantry Brigade (mot) had been a small and relatively self-contained unit, but at full strength it had only about one third of the manpower and less than one quarter of the equipment of a full

Panzergrenadier Division. The brigade arrived at the formation area for the new division in a very battered state and in possession of a miscellany of arms and vehicles.

The brigade's flak and infantry gun units had standard Wehrmacht-issue weapons, although these were probably in quite an advanced state of disrepair after two and half years of service. Its 75mm anti-tank guns were reconditioned and rechambered First World War French Schneider field guns. The artillery battalion was largely equipped with French 155mm howitzers. The heavy weapons were towed by a selection of aging tractors and heavy trucks of German, Czech and French manufacture, and Russian soft-skinned vehicles had also been added to the inventory wherever they could be acquired intact. Its infantry was truck-borne and its reconnaissance element consisted of a motorcycle company with, at best, a platoon of armoured cars. Given the age, undoubted unreliability and logistical problems caused by such an eclectic mix of equipment, it was clear that most of the equipment that the division already possessed would have to be replaced to bring it up to standard.

However, as stated above, 18.SS-Panzergrenadier Division was already being stripped of its new vehicles to replenish the more established Waffen-SS divisions even as they were being delivered from the factories, forcing alternative equipment for the division to be acquired from all manner of disparate sources.

Some of the less militarily useful units that had been raised in more hopeful times were coming under closer scrutiny as the German armies began to fall back towards the borders of the Reich, and the SS-Supply Department began to cast a covetous eye over any assets that they may possess. One such unit was Indian Infantry Regiment 950, more widely known as 'The Indian Legion'. This unit had been raised from prisoners of war from the Indian sub-continent who had been captured in North Africa. Propagandists had played on the idea of granting India independence from the British Empire should German win the war, and this idea had found favour with a small minority of Indian servicemen in captivity.

The Indian Legion had spent much of its existence in fixed defensive positions along the Atlantic Wall in France but had been withdrawn prior to the Allied invasion of Normandy due to the German High Command's distrust of its motivation, morale and fighting abilities.

On 8 August 1944, this unit, along with all other units raised from non-German personnel that remained under German Army command, was transferred into the Waffen-SS, and became the *Indische Legion der Waffen-SS*. The Legion consisted of about 2,300 men divided into three battalions and the troops possessed small arms but lacked a heavy weapons component, although an anti-tank company is reported to have had six guns of unknown calibre in its inventory. It possessed 81 motor vehicles and 700 horses. Hitler had little faith in this force, apparently remarking, 'The Indian Legion is a joke,' before ordering that its weapons and equipment be handed over to the 18.SS-Panzergrenadier Division.[59]

Welcome as these assets were to the division, they were a mere drop in the bucket for a Panzergrenadier division that was lacking more than 3,500 vehicles.[60] Much more was needed, but the supply problems continued to multiply. The Allied bombing campaign against Germany's support infrastructure was reaching its peak, and as the front lines edged ever closer to Germany Allied aircraft were able to roam for targets of opportunity including railway junctions, bridges and even locomotives delivering vital war supplies.

The 31.SS-Grenadier Division was also formed in the Batschka during the summer and autumn of 1944 from the pool of men that had been rejected as too old or infirm for the 18.SS-Panzergrenadier Division. They were stationed for initial training in the towns of western Batschka, supposedly far from the fighting front. The division experienced a great shortage of uniforms as the train bringing these supplies from the depots was attacked by Allied aircraft based in Italy and a number of wagons were destroyed.[61] This was just one small incident in an ongoing aerial bombardment, the effects of which were felt on every front.

On 2 July 1944, the Chief Operations Officer at OKH briefed his opposite number at Army Group Centre regarding reinforcements in the wake of the Soviet advance during Operation *Bagration*. After almost two weeks of desperate defensive action Army Group Centre was on its knees, with many of its divisions totally routed. Several divisions were stripped from other fronts or snatched from forming-up areas to add weight to the hastily gathered 'March' Battalions and 'Valkyrie' Regiments that were being rushed in to prop up the sagging front. The 18.SS-Panzergrenadier Division 'Horst Wessel' was one of the 'major formations' that was earmarked for frontline employment with the remnant of 4. Army, which was on the point of disintegration. By this stage of the operation three shattered German Armies were in full retreat and Minsk, the capital of Belorussia, was effectively lost, forcing German High Command into making ever more reckless sacrifices to stem the flood.[62] Common sense eventually prevailed and the tried and tested 3.SS-Panzer Division 'Totenkopf' was sent in its place.[63] However, this proved to be a very brief stay of execution as Army Group North Ukraine would find itself under heavy attack before the month was out, and the most battle-worthy elements of 18.SS-Panzergrenadier Division would be flung into action in defence of western Ukraine.

4

GALICIA

June 1944 was a particularly bad month for the German forces fighting throughout Europe. On 4 June, Rome fell to the US Fifth Army, closely followed by the Allied landings in Normandy two days later. Then, on June 22, the Red Army launched Operation *Bagration* against German Army Group Centre, which led to its near total annihilation within a few short weeks. As the whole German position in the east tottered and the German High Command stripped much needed troops and equipment from the east – including the bulk of the Luftwaffe's remaining aircraft – to contain the powerful Allied forces in northern France, the Russian 1.Ukrainian Front began a second strike against Army Group North Ukraine on 13 July, with the twin aims of gaining a bridgehead over the Vistula in the region of Sandomierz on the direct line of advance to Berlin and trapping the bulk of the army group on the eastern side of the Carpathian mountains. The opening moves of this assault broke over the junction between the German 4.Panzer Army and 1.Panzer Army and quickly gained significant ground.[1]

The Soviet plan called for a multi-pronged attack to initiate the collapse of the German front over a wide area. In the north the weakened German XIII.Army Corps was to be totally enveloped by a pincer movement, while in the middle of Army Group North Ukraine's front the capture of the important road junction and industrial centre of L'vov would mean that it could be used as a jumping-off point for forcing the Carpathian passes. The capture of these passes would both cut off 1.Panzer Army from its rearward communications and facilitate the Soviet advance onto the open plains of Hungary and Czechoslovakia. Following their standard practice, the Red Army also concentrated strong forces for attacks against non-German troops who were known to be ill-equipped and poorly motivated; in this case the Hungarian 7.Army Corps, on the Army Group's southern flank.[2]

Three days after the commencement of the offensive the German XIII Corps was indeed surrounded in the Brody-Tarnow pocket and the 1.Guards Tank Army had sliced through the German lines, separating the 4.Army and 1.Panzer Army. Meanwhile, the 4.Tank Army was forcing the approaches to L'vov.[3] In desperate fighting, the remnants of the four divisions and various attached troops of XIII Corps had fought their way out of the encirclement, but these units were shattered as a military force and the reduction of the Brody-Tarnow Pocket freed up the besieging units to continue their advance to the west. By 20 July, General Konev was urging his 1.Guards Tank Army to push on to the city of Przemy'l lying 54 miles west of L'vov.[4] With the situation growing more desperate by the hour, reinforcements of any sort were needed as a matter of the greatest urgency.

On the night of 6-7 July 1944 SS-Sturmbannführer Christians, the Waffen-SS liaison officer at the Führer's Headquarters (FHQu), telephoned the headquarters of 18.SS-Panzergrenadier Division with orders to ready all available forces for frontline action. Objections were raised about the unsuitability of the division for combat operations – that the division was only at half strength and was not mobile – but these objections were ignored as every soldier was needed to face the unfolding catastrophe on the Eastern Front and the Führer himself had ordered the deployment of the division.[5]

The division had reached about sixty per cent of its target strength, and most of these numbers were provided by the bulk of 1.SS-Infantry Brigade (mot) that had been transferred en masse to the division. Although there was a good balance in the ratios of officers, NCOs and men in each unit, there was a complete lack of equipment and armaments to expand the existing units to divisional strength; and the largely untrained ethnic German recruits rendered the unit as a whole combat ineffective.

SS-Oberführer Trabandt ordered the formation of a Kampfgruppe from the most combat-ready elements of the roughly 8,500 soldiers who had been assembled for commitment to action in Galicia.

The result was a 4,000-strong all-arms force which was arranged as follows:

I./SS-Panzergrenadier-Regiment 39 with 13. (Infantry Gun or I.G.) and 14. (Flak) Companies attached.

I. and II./SS-Panzergrenadier Regiment 40 with 13. (I.G.) and 14. (Flak) Companies attached.

I./SS-Artillery-Regiment 18.

Four Sturmgeschütz III assault guns from SS-Panzer Abteilung 18, which was actually a battery of guns that had been transferred from 6.SS-Gebirgs (Mountain) Division 'Nord'.

2. and 3.Companies from SS-Pz.Aufkl.Abt.18 along with parts of the signals, medical and supply units.[6]

The Kampfgruppe was to be attached to Army Group North Ukraine with the role of supporting the increasingly unreliable Hungarian units on the southern flank of 1.Panzer Army, but it was hoped that this would be more of a precautionary measure given the obvious weakness of the battle group.[7] The lack of a realistic alternative was recorded in the war diary of Army Group North Ukraine (la Tgb.Nr. 3285/44 g.Kdos. from 15 July 1944):

> 1.Panzer-Armee had to fight the defensive battle ... while forming new reserves from their own area. Use of the K.Gr. '18.SS-Freiw. Div.' in the front line in the quiet front section is authorised.[8]

The preparations to leave their cantonment in Hungary were met with bewilderment by the rank and file. SS-Oberscharführer Tieke who was an old hand was dismayed at the chaos:

> The order to march came suddenly overnight. The Abteilung is not even complete. Our company gets staff from other companies, our platoon gets a platoon commander, an Untersturmfuhrer... Two companies and the staff of the Abteilung are loaded... When we don't unload at the large military training area in Debica ... we old people know that we're going to the front... We unload in Stanislau [Ivano-Frankivsk] in Galicia.[9]

The fledgling division was so understaffed and unprepared for action that experienced men had to be temporarily transferred from the battalions that were staying behind to make up the numbers. Even so, forty trains were still required to move the Kampfgruppe to their deployment area in eastern Poland, where SS-Oberführer Trabandt reported its arrival to General Raus, commander of 1.Panzer Army in Czereze, on 17 July.[10]

There was much confusion and evasion on the part of 1.Panzer Army headquarters regarding the placement of the Kampfgruppe, as it was more concerned with the disaster that had overtaken its XIII. Corps on its north flank. Under its initial proposed deployment, it was to be attached to LIX.Army Corps, which had been expecting it to be sent to its sector of the Strypa River near Osowce,[11] but without warning it was subordinated to XXIV Panzer Corps instead. The Kampfgruppe was to take over the positions of the 371.Infantry Division, which was in turn needed to clear up another crisis unfolding further north as the Red Army broke through towards L'vov.[12]

While Army command rated the combat effectiveness of the Kampfgruppe as 'limited'[13] it still insisted on it fulfilling a frontline role. Protests from Trabandt about the inadvisability of using a brigade-strength unit to cover the positions previously manned by a whole, if understrength, division were brushed aside with the excuse that the position was in a quiet sector of the front and easily defended.

The Kampfgruppe began relieving the first units of 371.Infantry Division on 18 July and took over their positions on the Strypa River between Petikowce and Zlotniki, in what was grandly known as the 'Prinz Eugen' position, which seems to have been a defensive line along the western bank of the Strypa, probably consisting of not much more than a line of earthen bunkers behind barbed wire entanglements and mines.

I./SS-Panzergrenadier Regiment 39 was deployed at the southern end of the line with the two companies of SS-Pz.Aufkl.Abt.18 in the centre and the two battalions of SS-Panzergrenadier Regiment 40 to the north along an eight-mile-long front. The main German position ran along high ground, mostly on the western bank of the river and consisted of a trench line interspersed with bunkers constructed from wood taken from the houses of villages through which the frontline passed.

Although the Strypa front remained quiet, on 19 July the Russians were hammering at the German defences to the north attempting to break through to L'vov, which would leave the positions on the Strypa prone to encirclement. In view of this the 75.Infantry Division, 18.SS-Panzergrenadier Division's northern neighbour, withdrew from their positions at 14.00 that day, leaving Kampfgruppe's left flank exposed.

According to the orders of XXIV Panzerkorps, 18.SS-Panzergrenadier Division's own withdrawal was to commence at 20.00, but SS-Oberführer Trabandt refused to wait in such an exposed position and, despite being threatened with court martial, ordered the Kampfgruppe to begin the retreat at 15.00. SS-Sturmbannführer Bildstein, commander of SS-Panzer Abteilung 18, was tasked with ensuring that each unit received the withdrawal order, but he was killed while driving along the front when his car encountered a Russian reconnaissance unit.[14]

Soviet interrogation of German prisoners and extensive reconnaissance had revealed that the Germans were attempting to pull back from their positions all along the Strypa River and 1.Ukrainian Front was determined to thwart this move and the potential it had to free up mobile forces to block its thrust towards L'vov. It therefore launched an offensive across a broad front to pin both XXXXVIII. Panzer Corps and XXIV.Panzer Corps to their existing defences.[15]

For their part, the German forces south of L'vov hoped to force a delay upon the Russian advance by using a series of river lines as anti-tank obstacles, but the defence of these waterways was constantly undermined by the powerful Soviet westerly advance on L'vov that outflanked these positions, even while they were being assaulted frontally.[16] 18.SS-Division's Kampfgruppe was at a particular disadvantage as it lacked both infantry and artillery to effectively defend each river line, forcing it to leapfrog back from one water barrier to the next to avoid being outflanked and cut off from the main German frontline.

1.Ukrainian Front was able to keep up a constant pressure on the SS riflemen as they retreated. Russian troops had become adept at improvising river crossing, utilizing the simplest of materials to cross even major water obstacles – as they had proved the year before when they had forced the crossing of the Dnieper, the largest river in Europe. Assault troops lashed together planks, logs, and barrels to form crude rafts sturdy enough to carry heavy machine guns and light artillery.

With their support weapons safely across the river, the infantry could widen their bridgehead sufficiently for the engineers to construct pontoon bridges for the following armoured columns to cross.[17] In planning for operations in Galicia, Stavka had anticipated the number of river crossings that its armour formations would have to make, correctly anticipating that the retreating Germans would destroy as many bridges as possible to impede their progress. Therefore, 4.Tank Army that would spearhead the assault in the Strypa sector was provided with two additional sapper battalions and a pontoon bridging battalion to augment its own engineering resources.[18]

As the Russians rapidly followed up the retreat from the Strypa, a new defensive line was established on the line of the river Koropiec on 20 July, but the Russians crossed the river almost without a pause and captured the village of Bekersdorf (Velyka Novosilka) from units of SS-Panzergrenadier Regiment 40, with 3.Company in particular taking heavy losses, while SS-Panzergrenadier Regiment 39 fought for the ruins of Podhajce (Pidhaitsi). The loss of Bekersdorf undermined the whole position and as darkness fell the Kampfgruppe was ordered to disengage and fall back to the Narajomka River line, with SS-Pz. Aufkl.Abt.18 covering the retreat.[19]

Bridges across the Narajamka had been secured at Lipica-Dolna in the north and Swistelniki in the south, each by a company of SS-Pz. Aufkl.Abt.18, the rifle battalions retreating on foot from one position to the next for lack of vehicles. 2./ SS-Pz.Aufkl.Abt.18 was given the job of defending the Lipica-Dolna bridgehead, but they were too few to carry out this mission effectively and by nightfall they found themselves surrounded. Günther Friedrich, a young recruit in 2.Company remembered:

> The only hope was for us to break out by force of arms. While we were forming up in a wedge formation we could hear raucous singing from the Russian side, indicating that the Russians were drunk. On the firing of a 'white' flare, we stormed with loud hurrahs down the village street to the west, firing wildly to the sides. A platoon of 3.Kompanie received us.

By the time SS-Pz.Aufkl.Abt.18 caught up with the remainder of the Kampfgruppe on 23 July, it was digging in behind another water barrier, this time the Gnila-Lipa River. I.SS-Panzergrenadier Regiment

39 was positioned around the villages of Koniuszki (Konyushky) and Nastaszcyn (Nastashyne) to the south while SS-Panzergrenadier Regiment 40 fought for the villages of Rohatyn, Cercze and Potok to the north.[20] However, while the SS men were sighting their guns and digging foxholes, the armoured spearhead of Soviet General Grechko's 1.Guards Army was pushing past the confluence of the Dnestr and Gnila Lipa Rivers at Halych, essentially outflanking their position before their defence of it had even begun.[21] There was little option for the time being but to hold their ground until an orderly retreat could be organized.

I.SS-Panzergrenadier Regiment 39 initially suffered pinprick attacks against its defences around Koniuszki, where enemy patrols attempted to infiltrate through the line but were driven off with light howitzer fire. Repeated Russian incursions were driven back, at times in hand-to-hand fighting and two Russian 7.62cm dual purpose guns were knocked out by infantry gun fire, but by the evening of the 23 July mounting Russian pressure combined with the heavy losses incurred by I.Battalion were beginning to weaken the line.

L'vov fell on the night of 23-24 July to 3.Guards Tank Army with 60.Army coming up in support, by which point the northern front of Army Group North Ukraine was in full retreat. To plug the gap between German 4.Panzer and 1.Panzer Armies the headquarters of 17.Army, recently evacuated from the Crimea, was reactivated and took command of a rag-tag force initially amounting to only two-and-a-half divisions. Fortunately for the hard-pressed Germans, the flow of reinforcements coincided with a slackening of the pace of the Russian advance,[22] forced upon them as their logistics could not match the pace of their armoured formations, whose movements were also hindered by the torrential rain that made the roads all but impassable.[23]

The Russian armour may have been struggling to move forwards along sodden roads, but their infantry was much less hindered by the conditions or the terrain. Throughout 24 July, the Russians pumped more troops into fighting for Koniuszki. During the night a Russian fighting patrol had broken into the centre of the village and dug in around the church. This situation was only cleared up when the Battalion's reserve, its headquarters motorcycle platoon, was thrown in against them. At midday, a more powerful attack in company strength supported by three T-34 tanks reached the forward trench line and was only thrown back in close combat after the battalion's anti-tank guns had knocked out the tanks at near point-blank range.

Meanwhile, SS-Panzergrenadier Regiment 40 clung to the villages of Rohatyn, Cercze (Cherche) and Potok (Potik) but its two battalions were too weak to do more than hold these outposts as Russian units attempted to outflank them. Ultimately, they had little option but to fall back while the situation in SS-Panzergrenadier Regiment 39's zone of operations was also reaching crisis point. On the 25th the focus of the Russian assaults shifted a mile or so to the south to the river crossing at the village of Nastaszcyn. SS-Obersturmführer Gärtner, commanding a composite company made up from elements of the Division's *Begleit* (headquarters security) Company and 3./ SS-Panzergrenadier Regiment 39, was in the thick of the fighting for the village, which was attacked by a large concentration of infantry supported by five tanks. The first attack was successfully repulsed but the second gained a foothold in the village and, although Gärtner's troops managed to seal off the incursion, they could not eliminate it. The Kampfgruppe's four Sturmgeschütz assault guns were brought up for the counterattack but were driven off by accurate Russian gunfire, and even with further infantry reinforcement thrown into the battle the village could not be retaken. Accurate Russian artillery fire pinned the German troops to their foxholes while Russian infantry and armour forced an expansion of the Nastaszcyn bridgehead.[24]

Even worse was to follow for the infantry, as their armoured support covering their northern flank was stripped away. 1.Panzer Division was pulled back from the Gnila Lipa and Dnester to Stryi River line while 8.Panzer Division was dispatched south to try to shore up the defensive line around the vital railhead at Stanislau, both units struggling to obtain enough fuel to keep their armoured vehicles moving.[25]

By the morning of 26 July, the remnants of the Divisional Kampfgruppe were all pulled back behind the Swika, the final defensible water obstacle before the mighty Dniester River, and dug in to either side of Waslaczcyn (Vasyuchyn). However, by midday the new positions were already under attack by infantry and armour, and it was only through the intervention of the guns of I./SS-Artillery Regiment 18, under the command of SS-Sturmbannführer Hoffmann, that the position could be held at all.

That same day Stanislau in the rear of XXIV.Panzer Corps' southern wing fell to 1.Guards Army and, without pausing to regroup, Konev ordered its commander General Grechko to push on to the west. With the high peaks of the Carpathian Mountains clearly visible to the southwest, it was obvious to the Germans that they were running out of room to manoeuvre and although they tenaciously defended each ridge and water course, if 1.Panzer Army could not mount an effective defence of the mountain passes they would be surrounded and destroyed.[26]

1.Panzer Army's ability to resist the Red Army's onslaught was waning fast. It was forced to improvise again and again, juggling its armoured units from one flank to the other as breakthroughs occurred. Under these circumstances, divisions were switched between corps commands on an almost daily basis while battle groups of varying sizes and compositions were formed as the need arose. XXIV.Panzer Corps, which was itself subordinated to XXXXVIII.Panzer Corps, was directing the operations of four divisions, all of which were infantry units, as well as those of the 18.SS-Panzergrenadier Division Kampfgruppe. XXIV.Panzer Corps had responsibility for defending the front line from the mouth of the Swica River to the Dniester south of the town of Iscie, a distance of around thirty miles.[27]

The lack of mobility that characterized these divisions was heightened by the perennial shortage of fuel that was to hamper all Wehrmacht operations for the latter half of the war, which created problems for both the retreating combat troops and for their supply columns. Fuel consumption was also vastly increased by the exceptionally poor state of the roads and thick mud. Most of XXIV. Panzer Corps' units were now operating in isolation with minimal contact to their flanks and in their largely immobilized state localized encirclement was a constant threat.[28]

The Soviet 6.Guards Tank Corps, the vanguard unit of 3.Guards Tank Army, had reached the southern outskirts of Przemy'l, sixty miles west of L'vov, late on 26 July and began its assault on the city directly from the march. By 10.00 the following day most of the city was in Soviet hands. This rapid progress meant that the slower German infantry divisions were left far to the east and somehow had to establish a defensive line facing north as well as east as the Guards tanks threatened to sweep down into their rear areas.[29]

At this juncture, 1.Ukrainian Front was advancing on two divergent fronts which was severely complicating command and control over the separate armies. Recognising his need to concentrate his staffing efforts on developing the more important operation in the Sandomierz

Bridgehead, Konev applied to Stavka to have the southern portion of his front, which was thrusting towards the Carpathian Mountains, reassigned to another command. Stavka duly dispatched Colonel General Ivan Petrov and his Front administration, which had been unemployed since the recapture of the Crimea, to take over the newly designated 4.Ukrainian Front. Initially, this Front commanded 1.Guards Army and 18.Army, with fresh units being added in as required.[30]

By the end of July, German reconnaissance and interception of Russian radio traffic made it clear that the 1.Ukrainian Front intended to extend its advance directly westwards along the Przemysl-Dynow axis while the armoured spearheads of 4.Ukrainian Front were peeling off towards the southwest to cut the Sanok-Krosno road and rail link. Both of these manoeuvres were precursors to the seizure of the Dukla Pass, the main transport route through the Carpathian Mountains between Slovakia and Poland, which would cut off 1.Panzer Army from its supplies.[31]

These Soviet thrusts had effectively cut Army Group North Ukraine in two, with 4.Panzer Army falling back westwards into Poland and 1.Panzer Army retreating to the southwest with its back to the Carpathians.[32] As it fell back, 1.Panzer Army exposed the northern flank of 1.Hungarian Army, which, under heavy attack, rapidly showed signs of disintegration. Although some Hungarian units did their best to put up prolonged resistance, others swiftly collapsed and tried to flee to the Carpathian passes.[33] Unfortunately for the Germans, amongst those Hungarian troops that were routed were those units covering the strategically important town of Dolina, which was quickly captured by the Soviet 18.Army on the 29th, allowing access to a vital road through Wygoda and on into the German rear and the mountain passes that opened out onto the Hungarian plains.[34]

The 18.SS-Kampfgruppe had crossed the Dniester and was directed into new positions at Zurawno. Although many units of 1.Panzer Army were still in retreat and others were in the process of digging in, the next few days were relatively quiet as the Russian forces brought up heavy artillery and ammunition while also taking the opportunity to relocate their airfields closer to the frontline. The Kampfgruppe established a new trench line on either side of Zurawno with 359.Infantry Division to the north and 371. Infantry Division covering its southern flank.[35]

With the new defensive position established, the Kampfgruppe underwent reorganisation to take account of the heavy casualties it had sustained. The fighting elements of I./Panzergrenadier Regiment 39 were combined with the two battalions of SS-Panzergrenadier Regiment 40 to create 'Kampfgruppe Schäfer', named after SS-Sturmbannführer Ernst Schäfer, the commander of SS-Panzergrenadier Regiment 40, but still under the direct control of SS-Oberführer Trabandt. It is believed that the command staff of SS-Panzergrenadier Regiment 39 under SS-Standartenführer Petersen, being temporarily redundant, returned to Hungary to carry on with the constitution of the division.

An extract from SS-Oberscharführer Tieke's diary gives a flavour of conditions faced during their deployment on the west bank of the Dniester:

> As a Schwimmwagen kompanie, we are very mobile and are deployed wherever holes need to be closed, counterattacks are required, and reconnaissance is required. When the front calmed down a bit, our divisional combat group relieved army units in a position on the Dniester. The water is knee-deep in the ditch, and it's still raining, raining in July. We scoop the water out of the ditch, but it's not getting any less. The Russians are doing the same thing over there. Clothes are completely soaked.[36]

The quiet period ended on 30 July with probing attacks along the Brigade's whole eight-mile-long front. German artillery attempted to interfere with the Russian troop concentrations, but this only delayed the inevitable. 1./Panzergrenadier Regiment 39 defended the village of Wladzimirce in heavy fighting all day. A determined attack in company strength penetrated right up to the command post of 3.Company and SS-Obersturmführer Gärtner was obliged to counterattack with his radio operators and messengers and drive them away. All contact was lost with 371.Infantry Division on the right wing, while on their left flank SS-Panzergrenadier Regiment 40 was forced to abandon Dubrawka. However, a swift counterattack by SS-Pz.Aufkl.Abt.18 retook the village late in the afternoon.[37] SS-Oberscharführer Tieke fought at Dubrawka with 2.Company:

> Then the first counterattack, the first real baptism of fire, the first deaths. Somewhere the Russians crossed the river. Your own movements are at risk. The company attacks. My sMG group has taken up position at the edge of a row of alder trees and is

shooting like crazy. The Russians give way, the company follows behind with an impetuous attack. We make position changes with assembled equipment and go into position again at the river. The company fulfilled the task but paid a high price: several dead and wounded, including Untersturmführer Haak, who lost his sight. My men look thoughtfully at the dead Russians and are amazed to see that they are equipped with American weapons and equipment. The food comes from America, the meat cans bear the imprint: 'Meyer, Chicago'.[38]

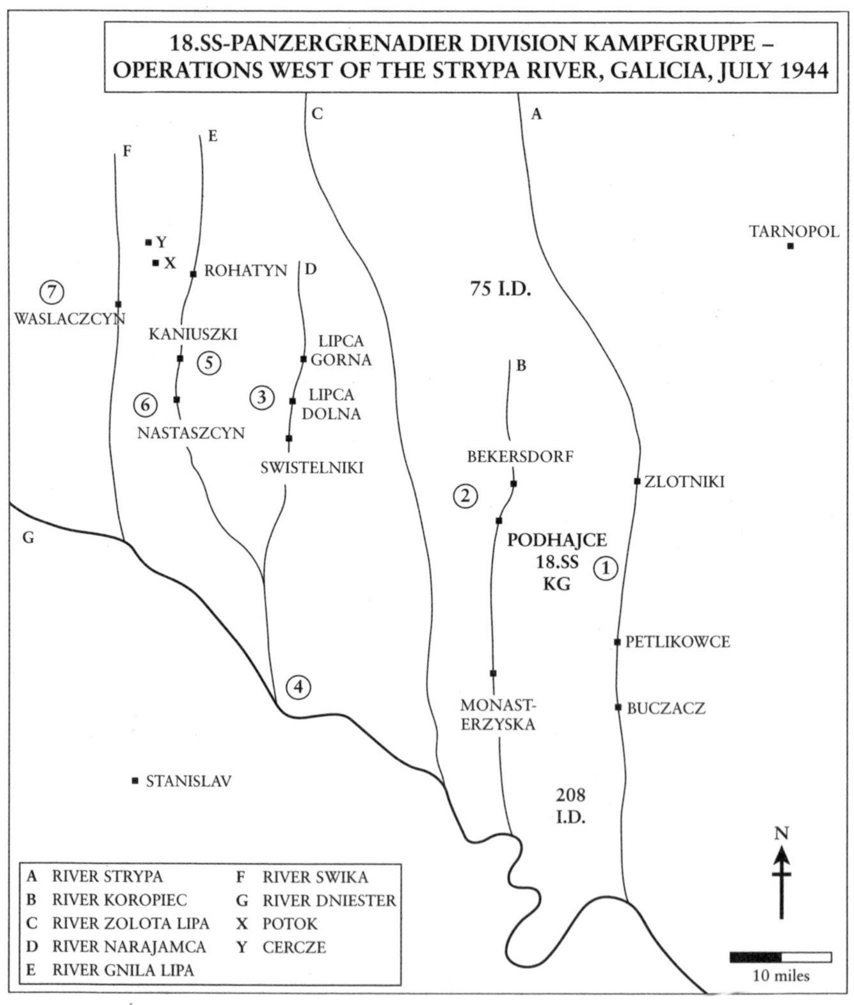

Galicia Map Notes

1 18.SS-Panzergrenadier Division Kampfgruppe began relieving units of 371.Infantry Division on 18 July and took over their positions on the western bank of the Strypa River between Petikowce and Zlotniki with 75.Infantry Division to their north and 208.Infantry Division to the south. On 19 July, the Red Army launched a major attack at the northern end of the Strypa line and the German defences were withdrawn later that day to avoid encirclement.

2 The Russians rapidly followed up the retreat from the Strypa and a new defensive line was established on the line of the river Koropiec on 20 July. However, the Russians crossed the river almost without a pause and captured the village of Bekersdorf from units of SS-Panzergrenadier Regiment 40, while SS-Panzergrenadier Regiment 39 fought for Podhajce. The loss of Bekersdorf undermined the whole position and at nightfall the Kampfgruppe was ordered to disengage and fall back to the Narajomka River line.

3 Bridges across the Narajomka had been secured at Lipica-Dolna in the north and Swistelniki in the south, each by a company of SS-Aufkl.Abt.18, but by 23 July the Kampfgruppe had been forced back behind the Gnila-Lipa River. I./SS-Panzergrenadier Regiment 39 was positioned around the villages of Koniuszki and Nastaszcyn to the south while SS-Panzergrenadier Regiment 40 fought for the villages of Rohatyn, Cercze and Potok to the north.

4 The armoured spearhead of Soviet General Grechko's Russian 1.Guards Army was pushing past the confluence of the Dniester and Gnila Lipa Rivers at Halych, essentially outflanking their position before their defence of it had even begun.

5 The Russians carried out aggressive patrolling to sound out the defences of I.SS-Regiment 39 around Koniuszki and throughout 24 July they steadily strengthened these attacks in a concerted effort to take the village. Meanwhile SS-Panzergrenadier Regiment 40 defended the villages of Rohatyn, Cercze and Potok to the north.

6 On 25 July, the focus of the Russian assaults shifted a mile or so to the south to the river crossing at the village of Nastaszcyn where, despite a desperate defence by the Kampfgruppe's last reserves, the Soviets made a breakthrough that outflanked the main defensive line.

7 By the morning of 26 July the remnants of the Kampfgruppe had been pulled back behind the Swika, the final defensible water obstacle before the Dniester River, and had dug in to either side of Waslaczcyn (Vasyuchyn), but it was clear that any further defence was unsustainable and 18.SS-Kampfgruppe crossed the Dniester the following day and was directed into new positions at Zurawno.

By the first week of August the 3.Guards Tank Army was poised to advance from the north east to take Krosno, Sedziszów Mlp, Mielec and Sanok and cut the connection between 17.Army and 1.Panzer Army,[39] while to the south the Soviet 1.Guards Army was advancing on Wygoda and threatening the railway line over the Carpathians to Skole, which was the principle supply route for both XXIV.Panzer Corps and XI.Army Corps. German forces counterattacked vigorously but by 30 July had lost their momentum and were wasting resources in a lost cause. Recognising the futility of trying to hold ground in the face of insurmountable odds 1.Panzer Army finally pulled back its troops between 5–7 August to the line of Stryj river, otherwise known as the 'Hunyadi Position'. A testament to the fierceness of the fighting was that the 357.Infantry Division had to be disbanded with its remnants being divided amongst neighbouring units.[40]

Fighting around Sanok

In the first few days of August the fast-moving mechanised troops of 3.Guards Tank Army turned south from their westwards advance with the aim of encircling the 1.Panzer Army in front of the Beskides Mountains, the range of foothills before the true Carpathians. Desperate to escape the net and keep their lines of communication open, the Germans folded back their left wing to the northwest to meet the threat and rushed whatever reinforcements that could be spared to the area. Heavy fighting developed around the town of Sanok, which was both an important railway junction and covered the approaches to the Dukla Pass, the main eastern access route through the mountains into Slovakia. To strengthen the line, 18.SS-Panzergrenadier Division Kampfgruppe was amongst those units ordered to move to the Sanok front, arriving in its new deployment area between 5–6 August.

It was during this move that the division learned that it was to be reinforced by a battalion of French volunteers from the French SS-Freiwilligen-Sturmbrigade, part of a force that was being gathered to break through the advancing Russian troops and re-establish contact with 17.Army that was being pushed away to the north.[41]

Anti-communist Frenchmen had been fighting for the Wehrmacht since the first winter of the war in the east, principally making up the bulk of the personnel within Army Infantry Regiment 638. On 30 August 1943, Hitler personally approved the creation of a French unit within the Waffen-SS and Französische SS-Freiwiiligen-Sturmbrigade (French SS-Volunteer Assault Brigade) was founded. It was initially formed of two battalions, each with three rifle companies and supporting heavy weapons unit and was undergoing training in Bohemia-Moravia when the order came for it create a battalion-strength battle group for immediate dispatch to the Eastern Front.[42]

I.Battalion, commanded by SS-Hauptsturmführer Cance, was selected for action and an exchange of personnel was made between the two battalions with the less experienced men from I.Battalion being swapped for the veterans in II.Battalion. It had three rifle companies; 1.Company under SS-Obersturmführer Noël de Tissot, 2.Company led by SS-Untersturmführer Léon Gaultier and 3.Company commanded by SS-Obersturmführer Henri Fenet. There was also SS-Obersturmführer Pleyber's 4. (heavy weapons) Company which, although its exact composition is unknown, definitely contained a towed Pak anti-tank gun platoon of three 7.5cm guns under SS-Oberjunker Kreis. It is likely that the balance of the personnel in 4.Company were employed as infantry.[43]

The French battalion had an overall strength of around 1,000 well trained, fully equipped, and motivated volunteers and their actions were documented by a P.K. (Propaganda Company) under the command of SS-Untersturmführer Le Marquer who was later killed in combat at Mokré, fighting as an infantryman.[44]

On 5 August, I.Battalion of the French SS-Sturmbrigade arrived at the town of Turka in Galicia after a week-long rail journey from Bohemia. Turka was some 40 miles east of Sanok, and the three rifle companies, without any transport of their own, had to march to the front through the scorching heat, but the position of the 18.SS-Panzergrenadier Division Kampfgruppe was becoming desperate so Trabandt dispatched lorries from the supply column to speed up their arrival.[45]

Upon his arrival, Cance, accompanied by his Chief of Staff SS-Obersturmführer Croseille, his orderly officer SS-Untersturmführer Scapula, and German liaison officer SS-Untersturmführer Reiche, was briefed by Oberführer Trabandt.[46] Trabandt painted a very bleak picture of the situation, which was deteriorating hourly. Sanok had fallen to the Russians on 4–5 August and a huge hole had been torn in the Wehrmacht-held lines to the west of the town.[47] With Sanok in their hands, the Soviets had refocused their main effort to the west of the town, cutting both rail and road connections to Krasno on 6 August and occupying the villages of Pisarowce and Sanoczek against weak German resistance from local security forces and parts of 208.Infantry Division.[48] Kampfgruppe Neumeister from 1.Panzer Division, consisting of Panzergrenadier Regiment 1, Pz.Aufkl.Abt.1 and II./Panzer Artillery Regiment 73,[49] had managed to recapture Sanok in a surprise coup that temporarily threw the Russians off balance, but the main road from Sanok to the west remained blocked and powerful Soviet forces were moving up for a counterattack.[50]

Consequently, 18.SS-Panzergrenadier Division Kampfgruppe received the order on 6 August to reinforce the defensive front hastily established by 96.Infantry Division to the southwest of Sanok. Once established in the area the Kampfgruppe was to clear the main road and railway line, seal the breach in the frontline, and re-establish communications between 1.Panzer Army and 17.Army, which was somewhere to the northwest. In Army Group North Ukraine's opinion, this was the most important objective, and they urged haste.

The OKW war diary reported that on the morning of 7 August: 'West of Sanok, an attack by parts of the 1st Panzer Division and 18th SS Volunteer Panzergrenadier Division to clear Sanok-Krosno [Krasno] highway failed to break through in the face of strong resistance.'[51]

This notation is terse in the extreme and gives no indication of the slaughter that occurred. I./SS-Panzergrenadier Regiment 39 commanded by SS-Hauptsturmführer Hoyer launched an assault on the village of Sanoczek as a prelude to reaching the highway, which was the Kampfgruppe's first objective. The battalion struck out from Malo-Stroze in a northwesterly direction but almost immediately ran into concentrated Russian artillery and mortar fire. With the Red Army holding the high ground and their artillery covering the approaches to Sanoczek, the German troops found it impossible to advance and were forced back by strong infantry counterattacks supported by armoured vehicles. With no cover and no way to immediately retaliate, casualties mounted at an alarming rate. SS-Obersturmführer Gärtner leading 3.Company was severely wounded in the stomach and had to be carried from the battlefield by his men. The battalion as a whole lost eight dead, fifty-six wounded and thirteen missing for absolutely no gain.[52]

As I./SS-Panzergrenadier Regiment 39 was driven back to its starting positions, SS-Panzergrenadier Regiment 40 and elements of 96.Infantry Division under Generalleutnant Richard Wirtz attempted another thrust from the south, the village of Sanoczek and the communications links west of Sanok again being the goals. However, these forces also proved to be insufficient for the task and were driven back with heavy losses, quickly finding themselves having to fight off a determined Russian counterattack.[53] The Russian attacks continued unabated and by the following morning Trabandt found that his rifle companies had been reduced to a strength of around thirty to forty men each, less than one third of their original strength. Under these circumstances he was unable to plug the breach that had been forced between SS-Panzergrenadier Regiment 40 and their left-hand neighbour, despite committing his last reserves, His position was now in danger of being completely swamped.[54]

SS-Pz.Aufkl.Abt.18 had been held in reserve during the first two attempts to capture Sanoczek, and its sector on the right wing of the Kampfgruppe had been relatively quiet throughout 7 August. The troops were occupying foxholes as the fluid nature of the fighting had not allowed time for more permanent defences to be constructed. Their positions were in rolling countryside in the foothills of the Beskides, in fields of ripening crops. They were overlooked by hills to the north. During the morning of 8 August their position was attacked by ground attack aircraft but to minimal effect as their fieldworks were small and placed far apart. Around noon Russian ground forces begin their attack. The platoons in positions on the forward slopes of the hills were taken under heavy machine gun fire while *Ratschbumm* (Russian 7.62 cm high velocity field guns) targeted any individual foxholes that they could identify.[55]

Günther Friedrich who fought with 2./SS-Pz.Aufkl.Abt.18 wrote an after action report:

> Things became noisy in the Russian positions already at 0400 hours. That was a sign for us that our opponents were drinking alcohol to get courage. Then the attacks started against our neighbour, SS-Panzer-Grenadier Regiment 39. But they collapsed in the defensive fire of our infantry and the barrier fire from our artillery. At approximately 1630 hours our positions were fired on by Ratschbumm and Stalin Organs. That fire was followed by an infantry attack at 1700 hours. About 80 Red Army men advanced stubbornly on our positions. Because I only had one belt of ammunition left we transferred the rounds to stripper clips and fired aimed shots with our rifles. Behind the position of our Gruppe, Oberscharführer Muth fired a Sturmgewehr [assault rifle] and Unterscharführer Hatzenbiller used a grenade launcher attachment.
>
> I suddenly received a powerful blow on my left elbow. The rifle was knocked out of my hand and the shot went into the air. My uniform and everything I had under it was blown off

> my body. I had a large wound between my shoulder blades and a splinter in my elbow. I ran back across the hill to the company command post, where I was bandaged... A little later I met Oberscharführer Muth who had lost an arm due to a wound. Only five men were left from our platoon.[56]

This attack was fought off with the aid of heavy and accurate artillery fire, but it was clear that the rifle companies were being depleted to the point of combat ineffectiveness. It was just at this moment of crisis that I.Battalion of the French SS-Sturmbrigade arrived as reinforcement. Trabandt immediately received SS-Obersturmführer Fenet's 3.Company from Cance, which was ordered to re-establish contact with 96.Infantry Division on the Kampfgruppe's left flank, but if it was unable to do so it should act as flank guard itself. As the area was being infiltrated by Russian infantry, Fenet was told to wait until dawn before starting out. The rest of the French battalion was held in reserve.

After much delay 3.Company set off on its appointed mission in the mid-afternoon of 9 August. Its route of advance was partially under Soviet observation and they had to run a gauntlet of artillery and mortar fire before making contact with 1./SS-Pangergrenadier Regiment 40 under the command of SS-Obersturmführer Tämpfer, whose 200-strong company had been reduced to just twenty effectives.[57]

SS-Obersturmführer Alfred Tämpfer was one of the very few SD officers to have served in an Einsatzgruppe who later made the transition to a Waffen-SS combat command. According to author French L. Maclean, Tämpfer (or Tempfer) was a member of Sonderkommando 7A, which formed part of Einsaztgruppe B operating in the northern sector of central Russia. Sonderkommando 7a cut a swathe across Eastern Europe from the commencement of Operation *Barbarossa* until well into 1942, operating as far afield as Vilnius in southern Lithuania to the Bryansk region of western Russia. A special report compiled by Einsatzgruppe B and dated 19 September 1942 noted that Sonderkommando 7a had 'specially treated' a total of 6,281 people by 31 August that year.[58] Tämpfer was active as an officer in a sub-unit within Sonderkommando 7a. He had joined the Waffen-SS in 1939 and in August 1942, following his service with Sonderkommando 7a, he was transferred to SS-Infantry Regiment 10.[59] Sonderkommando 7A was not disbanded until November 1944 and the reason for his transfer is unknown. Tämpfer was killed in action on 22 September 1944.[60]

Given the embattled state of Tämpfer's company and the total lack of information about what was happening on the exposed left wing, Fenet, who had undergone the training course at the Waffen-SS Officer's school at Bad Tôlz, felt that it was impractical to try and establish contact with friendly units and set up a defensive line facing west, covered by small fighting patrols.[61] As the situation on the left wing of the Kampfgruppe remained fluid, the decision was made to deploy the whole of the French battalion in this area with the additional duty of regaining and maintaining contact with scattered elements of 68. and 208.Infantry Divisions operating somewhere to the west and north of Pielnia.[62]

Clearly, it was tactically unsound to leave a gaping hole in the front line through which Russian infantry were infiltrating, and the French battalion was charged with capturing the village of Dundynce to effect a link-up with 208.Infantry Division. The attack went in on 10 August with 1. and 2.Companies forward and 3.Company in reserve. The village of Dundynce consisted of nothing more than a few hovels clustered around a church with a small stream running down the middle. It was flanked to the south and southeast by dense forest, with the village of Pielnia three miles to the west. Its importance lay in its proximity to Pisarowice a few miles to the north, situated on the main road and rail lines between Sanok, Krosno and Krakow.

De Tissot's 1.Company advanced through forested cover as far as possible, hugging the terrain as it circled the village to the northwest while Gaultier rashly led his 2.Company on the direct route to the village, northwards across open ground. Both columns were met with fierce resistance as soon as they set off, being hammered by artillery and heavy mortars, machine guns and snipers joining in at closer range.

SS-Untersturmführer Gaultier was struck in the chest by a large piece of shrapnel almost as soon as the advance started, and it took several hours and a large percentage of the company's assets to evacuate him. Edging up a ravine leading from the edge of the forest, de Tissot's company was observed by Russian spotters and suffered terrifying fire from mortars and mobile multiple rocket launchers know to the Germans as 'Stalin's Organ Pipes' (and to the Russians as *Katyusha* or 'Little Kate') which exploded in the treetops, adding lethal splinters of wood to the shell fragments raining down upon them and forcing the advance out into the open.[63]

1.Company reached the illusory safety of a group of farm buildings and in the sweltering heat of the day the French volunteers made to drink from the well, which proved to be the signal for Russian snipers, machine guns and mortar crews to hit them with a storm of fire. As the Frenchmen struggled to resume the advance, SS-Untersturmführer Pignard-Berthet was riddled with shrapnel. SS-Oberscharführer Mulier, who was hit in the stomach, tried to gather up his intestines in his helmet. As the slaughter continued de Tissot was left with no choice but to dig in on a ridge to the southwest of Pielna. As the wounded were dragged back to the battalion aid station in Wolica, the scale of the debacle became clearer. The casualties amongst platoon and squad leaders were devastating and by the time the assault companies were recalled they had suffered over 60 dead and wounded.[64]

General Balck re-emphasised the order for the 'Horst Wessel' Kampfgruppe to clear the Sanok to Krasno railway line at the earliest opportunity and the assault was to be renewed at noon on 12 August regardless of the fact that the Red Army had heavily reinforced the Sanok sector with 140. 183. 211. Rifle Divisions from General Moskalenko's 38.Army backed by tanks from 62.Guards Tank Brigade from General Lelyushenko's 4.Tank Army.

The Soviet defences were softened up with a 45-minute artillery barrage laid down by 10.5cm howitzers from I./18.SS-Artillery Regiment and Nebelwerfer rocket launchers provided by the army.[65] SS-Panzergrenadier Regiment 40 led the attack from its deployment area on the right wing of the combat group and was able to occupy Sanoczek. In the centre of the Kampfgruppe's line, I./SS-Panzergrenadier Regiment 39 also managed to push forward, but these were largely diversionary assaults. The main weight of the assault was delivered by the French SS Volunteer Battalion on the left flank. The still largely intact battalion resumed its thrust in the direction of Pisarowce, across the same ground where it had suffered so much two days previously, with elements of 68.Infantry Division advancing to their west.[66]

Attacking from south to north, II./Platoon of 2.Company, led by SS-Oberjunker Peyron, charged through a hail of Russian fire, his men throwing grenades and firing at the run. They stormed the village of Dundynce and advanced so rapidly that the artillery had to increase range to avoid hitting the French SS men. Meanwhile, 1.Company succeeded in capturing Pielnia. The Russians hastily fell back, abandoning their dead and wounded. As the first Russian prisoners were rounded up the attack pressed on, but the Russians threw fresh infantry units into the fight backed by tanks and, although the railway line was within sight, the Frenchmen were forced to dig in amongst the vacated Russian positions and postpone the next phase of the assault until the following day.[67]

The OKW daily reports from August 14, 1944 under the heading '1.Panzer Armee' recorded:

> XXIV Panzer Corps: In the course of their own attacks in the area west of Sanok, 96 Infantry Division pushed through on their left wing with subordinate battle group 18.SS-Panzergrenadier Division north to the Sanok-Zarszyn road and blocked it. South of this weaker enemy forces were surrounded; measures to destroy it are in progress.[68]

The 'official' version of events glossed over the heavy losses on the German side and the bitterness of the fighting for little actual territorial or strategic gain.

The attack was renewed on 14 August in sweltering temperatures. SS-Panzergrenadier Regiment 40 had initial success, but the Russians threw in counterattack after counterattack and because of the strength of this resistance they had to establish a defensive line to try and hold onto the ground they had taken. A company was formed from the combined remnants of I./SS-Panzergrenadier Regiment 39, under the command of SS-Obersturmführer Wagner, to fight its way forwards and maintain the link between the Cance's battalion and the stalled SS-Panzergrenadier Regiment 40. The company was to jump off from Dudynce at 1700 hours, but its attack was over an hour late in starting due to the need to expel infiltrating Russian infantry from its start line, all the while taking fire from Russian field guns. The French 1. and 3.Companies were unable to make much headway as every attempt to advance was met with a storm of artillery fire and heavy 120mm mortar rounds.[69]

However, on the following day, Tuesday 15 August, SS-Obersturmführer Pleyber's 2.Company resumed the advance towards Pisarowice with Oberjunker Peyron's II Platoon again seizing the initiative and leading the assault. As they approached the village of Pisarowice, the Russian fire intensified, with machine guns adding to the heavy weapons fire, but Peyron ordered his men to charge and, despite suffering many dead and wounded, they took the village in savage close quarters fighting with grenades and bayonets.

The French victory was short-lived though, as the Russians brought up more infantry in a two-pronged attack to encircle the village. Realising the danger of their position, Pleyber immediately ordered a breakout to the southwest before swinging back north onto their original course. German artillery and mortars quickly provided covering fire for the resumed advance, but the Frenchmen charged too quickly and became caught in their own supporting fire, a disastrous adjunct to the Russian barrage. SS-Oberjunker Peyron, refusing to wear his helmet, was struck in the head by fragments from a heavy mortar bomb and became the first French SS officer to be killed in action. After a brief pause to tend to their casualties, SS-Unterscharführer Andre Bayle assumed command of the twenty-five or so men that remained of II./Platoon and managed to press on for another mile until they reached the railway line and occupied a level crossing. But this was to be the limit of their advance and, horribly exposed, it was with some relief that they were relieved by German Army Panzer troops and could return to the battalion.[70]

On the left flank of Kampfgruppe Schäfer's sector, 1./SS-Panzergrenadier Regiment 40 under SS-Untersturmführer Kammer was surrounded by partisans and hopelessly pinned down. Lacking any sort of reserves of his own, Schäfer requested French help.[71] The order was received by telephone at the command post of SS-Obersturmführer Noël de Tissot's 1.Company at 04.00, and SS-Oberjunker Chapy with his platoon was sent to the aid of his German counterparts. The most direct route to Kammer's location involved negotiating a village occupied by Russian infantry, which was achieved by stealth during the pre-dawn hours before establishing contact with the beleaguered company. Kammer's men were in a bad way as their position was dominated by higher ground allowing the partisans to rake them with machine gun and mortar fire, which had already resulted in heavy losses. Dead and wounded were strewn across the position.[72]

Chapy and Kammer agreed that the only way to get out of the trap was to capture the dominating ridge in a frontal assault. The combined strength of the French and German units only amounted to about

100 men, but with fixed bayonets the screaming mass of SS men stormed the heights and dislodged the Soviets in savage hand-to-hand fighting. Following this victory, the wounded were evacuated and both units returned to their parent units without further loss of life.[73]

With all of the French Companies gathered at their battalion command post in Wolica, a roll was called. Accounts vary but it is likely that the battalion, which numbered over 1,000 men on 10 August, now had a total strength of less than 800 just one week later. It appears that 1.Company was hardest hit with sixty casualties in total, while 2.Company lost fifty men killed and wounded and 3.Company was missing twenty soldiers from its ranks. It is known that the 4. (heavy) Company also took casualties[74] as on 11 August, SS-Oberscharführer Kreutzer from the anti-tank platoon had been ordered to set up a 7.5cm gun on a ridge overlooking the village of Dundynce in full view of the Soviet artillery, which promptly hammered the gun position with large calibre shells, damaging the gun and wounding five of its crew.[75] The full extent of the battalion's losses around Sanok can only be estimated.

The result of these actions and the many casualties incurred was that the Krosno-Sanok railway line had been secured in places, but a stable front line connecting 1.Panzer Army and 17.Army could not be established. A solid junction between the two armies was only gained after the surrender of the Sanok area and subsequent shortening of the line.[76]

While 18.SS-Panzergrenadier Division Kampfgruppe and the French SS-Sturmbrigade had been fighting to restore the situation in the Sanok area, the overall position of Army Group North Ukraine had deteriorated drastically. Not only had the gap between 1.Panzer Army and 17.Army not been plugged, further north the Red Army's 1.Ukrainian Front had reached the Vistula River, the last great water barrier before the borders of the Reich, and crossed it on a broad front between the towns of Baranow and Sandomierz at the end of July. They spent the following weeks consolidating a hold on the bridgehead and amassing troops for an eventual breakout. 4.Panzer Army was desperately struggling to contain the western face of the bridgehead while 17.Army tried to gather sufficient troops to launch a counter stroke before the Soviet tank armada broke through in a south-westerly direction towards Tarnow and on into the Silesian industrial region. Resources were stretched everywhere, and Army

Group North Ukraine took the decision to cut its losses, abandoning the Sanok line, which was now seen to be of secondary importance, and concentrating its assets further north around the Vistula and Wisloka Rivers. As the German frontline contracted, it proved possible to squeeze out various units which were quickly redeployed to more sensitive areas.[77]

The Mielec Sector

Initially, LIX.Army Corps under the command of General Edgar Röhricht had been able to interfere with Russian ferrying operations across the Vistula as they transferred heavy tanks and artillery into the bridgehead. 23.Panzer Division was tasked to recapture Baranow and the crossing points to the northwest of the town. However, after months of heavy fighting, this division was at the end of its strength and was unable to carry out such an optimistic mission.[78]

The Russian 9.Mechanised Corps had been intended to cross into the Baranow bridgehead, but in the face of the attack by 23.Panzer Division had launched immediate and powerful counterattacks, supported by elements of 13.Army, to protect the southern flank of their Vistula bridgehead. With this counter thrust unexpectedly gaining momentum, the Soviet command quickly altered its plans and began an advance on both sides of the Vistula towards the town of Szczucin, far in the German rear. 24.Panzer Division was sent to the aid of its hard-pressed comrades, but German aerial reconnaissance identified seven fresh divisions from 5.Guards Army approaching the Wisloka River, a north-south running tributary of the Vistula, and both Panzer divisions were forced to pull back or be trapped on the wrong side of it. By 5 August, the Wisloka River line had been crossed at several points and the city of Mielec, which had been an important staging post and supply centre for the Germans, had been lost.[79]

By the middle of August the LIX.Army Corps was having to defend the Wisloka River line with very weak infantry forces, in both quantity and quality, deployed in a string of outposts as there were insufficient troops to form a coherent front. 78.Grenadier Division had been rebuilt for the second time in the war after previously being annihilated at Stalingrad and then again during Operation *Bagration* just two months earlier. 544.Grenadier Division was one of the new wave of Infantry Divisions, hastily raised and poorly equipped, especially to fight tanks. Infantry elements of 5.Guards Army had been able to cross the river with little resistance at multiple points and had captured the last German bridge at Przeclaw. This frontal assault was matched by a threat to the Corps' rear from the Vistula crossing at Szczucin, which necessitated a defence on two fronts, one facing east and the other north. 23.Panzer Division was joined by 17.Panzer Division, on temporary attachment to LIX.Army Corps, in the area to the west of Mielec to act as a buffer to further Soviet advances in the short term but with a view to advancing in concert with III. Panzer Corps further north to eliminate the Baranow / Sandomierz bridgehead.

The battle see-sawed throughout the second week of August. A Russian bridgehead across the Wisloka at Przeclaw was eliminated, while the Russians gained ground to the west of the Mielec-Wisloka estuary along the south bank of the Vistula, which effectively pinned the two Panzer divisions to a holding role until infantry reinforcements could be brought in to free them up once again for mobile operations.[80]

On 16 August, 18.SS-Panzergrenadier Division Kampfgruppe, with the French SS volunteer battalion still attached, received the order to relocate to Radomysl, sixty miles to the north of their positions, where they would come under the command of LIX.Army Corps in 17.Army's zone of operations. The redeployment had to be carried out with some urgency[81] and the change of positions was conducted in daylight. The Russians were obviously alerted to the movement of the departing troops. During their harassing fire a mortar round killed SS-Untersturmführer Hartmann of I./SS-Panzergrenadier Regiment 39.[82]

This movement order produced an unexpected lull in combat operations which allowed time for a reorganisation of the Kampfgruppe's decimated units. Those heavily reduced companies which still retained a core of effectives were merged and strengthened with new recruits, while those that were deemed to be totally burnt out were sent back to the division's formation areas in Hungary for reconstitution.[83] The overhauled Kampfgruppe Schäfer consisted of two composite battalions from 18.SS-Panzergrenadier Division, one infantry gun company, one Flak company, an amalgamated reconnaissance company and a reduced I./SS-Artillery Regiment 18 with two batteries of six guns each.[84] The first makeshift rifle battalion consisted of the remnants of I./SS-Panzergrenadier Regiment 39 padded out with elements of SS-Panzergrenadier Regiment 40 and was commanded by SS-Sturmbannführer Hoyer. The second battalion, led by SS-Sturmbannführer Riepe, was an amalgamation of I. and II./SS-Panzergrenadier Regiment 40. The battalion of French SS volunteers remained subordinate to the Kampfgruppe. The whole unit was reinserted into the line in the area of Przeclaw on 19 August near the old Waffen-SS training ground at Debica, where Riepe's battalion replaced elements of 371.Infantry Division on its left flank and Hoyer's men and the French contingent relieved parts of 78.Grenadier Division on the right.[85] The combined reconnaissance company was placed to the rear as the Kampfgruppe's only reserve, while the main dressing station was established in Radomysl under the direction of SS-Oberartz (Senior Doctor) Doctor Krämer. Despite the Kampfgruppe's designation, SS-Oberführer Trabandt remained in overall command.[86]

The French relieved troops of a weak Wehrmacht battalion along a long stretch of the Wisloka River south of Przeclaw, and although the sector was relatively quiet, SS-Hauptsturmführer Cance had to spread his men out very thinly to cover his allotted sector. The platoons of de Tissot's 1.Company took over more than half a mile of front line each, with an average French deployment of around 100 men per mile.[87]

18.SS-Panzergrenadier-Division Kampfgruppe was again being required to take over a section of frontline that would ideally have needed a full infantry division to defend with any hope of success. LIX.Army Corps recognised the Kampfgruppe's obvious weakness in all arms but especially in artillery and ordered Arko.103, an artillery command which co-ordinated most of the artillery assets within the corps command structure, to cooperate closely with the Kampfgruppe, anticipating that the weight of fire that it could produce would counteract any large-scale attack.[88]

Towards midnight on the night of 19–20 August, the Soviet artillery commenced shelling the German positions on either side of the French battalion. As the light improved towards dawn the fire intensified, batteries of Katyusha rockets adding their weight to the devastating barrage. The French battalion was spared the worst of the destruction, but SS-Untersturmführer Bartolomei was wounded by shrapnel and had to be evacuated.[89]

The heaviest bombardment lasted for two hours and heralded the opening of the 5.Guards Army's offensive against the right wing of

LIX.Army Corps. The shelling was closely followed up by strong infantry and tanks attacks and strafing runs by ground attack aircraft. This attack was aimed at the junction between 371.Infantry Division and SS-Sturmbannführer Riepe's battalion that abutted it, but was extended to envelope the Kampfgruppe's entire front.[90]

As the Russian attack unfolded, Kampfgruppe Schäfer quickly began to lose control of events in its sector. By 07.00 Russian tanks were reported to be advancing unopposed towards Radomysl where the Kampfgruppe's service elements were situated, but with the German companies pinned to their trenches by the heaviest of the bombardment and expecting a ground attack imminently, none of them were able to intervene. SS-Sturmbannführer Schäfer contacted Cance and urgently requested the dispatch of his anti-tank platoon to Radomysl to take control of its defence.[91]

SS-Oberjunker Kreis and about thirty men of the PAK platoon arrived in Radomysl at 09.00 hours, where Kreis had been ordered to hold the town until 16.00 hours at all costs.[92] The platoon's equipment status as it set off on this mission is in doubt, but it is likely that it had been obliged to hand over its two remaining serviceable anti-tank guns to one of the two German battalions of the Kampfgruppe and had drawn *Panzerfaust* single-shot, hand-held anti-tank missiles instead.[93]

Kreis was named 'Battle Commander' of the town and his handful of men covered the roads into Radomysl from the north and east. Although his new title was clearly preposterous under the circumstances, it gave Kreis the authority to integrate any personnel retreating through the town into its defence until the garrison had swelled to approximately one hundred men, strengthened by a lone assault gun.

The Russians had been slow to follow up their initial thrust and it was only at midday that they put in their first attacks against Radomysl using unsupported infantry. As the afternoon wore on, more infantry units were thrown at the defences until they may have been facing several thousand men. Although the Russians brought up tanks in the middle of the afternoon the defenders were initially able to fend them off with their *panzerfauste*, but the weight of the attacks mounted steadily and with ammunition running low the defenders fell back from house to house to the last defensible spot at the cemetery.

As his 16.00 hours deadline approached, SS-Oberjunker Kreis was seriously wounded while tackling a Russian tank with one of the last remaining panzerfauste and it was his second in command who gave the order for the platoon to withdraw along the Radomysl-Przeclaw road to the area west of Ruda, where they were temporarily incorporated into Riepe's battalion as it retreated southwards.[94] Despite the desperate resistance of all the units involved, and at considerable cost to the attackers, the Russians had captured Radomysl by the evening and were consolidating their position.[95]

SS-Sturmbannführer Hoyer's battalion spent the morning of 20 August enduring concentrated shelling from artillery and heavy mortars across its whole sector while dual-purpose 7.62cm field guns targeted specific strongpoints, including the battalion command post in Rydzow. Initial infantry probing was driven back by the battalion's supporting heavy infantry guns.

The situation had been similar for Riepe's battalion on their left; heavy artillery fire continuing throughout the morning interspersed with strafing runs by ground attack aircraft. Towards noon, a company-strength attack by Russian infantry penetrated the right-hand side of the battalion positions and the Kampfgruppe's reserves had to be thrown in to clear up the incursion. SS-Pz.Aufkl.Abt.18 launched a surprise counterattack on the village of Pietcowiec to relieve the pressure on the main line of resistance and threw the Russians back for a while but were unable to halt their advance along the Mielec-Radomysl road, and the company found itself surrounded. Fortunately for them, with the fast-moving front remaining so fluid, they were able to conduct a successful withdrawal at nightfall.[96]

In their foxholes along the Wisloka River the French SS companies were not spared the onslaught for long. A wall of fire erupted over them, ripping up trees, shredding telephone lines and caving in bunkers, while Soviet infantry used the barrage to mask their movement across the river. They established a bridgehead on the French side near Rzochow and had little difficulty in penetrating the flimsy defences of their over-extended line. Russian snipers were active in the forward lines and the platoon positions contracted as their casualties mounted.[97]

Meanwhile, the Russians continued to attack up and down the line and in the early afternoon approximately 120 men broke through the thinly manned frontline on the left of Hoyer's battalion, and again it was only the intervention of the reconnaissance company that saved the situation, but it was clear that the Kampfgruppe's position was becoming untenable, with Russian troops infiltrating through the line almost at will. With a gaping hole in the line between the Kampfgruppe and 371.Infantry Division and no communication between the two battalions, a withdrawal to the south was ordered to avoid being surrounded.[98]

Trabandt ordered his battalion commanders to disengage with the utmost urgency and fall back to the line Radomysl-Pouby-Przeclaw. The French companies, suspecting that they were surrounded, stealthily withdrew through the dense forest that backed their position with Lambert's 2.Company and the headquarters group and pioneer platoon in the lead, followed by Fenet's 3.Company and de Tissot's 1.Company bringing up the rear, their line of march silhouetted by the burning hamlet of Dzilec. SS-Oberjunker Chapy's platoon acted as rear-guard.[99]

As the Kampfgruppe retreated south and west, the Russians followed up closely and by nightfall both Ruda and Radomysl had been lost. Following their capture of Radomysl, the Soviet units divided, the main body carrying on the assault to the southwest while strong elements peeled off to roll up the lines of the Kampfgruppe from west to east.[100]

The retreating French column quickly broke up into company sections and became scattered. Lambert's 2.Company came under fire as it approached its designated positions because Russian troops had reach the area ahead of them and a running battle ensued in pitch darkness. As the Russians closed in from both flanks, the company splintered into smaller and smaller groups. SS-Untersturmführer Bartolomei was wounded in the leg but still managed to lead thirty dirty and shell-shocked survivors out of the trap towards the south where they eventually established contact with friendly units in Dubrowka, but for the moment there was no news of the fate of the rest of the company.

De Tissots 1.Company bringing up the rear quickly lost contact with the rest of the battalion. His men were made less cautious by a chronic lack of sleep and as they paused to rest, they failed to notice that an approaching motorised column consisted of Russian troops. All hell was let loose as machine guns opened fire on the dazed Frenchmen and grenades exploded in their midst, scattering them into the surrounding forest. Chapy's rear-guard platoon was spared the worst of the debacle, but SS-Obersturmführer de Tissot was killed in the melee. Accounts vary as to the circumstances of his death.

Chapy took command of the company and after rounding up those men that could be found, retreated in a westerly direction after abandoning all heavy equipment. They eventually worked their way back to Dubrowka where the battalion command post was temporarily situated.[101]

3.Company's retreat had begun uneventfully, and they were able to man their new defensive line without incident and dig in around the village of Pouby. The Russians launched their first attack at dawn when a full Guards battalion penetrated the company's positions and had to be ejected in hand-to-hand fighting. As the day wore on the Frenchmen were subjected to an increasingly heavy mortar bombardment and direct fire from field guns. As the Guardsmen struck again, Fenet's company began to disintegrate under the weight of the combined arms attack, and when his 2.Platoon was overrun around midday he gave the order to fall back to the south towards Mokra.[102]

On 21 August, the Russians continued to hammer at 18.SS-Panzergrenadier Division Kampfgruppe which had suffered heavily on the previous day. Evicted from its defensive positions, its right wing was forced back almost five miles to the southwest of Przeclaw while 371.Infantry Division also had to retreat over a mile at its junction with the SS-Kampfgruppe before it was able to seal off the Russian penetration. Counterattacks to recapture Radomysl from the southeast by the Army's Grenadier Brigade 1134 and a Kampfgruppe from 8.Panzer Division after some initial success were thrown back to their starting point by numerically superior Russian forces supported by tanks.[103]

As it fell back southwards on a line roughly parallel with the Przeclaw-Radomysl road, 18.SS-Panzergrenadier Division Kampfgruppe's retreat was threatening to turn into a rout. Fenet's 3.Company tried to make a stand to allow the rest of the French battalion to catch up, and Hoyer's battalion held out for a time around the villages of Laszki and Brzeskie, but the Kampfgruppe's envisaged new front line was more of a fantasy than a reality. The Russian spearheads had already pushed past this projected boundary even before some of the SS units had reached it.

By 16.30 hours Hoyer's battalion positions were being bracketed by Soviet heavy artillery fire and an infantry attack was in the offing, supported by four T-34 tanks. Within an hour the Russian assault troops were within 50 metres of the battalion command post in Brzeskie and every dispatch rider, messenger and orderly had been called upon to mount a defence before the battalion disengaged and continued its retreat to the south. A testament to the last-ditch nature of the fighting was that SS-Unterscharführer Hammer, commander of a radio troop with SS-Nachrichten Abteilung 18 (SS-Signals Detachment 18) and a specialist who technically should have been well away from the fight, was awarded the German Cross in Gold for his leadership in this action.[104]

SS-Hauptsturmführer Cance arrived in Dabrowka in the night of 21-22 August with just a handful of his men after an exceptionally fraught retreat. With his soldiers scattered and no heavy weapons or communications, the French battalion was virtually combat ineffective, but as the Russian offensive continued unabated SS-Sturmbannführer Schäfer ordered Cance to move his unit to Mokre and hold it for the next 12 hours. Although Schäfer appreciated Cance's predicament, both Hoyer and Riepe's battalions were also almost at the end of their resistance, and with no reserves and no prospect of reinforcement it was hoped that the defence of Mokra could stabilise the line.

Cance arrived on the outskirts of Mokre in the middle of the night with just 70 of his men to discover that it was already held by the Russians, but a spirited attack drove them out again and the Frenchmen dug in around the village. Later that night, SS-Untersturmführer Lambert arrived in Mokre with some of the dispersed elements of 1. and 3.Companies who were able to rejoin their comrades.[105]

Now it was just a question of establishing defensive positions for the remnants of the three companies in total darkness on ground that none of them knew, and with little idea where other friendly troops were situated. Cance took Fenet by car and dropped him off alone in the middle of nowhere to await the arrival of the rest of 3.Company, whose mission was to plug the gap between the rest of the French battalion and Hoyer's Battalion, which was supposed to go into the line on their right. In the darkness, in completely unknown territory, Fenet began to calculate the firing ranges for his automatic weapons, should they ever arrive.

Lambert's 2.Company was installed on the right flank of the battalion, but it was stretched so thin it barely justified the name of a frontline and Lambert clearly had no illusions about his ability to hold against an attack. 1.Company was slated to take up position on 3.Company's right, but before it could even find its allotted area it found itself caught up in a Russian night attack. Disorientated and surrounded, the company has no choice but to slip away unnoticed.[106]

Meanwhile, Hoyer's men had been holding Nagoszyn and had been able to integrate some of the dispersed Frenchmen into his defence, but they were hit by a Russian force advancing down the Przeclaw-Debica road and had to give it up that night, despite relief efforts by SS.Pz. Aufkl.Abt.18. Covered by their rear-guard they loaded their wounded on to their remaining transport and prepared to break contact with the Russian forces that were penetrating their positions.[107]

As Russian infantry began to infiltrate through to the German rear, SS-Obersturmführer Wagner of I./SS-Panzergrenadier Regiment 39 led the breakout in a lorry filled with men armed with automatic weapons that blazed a path for those on foot to follow. Hoyer's battalion and his new French contingent numbered a mere hundred men by the time they reached the relative safety of Mokre, where Hoyer's men occupied positions on the left flank of the French battalion. Losses had been extremely high all round and the companies of the Kampfgruppe were again reduced to platoon strength.[108]

The Soviets were keen to take advantage of the evident weakness of the right flank of LIX.Army Corps and gave the depleted companies of Kampfgruppe Schäfer no time to rest. On 22 August, Soviet troops forced another crossing of the Wisloka northwest of Debica under cover of artillery fire and sorties from ground attack aircraft. With the Kampfgruppe significantly reduced in strength it could not contain this latest thrust, which quickly reached the outskirts of Starzecin, two miles to the east of Debica.[109]

At first light on the same day, despite direct observation being obscured by thick fog, a massive volume of fire from concentrations of heavy weapons targeted the entire Kampfgruppe sector from Dabic to Zassow, Mokre and the banks of the Wisloka. As the morning wore on, infantry attacks supported by armour were thrown against the forward field positions. SS-Sturmbannführer Hoffmann's Artillery Abteilung with its two batteries of 10.5 cm light howitzers hammered at the attackers but lacked the numbers required to cover the whole front, which was comprehensively breached by noon, creating a gap between Hoyer and Cance's battalions. The Kampfgruppe's light flak guns covered the withdrawal to a new defence line between Roza and Wiewiorka – but Hoyer and Riepe's battalions were now on their own.[110]

In Mokre, the French battalion quickly found itself isolated, with Soviet scouts taking advantage of the fog to infiltrate through the thinly held line. SS-Hauptsturmführer Cance's command post that was situated in a peasant's house became a target for Russian snipers, and Cance himself took a bullet through the arm while directing operations. Schäfer had demanded that Mokre be held for 12 hours, and as the situation deteriorated Cance ordered SS-Untersturmführer Lambert to lead 2.Company in a limited counterattack to drive off the Russian patrols and buy them some breathing space.

Lambert led his men into the fray, which rapidly degenerated into desperate close combat fought with knives, bayonets and spades. The Russians fell back and 2.Company held their ground, but it had sustained such high casualties that it was essentially finished as an effective fighting force, and its morale took a heavy blow when Lambert was killed by a mortar shell.

The Russian barrage was relentless, and the timber-framed houses burned all around. SS-Untersturmführer Reiche and SS-Untersturmführer Binder, the German liaison officers, along with SS-Obersturmführer Le Marquer were all killed when the command post received a direct hit from a large-calibre shell. By early afternoon the defenders of Mokre were running out of ammunition and the Russians were preparing to send tanks in against them. Lacking anti-tank weapons, the Orderly Officer SS-Untersturmführer Scapula broke out of the loose encirclement in a Kübelwagen jeep and drove to Debica to the battalion's supply train. Here he stacked his vehicle with ammunition and started the return run, but on approaching Mokre the car came under a barrage of fire which is thought to have ignited the load of ammunition aboard. The vehicle exploded killing Scapula and his German driver instantly. With the loss of the desperately need ammunition, the defence was doomed.

The Frenchmen continued to resist stubbornly and isolated groups were caught up in savage hand-to-hand fighting amongst the blazing buildings. Cance was wounded again and had to be carried off the battlefield. The attrition rate amongst the battalion's leadership had reached such a level that SS-Oberscharführer Boyer, with a rank equivalent to a Sergeant, had to take command of its shattered remnants. The defenders were prepared to make a last stand around the wrecked command post, but when the Russians threw tanks against it the surviving Frenchmen escaped as best they could.[111]

As they withdrew, the army troops from Sturm-Regiment Panzerarmee Oberkommando 1 counterattacked into the flank of the attacking Russians and were able to slow but not stop their advance.[112] The survivors of the battle for Mokre regrouped near Debica from where they were transferred by lorry to Tarnow, [113] but the battalion had been effectively destroyed. Of the estimated 980 French SS troops engaged some two weeks before, 130 were killed, around fifty were missing, and more than 660 were wounded. Of the battalion's original fifteen frontline officers seven were killed and eight wounded.[114]

As the day progressed, the right wing of LIX.Army Corps was comprehensively penetrated by Russian forces between the Wisloka River and Zassow, their spearheads advancing south and reaching the Wisloka crossing to the northwest of Debica. Simultaneously, Russian armoured formations broke out to the southwest from Radomysl forcing 8. Panzer Division farther back towards Dabrowka. It was clear that 5.Guards Army intended to exploit two main axes of advance: one directly south toward Debica that was threatening to overwhelm 18.SS-Panzergrenadier Division Kampfgruppe, the other along the Radornysl road toward Tarnow, a major communications centre housing the headquarters of Army Group North Ukraine and many attendant command posts and supply depots. Only 371.Infantry Division on the 18.SS Kampfgruppe's left wing was holding its own, but it was becoming increasingly isolated.[115]

By the evening of 22 August the French battalion and Grenadier Regiment 14 from 78.Grenadier Division on the right flank of the SS-Kampfgruppe had been smashed, and the Soviets now released 4.Guards Tank Corp to make the breakthrough to the west towards Tarnow. Sturm-Regiment Panzerarmee Oberkommando 1 (hereafter referred to as Sturm Regiment 1 AOK) had to try and forestall the advance of these powerful motorized forces until it was relieved by

Grenadier Brigade 1136 supported by Grenadier Regiment 1070 as they established a new line to the west of Debica.[116]

The two remaining battalions of Kampfgruppe Schäfer conducted a fighting withdrawal to the area around Borowa under heavy Soviet pressure. After suffering serious attrition from machine gun and direct anti-tank fire which targeted the grenadiers in their individual foxholes, they were forced to give up Roza and fell back by blocking positions until they linked up with elements of 24.Panzer Division advancing from the southwest.[117]

On the afternoon of 23 August, 24.Panzer Division's armoured group with attached infantry from 18.SS-Panzergrenadier Division Kampfgruppe successfully counterattacked and retook both Roza and Borowa. Using these two villages as an anchor, the panzer units under the command of General Major Freiherr von Edelsheim continued to attack towards the Wisloka River over the next two days, totally dislocating the advance of the Soviet IV.Tank Corps, which was forced to abandon its attacks on this front.[118]

However, even with such strong reinforcements, 18.SS-Panzergrenadier Division Kampfgruppe struggled to maintain a hold on their defensive line. SS-Sturmbannführer Riepe's battalion, dug in around the village of Jazwiny, came under strong infantry attack on the morning of 24 August but initially managed to hold its positions while Hoyer's men held the key position of Borowa situated on the main highway from Frystak to Krosno. As the day progressed the Soviet attacks became heavier with tank attacks supported by artillery and aircraft. During the afternoon, Hoyer was wounded but was treated on the battlefield and remained in command. Meanwhile Riepe was surrounded and forced to breakout in the face of overwhelming force. By the evening of 24 August both positions had had to be abandoned.

Following a night of planning and regrouping, the entire Kampfgruppe Schäfer went over to the attack on 25 August and following closely behind a short, sharp artillery barrage, stormed the Russians occupying their old positions. Within two hours the villages of Jazwiny and Borowa were again in their hands, while a concentration of Russian troops assembling for another assault near Roza was smashed by the full weight of LIX.Corps artillery. Over the next four days the troops of Kampfgruppe Schäfer maintained their positions in the face of small-scale local attack and harassing artillery fire, but the main thrust of the fighting had moved away from their sector by the end of August.[119]

During the night of 29–30 August, army units took over the positions of 18.SS-Panzergrenadier Division Kampfgruppe outside Debica and its shrunken units were able to use their own transport to motor to Tarnow where they briefly rejoined what was left of the French Volunteer Battalion. However, this was to be the end of their acquaintance. The French unit was moved to West Prussia for rebuilding while SS-Oberführer Trabandt and selected elements of his command returned to Hungary to supervise the expansion and training of 18.SS-Panzergrenadier Division. For Kampfgruppe Schäfer there was to be no rest. It was briefed for its next mission, to help to subdue the Slovak Uprising which was already threatening the rear of Army Group North Ukraine.[120]

5

SLOVAKIA

In the aftermath of the German occupation of Czechoslovakia the country was partitioned into the German-controlled Protectorate of Bohemia and Moravia and the quasi-independent Slovakia. Hitler's abiding hatred for the Czech people resulted in a brutal occupation aimed largely at keeping the country subdued while the economy was exploited for the benefit of the German war machine.

In Slovakia, the Germans had similar interests but used alternative methods to achieve their ends. Instead, they created an independent puppet state under Monseigneur Jozef Tiso and his ruling Slovak People's Party, which was used to demonstrate that Germans and Slavs could prosper together under the New Order. Despite German protestations of its independence, the Slovak government proved its subservience by entering the war as an ally of Germany, by providing troops for the Eastern Front and by supporting Hitler's policies towards the Jews.[1]

During the bitter fighting on the Eastern Front the small but professional Slovak Army had avoided the annihilation suffered by the Romanians, Hungarians, and Italians by limiting the size of the force that they committed to the Russian campaign to one that they could sensibly supply and maintain. This force amounted to a standard infantry division on foot and with a horse-drawn artillery element and a Fast Division, which was essentially a motorised infantry division with a small complement of light armour. The infantry division was poorly suited to mobile warfare and largely undertook occupation duties while the Fast Division fought well, advancing with Von Kleist's

1.Panzer Army into the Caucasus where it was highly regarded by its German allies.

However, the Slovak Army was not slow to recognise the reversal in fortunes that the German military had suffered since the disaster at Stalingrad. The Fast Division was badly mauled during the long retreat to Rostov and its remnant was airlifted home minus its heavy equipment, its morale shattered. Throughout the autumn of 1943 the Germans had gained ample proof of the increasing unreliability of their Slovak allies, which had culminated with a full regiment of the Slovak 1.Infantry Division deserting to the Soviets: 2,000 men in total, led by their officers.[2]

Following the German setbacks of 1943, elements within the Slovak High Command and government had tentatively approached the Soviets for material aid to enact an armed revolt against the Germans and their own collaborationist government. The plotters well knew that the revolt could only succeed if it was co-ordinated with the advance of the Red Army up to the borders of Slovakia. Although theoretically they had powerful forces at their disposal, as the bulk of the army had been preserved intact, the leaders of the revolt knew that the Germans would not tolerate a hostile force in the immediate rear of their fighting front and would bring all of their available forces to bear to crush any uprising. Therefore, a swift link-up with Soviet forces was a necessity. It was hoped that the proximity of Russian forces would allow for both Russian air cover for the uprising and aerial resupply.[3]

By the late spring / early summer of 1944, General Ferdinand Catlos, the Slovak Minister of Defence, had masterminded a plot for Slovakia to defect from the Axis and join the Russians. The plan was to be mutually beneficial, allowing the Czech and Slovak contingents to liberate their country from Fascist oppression while fulfilling the Soviets' strategic objectives. If Russian troops could cross the Carpathian Mountains in one swift move, they would outflank the German armies in Romania and Hungary and render the whole German position in the Balkans untenable.[4]

As far as the collaborationist government was concerned, the only forces truly loyal to the Tiso regime were poorly equipped militia units of the Slovakian People's Party, the Hlinka Guard, which protected senior government figures and buildings, and some police and Gendarmerie units grouped around the capital, Bratislava. These forces were in no position to put down any significant internal opposition and would be obliged to request help from the German military. It was a race for the rebels to grab the country and allow the Soviets in before the Germans could flood Slovakia with their own troops.[5]

General Catlos' plan envisaged that the 22,000 men of Slovak 1.Corps consisting of 1.Infantry Division and 2.Security Division, which were at that time engaged in constructing fortifications along Slovakia's eastern border, would attack the Germans in the rear and clear a path for the Russian 1.Ukrainian Front through the Carpathian mountain passes in the area of Bardejov and Medzilaborce including the strategically vital Dukla Pass. The Slovak Rear Army of 10,000 garrison troops would secure central Slovakia by concentrating around the key towns of Zvolen, Banska Bystrica and Brezno. These units were to seize vital installations, mobilise reserves and assist in partisan operations.

Partisan groups were to launch diversionary attacks in central Slovakia to draw off German and local Fascist forces.[6] These native forces were greatly augmented by resistance groups that filtered in from Bohemia and Moravia while others infiltrated over the mountains from Poland and Russian military advisors and technical staff were airlifted in.[7]

The uprising had been planned to start with a pre-arranged radio signal from the Russian high command, or if German forces attempted to occupy the country; whichever came first. Unfortunately for the plotters, the strength and aggression that made the partisan groups such formidable adversaries became their undoing almost immediately.[8] Volunteers had flocked to fill the partisan ranks and although many would remain unarmed until the Red Army could organise a dependable flow of arms and ammunition, the pressure for action was overwhelming and the regular army quickly found itself in a position it was unable to control.[9]

Partisan attacks began in earnest on 23 August and the rebellion spread rapidly, with the army either looking on impassively or actively co-operating with the partisans. People's Party officials were murdered, and ethnic German communities attacked. On 28 August, twenty-two members of the German military mission to Romania, which was being evacuated back to Germany, were dragged off a train at Turc Sv. Martin in central Slovakia and shot by a partisan group directed by a Soviet military advisor. This incident, combined with a significant increase in partisan activity in the rear areas of the German frontline, was the catalyst for a German reaction and with Tiso begging for help the German reserve army mobilised all available motorised units for an immediate incursion.[10]

While the German reserve army scraped together whatever forces it could find for the occupation of Slovakia, Army Group North Ukraine took matters into its own hands. With its rearward communications and transport disrupted by partisan actions and the shock defection of Romania to the Allied cause on 24 August, the Army Group command staff promptly prepared operational plans for the disarmament of the Slovak 1.Corps under the codename *Kartoffelernte* or Potato Harvest, thereby threatening the key part of the rebel plan to facilitate the Red Army's advance into Slovakia.[11]

The first clashes took place between the advancing German occupation troops and Slovak army units on 29 August at Cadca, Zilina, Povaiská Bystrica, and Trenéin and that same evening the code word was sent out to all garrisons to trigger the revolt, followed the next morning by a broadcast to the nation on the Free Slovak Radio Station calling on the people to revolt against their oppressors. Taken by surprise by the abrupt start of the revolt, the activation of most military units failed almost immediately. It quickly became apparent that only a few high-ranking officers in the high command had been admitted to the plan and that the Slovak divisions in the Carpathians were wholly unprepared to fight.[12]

This hesitation was quickly capitalised upon by Army Group North Ukraine which launched *Kartoffelernte mit prämie* or 'Operation Potato Harvest with Bonus' on 30 August, the suffix indicating that the Slovak troops were to be interned after disarmament. 1.Panzer Army formed Kampfgruppe Mathias, a mixed arms motorised force of 1,200 to 1,300 men drawn from the 68. 96. and 208. Infantry divisions, which moved to secure the Dukla Pass and disarm the Slovak 1.Infantry Division. The speed and efficiency of this action meant that very few Slovak soldiers escaped the net to join the rebellion in central Slovakia.[13]

The Slovak 2.Infantry Division was also swiftly dealt with, which resulted in both the loss of a large proportion of trained soldiers and also the capture of huge quantities of weapons and ammunition when the Germans occupied the town of Kvetnica. The haul of munitions

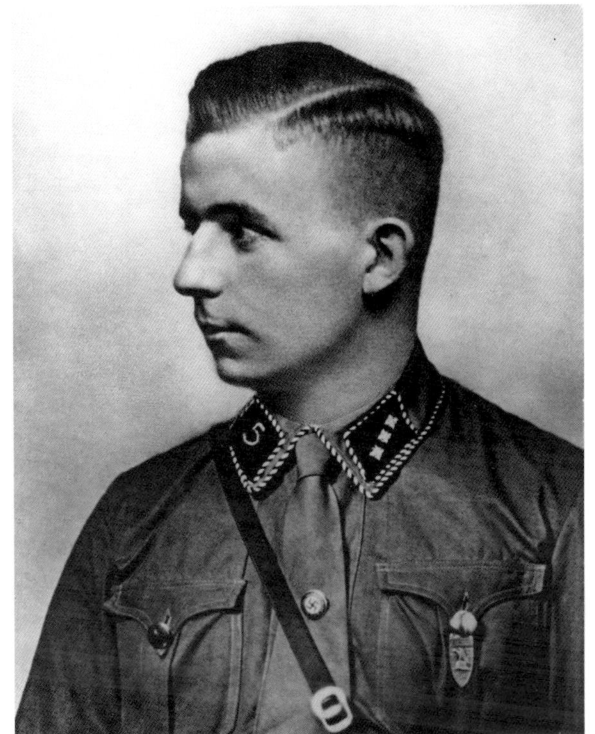

A studio portrait photograph of Horst Wessel in the uniform of an SA-Sturmführer of SA-Sturm 5, taken in 1930. (Bundesarchiv, Bild 146-1978-043-14 / Heinrich Hoffmann / CC-BY-SA 3.0 Wikimedia Commons)

Period mass-produced postcard with music and lyrics of the 'Horst Wessel Lied' that Horst Wessel wrote as a marching song for his comrades, which became an unofficial national anthem following his death. (Private Collection)

Left: Karl Maria Demelhuber seated on the left, first commander of the 1.SS-Infantry Brigade (mot) (NIOD Institute for War, Holocaust and Genocide Studies)

Below: SS security troops checking civilian documentation at a checkpoint in Russia, July 1941. (Wydawnictwo Prasowe Kraków-Warszawa, Wikimedia Commons)

A Russian captain from a Red Army reconnaissance unit instructs partisans in the operation of a German MP-40 sub machine gun. August 1941. (Георгий Петрусов, Wikimedia Commons)

Anti-partisan sweep. White armbands are worn to aid identification of friendly forces in a landscape with such poor visibility. (Wydawnictwo Prasowe Kraków-Warszawa, Wikimedia Commons)

SS-Gruppenführer Erich von dem Bach-Zelewski at a map briefing in Russia. (Bundesarchiv, Bild+101III-AhrensA-020-31A, Wikimedia Commons)

A Waffen-SS patrol in Russia, 1943, passes anxious civilians. (Wydawnictwo Prasowe Kraków-Warszawa, Wikimedia Commons)

Officers and men of 1.SS-Infantry Brigade (mot) paraded for inspection by the brigade commander, SS-Standartenführer Trabandt, autumn 1943. The third figure from the left, closest to the camera, is SS-Sturmbannführer Ernst Schäfer who commanded III./SS-Infantry Regiment 10 during this period. (Bundesarchiv, Bild 101III-AhrensH-093-15 / CC-BY-SA 3.0 Wikimedia Commons)

Wehrmacht Generalfeldmarschall Günther von Kluge (seated) discussing the frontline situation. Kluge ordered the withdrawal of Army Group Centre behind the Dnieper River, which forced the abandonment of Smolensk. (Wydawnictwo Prasowe Kraków-Warszawa, Wikimedia Commons)

Left: Marshal of the Soviet Union Vasily Danilovich Sokolovsky, liberator of Smolensk. (Ministry of Defence of the Russian Federation, Wikimedia Commons)

Below: Soviet troops forcing a crossing of the Dnieper River, 1943. (LOC)

SS Squad Leader in action. (Wydawnictwo Prasowe Kraków-Warszawa, Wikimedia Commons)

A German late production Sturmgeschutz III Stug 40 Ausf G assault gun. These vehicles were issued to both SS-Panzer Abteilung 18 and SS-Panzer-Jager Abteilung 18 in lieu of traditional turreted gun tanks. (Vassia Atanassova, Wikimedia Commons)

Above: Russian troops improvise a river crossing of the type used to outflank the 18.SS-Panzergrenadier Division Kampfgruppe time and again on the Strypa River sector. (Леонид Великжанин, Wikimedia Commons)

Opposite, top: Slovak Army officers involved in the uprising against their former allies. (Wikimedia Commons)

Opposite, bottom: A view of the Slovak town of Ružomberok, captured by SS-Kampfgruppe Schäfer on 6 September 1944. This image shows the mountainous nature of the terrain through which the Kampfgruppe fought. (Fortepan ID-96059 donated by Schermann Ákos, Wikimedia Commons)

Left: Hungarian leader Miklós Horthy and Adolf Hitler. (Ladislav Luppa, Wikimedia Commons)

Below: László Bárdossy, Hungarian Foreign Minister, with German Ambassador to Hungary Dietrich von Jagow. Von Jagow, as a senior SA officer, hindered SS recruitment in Hungary to the best of his ability. (Wikimedia Commons)

Eigenhändige Unterschrift des Inhabers

Kommandobuch

zugleich Personalausweis

Nr. 1838

für

den SS-Hauptsturmführer
(Dienstgrad)

ab .... (Datum) .... (neuer Dienstgrad)

ab

ab

Heinrich Böltz
(Vor- und Zuname)

Beschriftung und Nummer der

1

Above: Kommandobuch issued to Heinrich Boltz, a member of the Volksdeutsche Mittelstelle (VoMi) It is interesting to note Boltz's SS rank and issue stamps on the document, even though VoMi was never officially part of that organisation. (Huddyhuddy, Wikimedia Commons)

Below: Waffen-SS patrol in Hungary, November 1944. The soldier closest to the camera has an Army issue helmet cover, suggesting shortages of even basic uniform items. (Wydawnictwo Prasowe Kraków-Warszawa, Wikimedia Commons)

Hungarian General Karolyi Beregffy at the command point of an SS-Cavalry Regiment on the outskirts of Budapest. Probably part of the 'Attila Line', this image clearly shows the weakness of the prepared defences around the city. (Fritsch, Wikimedia Commons)

Soviet troops in the ruins of Budapest following its capture in February 1945. The failure of LVII.Panzer Korps to hold the southeastern approaches to the city directly contributed to its encirclement and loss. (FORTEPAN / X.Y. adományozó, Wikimedia Commons)

Right: SS-Obersturmführer Dr Hans Lipinski, commander of 1.SS-Flak Abteilung 18 who won a Knight's Cross for his unit's performance in the defence of Szécsény. (Wikimedia Commons)

Below: German 88mm anti-aircraft gun, used to devastating effect against Russian tanks by 1./SS-Flak Abteilung 18 at Szécsény. (Mohit S, Wikimedia Commons)

Left: The leaning tower of Szécsény was built as a fire tower in the 18th century. Miraculously surviving the battle, as one of the highest points in the town it undoubtedly acted as a convenient aiming point for Soviet artillery. (HoremWeb, Wikimedia Commons)

Below: A Sturmgeschutz III Stug 40 Ausf G assault gun of 18.SS-Panzer Abteilung loaded with panzergrenadiers negotiating a mountain road in Slovakia following the Division's general retreat from northern Hungary, December 1944. (Narodowe Archiwum Cyfrowe, Wikimedia Commons)

A German Sd.Kfz 142/2 Sturmhaubitze 42 Ausf.G with 105mm howitzer main armament built by Alkett in Berlin. SS-Panzer-Jager Abteilung 18 received eight of these vehicles in February 1944. (Alan Wilson, Wikimedia Commons)

Abandoned German vehicles in Silesia, April / May 1945. This was the fate of virtually all of 18.SS-Panzergrenadier Division's equipment in the final days of the war as individual units scrambled to reach the demarcation line and surrender to the US Army rather than fall into the hands of the Red Army or Czech partisans. (Donated to Wikimedia Commons by Vitězslav Kollmann)

German 'Hetzer' tank destroyer. (Roman Mifek, Wikimedia Commons)

Above: Soviet SU-152 assault gun. It was a battery of these powerful tank destroyers that broke up the combined Army and Waffen-SS attack towards Breslau on the last day of the war. (Wikimedia Commons)

Left: Heinrich Sonne, commander of SS-Aufklärungs Abteilung 18, in the uniform of an officer in the postwar Bundeswehr. Sonne was one of the very few Waffen-SS veterans allowed to serve in the reconstituted West German Army. (Wikimedia Commons)

that were lost to the uprising included well over forty million rounds of small arms ammunition, 112,000 hand grenades and more than 60,000 artillery shells and several hundred machine guns of various calibres.[14]

Confusion also reigned in western Slovakia where many of the garrisons, including those in the major cities of Bratislava, Nitra, Hlohovec, Nové Mesto and, Váhom, Trenéin, and Keimarok, failed to join in the rising (and may not even have been informed that an uprising was about to happen), allowing the German forces to concentrate on crushing the rebel forces already largely penned in the centre of the country.[15]

With fighting lines crystallising across the country, Army Group North Ukraine continued to act aggressively to the threat to its rearward communications. It quickly formed a combat group consisting of the battered remains of SS-Kampfgruppe Schäfer, still reeling from its losses in Galicia but for the moment unable to rejoin the bulk of 18.SS-Panzergrenadier Division, and a reinforced battalion consisting of the mobile elements of 86.Infantry Division supported by I./SS-Artillery Regiment 18 (three batteries of light field howitzers under SS-Sturmbannführer Hoffmann) and an armoured car squadron from 24.Panzer Division. The Kampfgruppe was tasked with penetrating down the Váh (Waag) and Hron Valleys with the ambitious aim of capturing the towns of Ružomberok (Rosenberg) and Banska Bystrica and effecting a link-up with Kampfgruppe von Ohlen from Panzer Division 'Tatra', which was advancing south eastwards across the Polish border.[16]

The 2,400-man-strong force was formed at Nowy Targ in the General Government region of Poland on 30 August and its initial objectives were the capture of the towns of Kežmarok and Poprad prior to reopening the main east-west railway line that ran through the Waag valley and supplied the German Carpathian front.[17]

Given the extent of the casualties suffered by the Divisional Kampfgruppe in the recent fighting and the slow pace of recruitment and training being carried out by the bulk of the division in Hungary, Kampfgruppe Schäfer was relatively weak in all arms, and its strength probably only amounted to around 1,200 men at this date. At its inception it consisted of a mixed Grenadier battalion with two infantry companies from SS-Panzergrenadier Regiment 40 and one company from SS-Panzergrenadier Regiment 39. There was also the

13.(Infantry Gun) Company from SS-Panzergrenadier Regiment 39 and the 14.(Flak) Company from SS-Panzergrenadier Regiment 40 and a 'Heavy' Company from SS- Panzergrenadier Regiment 39 with heavy machine guns and mortars. Added to this was a mixed support company with a platoon of motorcyclists and a platoon of 7.5cm anti-tank guns from SS-Panzergrenadier Regiment 40 alongside a reinforced platoon from 2./SS-Pz.Aufkl.Abt.18. An artillery complement drawn from I. and II./SS-Artillery Regiment 18 comprised of light field howitzers was added to provide punch to the Kampfgruppe, which was rounded out with small medical, signals and supply units.[18]

The activation of Operation *Potato Harvest* was the signal for the Kampfgruppe to prepare for action where it would be subordinated to the ad hoc Sturm Regiment 1 AOK. Both units advanced from Skryzow in Poland towards Poprad on 1 September with the mixed company, led by SS-Untersturmführer Wischmeyer, acting as vanguard for the Kampfgruppe.

The area around Kežmarok and Poprad was home to a large and well organised Volksdeutsche population, who had made efforts to arm themselves as the threat of partisan action against them increased. Although the Volksdeutsche in Poprad were disarmed by local partisans, in Kežmarok members of the ethnic German population skirmished with troops from the Slovak Artillery Regiment 12, who garrisoned the town, and prevented their retreat in the face of the advance of Kampfgruppe Schäfer. The battle group suffered its first casualties while trying to oust Slovak regular army soldiers manning a barricade in the main street before accepting the town's surrender on 31 August without further resistance.[19]

From the very beginning of the insurgency, the ideological struggle between Nazi Germany and its Communist adversaries incited the type of brutality that had become commonplace on the battlefields of the Eastern Front. Beyond the obvious strategic necessity of suppressing an uprising behind his front lines, Hitler had an ulterior motive for suppressing the rebellion. He had the dual aim of crushing the Communist elements in Slovakia and bringing the country back into the Axis fold while forcing the Slovak leadership to deport the 35,000 Jews whom they had previously refused to hand over.[20] To this end, SS-Reichsführer Himmler assumed responsibility for crushing the uprising in his role as commander of the German Replacement Army and he ordered that the rising should be promptly put down and communications in Slovakia restored.[21]

On 1 September, SS-Obergruppenführer Gottlob Berger, the former head of SS recruitment who had recently been appointed as Higher SS and Police leader (HSSPF) for Slovakia, arrived in Bratislava to assume command of all German forces in western and central Slovakia.[22] Encouraged by the patchy resistance encountered in the west of the country Berger confidently predicted on 2 September that he could subdue the rising in just four days and suborned every available SS unit into his command in an attempt to ensure his success.[23] In the face of this force it was the Jews and ordinary peasants who suffered the worst reprisals and the Soviet led partisan groups reacted in kind, deliberately targeting ethnic German settlements, leading to large-scale killings of unarmed civilians.[24]

Part of the reason for the escalating violence against the civilian population was the lack of progress made in advancing towards the centres of the rebellion. SS-Obergruppenführer Berger had virtually no experience of commanding large military formations in combat and his forces were in a particularly poor position for putting down an armed insurrection. His command consisted of a mixed bag of training units, occupation troops and burnt-out battle groups, hurriedly withdrawn from the Carpathian front, totalling only 15-20,000 men. This meagre and widely dispersed force had to attack through some of the most mountainous country in Europe, which was ideal for defence. With the troops at his disposal, all that Berger could do was aim at restoring the most important lines of communication through rebel territory.[25]

Army Group North Ukraine appeared to have little faith in Berger's command of the situation, as it continued to exercise operational control in its own rear areas. On 3 September, Army Group ordered SS-Sturmbannführer Schäfer to advance westwards along the Váh Valley with the objective of occupying Ružomberok and linking up with Kampfgruppe von Ohlen advancing from the northwest.[26]

Kampfgruppe von Ohlen was based around the Panzer Grenadier Replacement and Training Regiment 82 and was a motorised force of around 2,400 men, which included a Panzer company and motorised artillery battery and was one of the major components of Panzer Division 'Tatra' alongside Kampfgruppe Junck, built around Panzer Grenadier Replacement and Training Regiment 85.[27]

Following the capture of Poprad, Kampfgruppe Schäfer and the reinforced battalion of 86.Infantry Division separated, the former advancing on Liptovsky Sv. Mikuläs while the latter was directed up the Hron Valley towards Cervena Skala.[28] As Schäfer's march continued, a new defensive position was encountered just three miles west of Poprad. Slovak forces had blocked the road and the terrain was such that it could not be bypassed by vehicles. Howitzers were brought forward and hammered the position before SS-Untersturmführer Wischmeyer's vanguard company stormed the barrier. The advance continued with barrier after barrier having to be overcome in a similar fashion.

Quite unexpectedly, the column of German vehicles came under machine gun attack from several obsolete Slovak Š-328 biplanes that also dropped hand grenades on the troops below, which, although doing little damage, sought to unnerve the attackers who had little or no air support of their own.[29]

Tension mounted, the grenadiers expecting an ambush at every turn in the road. While traversing a deep ravine two miles beyond the town of Hybe, the head of the motorised column came under heavy machine gun and artillery fire that was followed up by a determined infantry attack driven off by the combined fire of 2cm flak guns. But even as the head of the column continued to make progress, there was trouble to the rear:

> According to reports from Fritz Krumrey, gun commander in 2./SS-Artillerie Regiment 18, the following ammunition Staffel was ambushed by partisans on that 4 September, resulting in the Muni-Staffel-Führer, an SS-Unterscharführer, and two of his drivers being killed.[30]

5 September followed the same pattern as the previous day, with small surges of progress followed by ambush, artillery fire, attack and a resumption of the advance. By the early morning of the 6th the Kampfgruppe was in a position to liberate Ružomberok. The attack began early in the morning with reconnaissance troops probing the outskirts of the town. They took fire almost immediately and a battery of light howitzers moved forward to put identified rebel positions under direct fire, closely followed up by an infantry attack by two rifle companies supported by a reinforced platoon from 2./SS-Aufkl. Abt.18. Meanwhile, the rest of 2./SS-Aufkl.Abt.18 assaulted the heights to the south of the town, neutralising several Slovak artillery

positions in hand-to-hand fighting before securing the southern approaches to the town. By 09.00 hours the town was secure.

The ethnic Germans of the town received the troops with open arms, as they had witnessed the massacre of the many of their own people. They reported that seventy Volksdeutsche had been shot on the orders of Soviet Commissars and that a further forty to fifty people had been led away and were presumed to have met the same fate.[31]

The capture of Ružomberok was a significant coup for the occupation forces as the town had become an important industrial centre for the war economy of the Reich, far removed from the Allied bombing of Germany. Amongst the liberated industrial complexes, 982 completed artillery carriages were discovered that had been destined for shipment back to Germany before the uprising and which the insurgents had failed to destroy.

However, the wider strategic victory, that of opening the Váh Valley to German railway traffic, remained elusive as Slovak artillery continued to dominate the area, and events elsewhere were proving that the German forces deployed throughout the rest of Slovakia were far too weak to suppress the rebellion. Progress almost everywhere else was desperately slow.[32]

At the beginning of September, approximately 47,000 rebels were involved in the uprising including over 18,000 Slovak frontline soldiers. There were also an assortment of large and small partisan groups totalling more than 15,000 combatants made up of men and women from more than 24 European nations, including escaped forced labourers, ex-prisoners of war and Soviet technical advisors. Additionally, the Russian High Command had authorised the airlift of the 2,000 men of the Czechoslovak 2.Airborne Brigade into the combat zone in the second half of September where they joined the 1.Czechoslovak Air Fighter Regiment in the fighting.[33]

From the start of the uprising, the insurgent army had been divided into two defensive areas, with groups of infantry battalions and artillery batteries in areas surrounding the larger towns in the rebel-held zone. However, this division of forces quickly proved itself to be too unwieldy for effective command and control and on 9 September Colonel (later General) Ján Golian created six tactical groups of approximately brigade strength to take their place. The tactical groups were now combined arms units with, at least at the outset, their composition corresponding to the individual tactical requirements and geographical conditions of their assigned combat sectors.

Tactical Group One was based around the rebel capital of Banska Bystrica and served as the strategic reserve for the insurgent army. It had a strength of 4,000 infantrymen and four artillery batteries.

Tactical Group Two was centred on Brezno in the Hron valley and was tasked with the defences of the east and south-east of the country. This was the strongest group with 16,000 infantrymen and twelve artillery batteries of various calibres.

Tactical Group Three had its command post in the city of Zvolen and its forces covered the south and southwest, principally the long border with Hungary. It initially benefitted from the Hungarian policy of non-aggression towards the uprising. It possessed around 10,000 infantrymen, fifteen artillery batteries and fifteen tanks.

Tactical Group Four covered Zemjanske Kostolany in western Slovakia with 5,000 infantrymen, four artillery batteries, two anti-tank guns believed to be German-manufactured Pak 40, and five tanks. This group was commanded by Colonel of Cavalry Augustin Malar who had served with distinction with the Slovak Fast Division in Russia and had earned the German Knight's Cross for his division's achievements there.

Tactical Group Five was responsible for the defence of northwestern Slovakia around Turc. Sv. Martin. It had 4,000 infantrymen, four artillery batteries, five anti-tank guns and ten tanks.

Tactical Group Six defended the north routes into the country including the country around Ružomberok. This was numerically the weakest tactical group with 3,500 infantrymen, three artillery batteries, ten medium mortars and several tanks, although the terrain in this region markedly favoured the defenders.

Added to these were around 2,000 specialists from the pioneer, intelligence and medical branches centralised under the army high command.[34]

The loss of Ružomberok was a big strategic blow to the uprising, being the northern anchor of its defences and only thirty-two miles from the rebellion's provisional capital in Banska Bystrica. Therefore, Colonel Golian ordered an immediate counterattack from the north and brought up more reinforcements from Zvolen to the south. These counter attacks were fought off with heavy and accurate artillery and mortar fire, but the Kampfgruppe was likewise unable to make further headway as more Slovak troops concentrated upon the town. Slovak possession of the high ground at Biely Potok approximately two miles from the southern outskirts of Ružomberok allowed them to dominate the town and railway line with their own artillery.[35]

Following Colonel Golian's orders Tactical Group 6, led by Colonel Cernek, made the first determined attack on Ružomberok from the wooded country to the south of the town and although this assault was repulsed, the Group continued to use small units to probe the defences while keeping up a wearying and persistent harassing fire with mortars. The grenadiers of Kampfgruppe Schäfer attempted to keep their opponents at arm's length with aggressive patrolling of their own to deny the Slovaks possession of the outlying villages. These patrols brought back quantities of captured ammunition and military equipment but met with little real opposition.[36]

On 9 September, a larger operation was launched along the road towards Banska Bystrica. Two platoons led by SS-Untersturmführer Radtke advanced south but upon reaching Biely Potok they came under heavy artillery fire from the hills around the town and the advance was further blocked by a strong anti-tank barrier covering the road. Realising his inability to advance while under observation from an entrenched and powerful enemy force, Radtke took his small unit back to Ružomberok.[37]

As the value of possession of Biely Potok became fully realised, the Slovaks quickly strengthened its dominating position in the hills with tank traps, bunkers and a trench system. The Slovak regular army troops deployed here were professionally led by Major of Artillery Mild Vesel and were able to establish positions on both sides of the only approach road, which they covered with artillery and mortars.

The inability of the battle-worn Kampfgruppe Schäfer simultaneously to hold Ružomberok and keep its supply lines free from partisan attack whilst attempting to breach the fortified positions at Biely Potok was symptomatic of the wider problems faced by the disparate German units trying to contain the rebellion. These units were simply too weak and poorly equipped to swiftly overcome a determined enemy entrenched in mountainous terrain. The attacking forces were also handicapped by a dislocated command and supply structure with units advancing from the west being directed by German Command Slovakia and those operating in the northeast and east, including Kampfgruppe Schäfer, still being controlled and provisioned by Army Group North Ukraine.[38]

Nevertheless, by 10 September the East Slovak Army had been disarmed and the eastern region of Slovakia pacified, Army Group North Ukraine withdrew the bulk of its troops, leaving only the reinforced battalion-sized Kampfgruppe drawn from 86.Infantry Division to cover Telgárt and Poprad in its immediate rear on a purely defensive footing, leaving German Command Slovakia to conduct the final suppression of the uprising.[39]

For the moment there was stalemate around Ružomberok as both sides continued to probe each other's defences. Between 10–12 September Kampfgruppe Schäfer conducted search and destroy missions in the surrounding villages to keep the rebels from concentrating their forces and to prevent them from encircling Rosenberg too closely. Platoon-sized patrols of 25-30 men under SS-Untersturmführer Gammer and SS-Obersturmführer Bachler exchanged fire with rebel troops who took advantage of the high peaks surrounding the town to snipe at passing traffic and destroyed their position whenever they had the chance,[40] but it was clear that a more concerted effort was necessary.

Orders were issued by Berger's command staff in Bratislava that tasked Kampfgruppe Schäfer with clearing the railway line from east to west with the aid of the 1,000-man-strong Kampfgruppe Volkmann attacking in a southward direction on a converging line from Trstená. Kampfgruppe Schäfer launched a surprise attack to the west on 13 September, which gained some ground and captured an LTvz38 light tank, one of the very few armoured vehicles remaining to the insurgents. This success was followed up by the seizure of the important road and rail junction at Kral'ovany, although the attack was brought to a halt just beyond by strong Slovak forces entrenched at Šútovo.[41]

In northern Slovakia the bulk of Lieutenant General Friedrich-Wilhelm von Loeper's ad hoc Panzer Division 'Tatra' had been manning holding positions when it was belatedly ordered south on 10 September to assist in the clearing of the Váh Valley and to affect a link up with Kampfgruppe Schäfer. The division's advance had been delayed by the need to wait for reinforcements, which allowed 5 Tactical Group to prepare its defences in some depth ahead of it, but forward elements of the division were able to push on into the Váh Valley by 13 September and made contact with a combat patrol from Kampfgruppe Schäfer two days later. On the face of it, this appeared to be a significant German victory, but the connection between the two units was tenuous, the line of the valley at best only covered by thinly spaced outposts under the guns of Slovak artillery on the hills all around. With the heights of Biely Potok still firmly in Slovak hands, it would be more than a month before rail traffic could safely traverse the line.[42]

Elsewhere, intense battles had taken place in the southern part of central Slovakia around the city of Telgárt during the first two weeks of September, the Germans initially taking the initiative and capturing the town, only for Slovak units to counterattack and regain the lost territory. However, the Germans could not maintain the pressure as they were forced to transfer troops to the Carpathians where a combined Soviet and Czechoslovak force began operations to force the Dukla Pass on 8 September. As a result, the whole southern sector of the rebel-held area was also relatively quiet for almost a month, which was aided by Hungarian's policy of neutrality toward the uprising.[43] By mid-September there was relative stability on most parts of the rebel front with only small-scale battles being fought on the northern slope of Mount Ostrô, on the western fringe of the rebel area round Kremnica and Jánova Lehota, where the Germans tried to force their way through to the city of Zvolen.[44]

Although the German units initially deployed to Slovakia had a very mixed composition, they still had a distinct advantage over their opponents in terms of training, combat experience and quality of equipment. However, the rebellion was much larger in scale than the Germans appreciated, which frustrated their attempts to quell it quickly. Ineffectual command and control stemming from the inexperienced SS-Obergruppenführer Berger and his staff required Himmler to replace him with General of Police Hermann Hofle on 14 September and increase the commitment of troops to the region to a strength equivalent to seven divisions, including the improvised Panzer Division 'Tatra'. This gave the German occupation force a combined total of 45,000 soldiers supported by tanks, artillery, and ground attack aircraft,[45] but the deployment of so many troops was hampered by the poor road network which hindered the resupply of large, mechanised forces and limited the width of the front on which they could advance.

Despite these difficulties, Hofle appreciated that the rebels had benefitted from Berger's lack of aggression and ordered Panzer Division 'Tatra' to attack from the west on the 20 September down the Turiec Valley to link up with Kampfgruppe Schill, which was advancing from the southwest. The next day the Panzer Division 'Tatra' captured Turc Sv. Martin where it smashed a rebel brigade, killing and capturing over 1,000 men.[46]

On 23–24 September Panzer Division 'Tatra' finally broke through to the Váh Valley in strength as their Slovak opponents abandoned their positions and a solid link-up was made with Kampfgruppe Schäfer at Šútovo. This union allowed the Kampfgruppe to seize a vital railway bridge over the Váh River to the east of Vrútky, which allowed the railway line to be reopened on 11 October; although even at this date it still came under sporadic artillery fire.[47] This artillery fire was still being laid down by the stalwart Major Vesel and his men atop Biely Potok, who held out in their positions for seven weeks against fourteen separate assaults. Casualties were very high on both sides. Given the numerical weakness of 6 Tactical Group it proved necessary to draw in reinforcements from quieter areas to maintain a coherent defence. Support arrived from both 2 and 3 Tactical Groups, although the weakening of their sectors was to have serious consequences later in the battle.[48]

In addition to confronting Slovak regular army forces to the south and west of Ružomberok, Kampfgruppe Schäfer were forced to continue their patrolling activities to keep their lateral and rearward communications open in the face of aggressive partisan activity. The actions of one of these patrols resulted in an atrocity against civilians that is directly attributable to the 18.SS-Panzergrenadier Division (rather than to the 1.SS-Infantry Brigade (mot)). It concerns the fate of eight Jewish people who were captured near Stara Cernova, approximately two miles to the west of Ružomberok up the Váh Valley, on 28 September. These people were presumably denounced by the local Volksdeutsche population and reportedly handed over to the divisional Feldgendarmerie (military police) Company for 'special handling', which almost inevitably led to their execution.[49]

On 2 October Kampfgruppe Schäfer resumed its attempts to storm the high ground at Biely Potok, making several efforts over the next few days but suffered heavy losses for little gain. Finally, after days of battering away and sustaining irreplaceable losses, Schäfer's men broke into the defences on 8 October. SS-Untersturmführer Radtke, commanding a company of men from I./SS-Regiment 39, led a dawn attack on the position under cover of artillery fire provided by light howitzers from 2.Battery of II./SS-Artillery Regiment 18 under SS-Untersturmführer Fiedler and by 08.00 had captured the main position and the dominating height of Hill 1102 in a direct frontal assault that caught the defenders completely by surprise. This attack was carried through at the cost of two dead and nine wounded to the assault company, casualties matched by the covering artillery battery, which suffered from Slovak counter-battery fire.[50]

Major Vesel was not to be bested so easily though, and this success was undermined on the following day when he personally led two companies to recapture the Sidorov, a dominant hill just one mile to the northwest of Biely Potok from which he could again dominate the surrounding countryside. This attack coincided with the onset of the autumn rains, which made all movement in the hills away from paved roads a near impossibility.[51]

By the end of the first week of October it was clear that the original German forces committed to putting down the uprising had been fought to a standstill and that fresh units were needed. This resulted in a pause in the fighting which lasted until mid-October and was used by Hofle to tighten his stranglehold around central Slovakia while he prepared to carry out the decisive push into the centre of the rebel enclave in the south-east. He was reinforced by the 271.Volksgrenadier Division and three further battalions of 14.SS-Grenadier Division 'Galicia' which were deployed along the Váh Valley, while the 708.Volksgrenadier Division was sent to Nitra. Additionally, various anti-aircraft, mountain, and pioneer units were transferred to Slovakia alongside several security and military police formations. In total Hofle received approximately 35,000 extra troops but in return he was supposed to release SS-Kampfgruppe Schill and Panzer Division 'Tatra' for urgent re-assignment to the Carpathian Front but as these represented his most able fighting troops, he felt obliged to ignore the order.[52]

Hofle planned to administer the coup de grâce with a thrust into the soft underbelly of the rebellion, using the full 18.SS-Panzergrenadier Division in a surprise attack from northern Hungary into the hitherto quiet zone of 3 Tactical Group. In preparation for this action the infamous SS-Brigade 'Dirlewanger', fresh from the slaughter that it had wrought subduing the Warsaw Rising, marched south over the border from Poland where it was to replace Kampfgruppe Schäfer in the Ružomberok area, which was in turn ordered to rejoin its patent unit to bolster it for its upcoming baptism of fire in Slovakia. The Kampfgruppe left Ružomberok on 10 October and was transferred by train to a divisional staging post around Losonc in northern Hungary where its elements arrived over the next three days. Given both the professionalism with which the insurgent army had been led and the ferocity with which the partisan war had been fought, much was being asked of the untried 18.SS-Panzergrenadier Division. Its mission was to advance across the Hungarian-Slovakian border on a broad front almost 40 miles wide between the towns of Lučenec to Plešivec and fall on the Slovak defenders from the rear, aiming to capture the rebel held strongpoints of Telgárt, Banská Bystrica, and Zvolen.[53]

In concept the plan was relatively straightforward but events elsewhere conspired to throw it off course. For some time, the German high command had become increasingly agitated by both Soviet advances towards eastern Slovakia and the political situation in Hungary, where it was an open secret that Admiral Horthy wanted to remove his country from the war. Given the deteriorating military situation in southeast Europe, the strategic value of Slovakia continued to increase, and it was essential for the Germans to end the rebellion as quickly as possible.

Admiral Horthy made a radio address to his people on 15 October during which he announced that he was to conclude a peace with the Allies, but the German authorities in Hungary acted with enterprise and efficiency and promptly deposed Horthy and installed the Fascist 'Arrow Cross' organisation in government. This move initially strengthened the German strategic situation in Slovakia as they could now move troops at will throughout the country, but it failed to consider the will of the Hungarian people.[54]

SS-Oberführer Trabandt had received a direct order from Himmler himself to mobilise his division and begin the final suppression of the insurgency no later than 2 October, but this order was more easily issued than executed. Himmler seems to have had as little consideration for Hofle and his chain of command as he had for Hungarian national autonomy, but his scheme for early action was scuppered by the Hungarian railway system.

Upon approaching the Hungarian transport officer responsible for providing trains to move the division to its staging areas, the divisional staff were informed that it would take three weeks to move the entire division, not the three days that had been anticipated. Disruption due to allied air attacks on bridges and junctions was cited as the official reason for the delays but, with trains being mysteriously misdirected or rolling stock failing to appear at all, it was obvious that the Hungarian authorities were being as obstructive as possible.[55]

Most of the divisional units were eventually assembled in the border area by 14 October, but large portions of the new raised force were in a very poor condition. With the reintegration of the soldiers from Kampfgruppe Schäfer, the division now mustered around 8,000 men, which represented less than half of its authorised strength. Some units had received no uniforms and virtually no training. The grenadier regiments were woefully undermanned and lacked key specialist staff in command and communications roles. Morale amongst the conscripts was exceedingly low and the division reported that 100 recruits had deserted during the three-day journey.[56]

Many of the infantry and anti-tank gun companies had not arrived from their training areas and the reconnaissance unit had no armoured cars. Only a third of the artillery batteries had been formed by this time and those gunners that had seen no previous action only fired their weapons for the first time on 14 October. Fuel and food were in very short supply. The division's only saving grace was its Panzer battalion, which was equipped with Sturmgeschütz III assault guns, although how many guns the battalion actually possessed is unknown.[57]

Both General Höfle and his chief of staff, Lieutenant Colonel Uetritz, were shocked at the state of the division upon which they had place such high hopes.[58] Indignantly, Höfle sent the following telex to the Reichsführer SS Himmler:

> Given the inadequate equipment, the poor level of training and the unstable internal status of the unit, there are at least two days needed to prepare the troops for the attack. Although I am fully aware of the need for an immediate advance due to the overall situation and am also making the greatest efforts to establish readiness, the attack cannot take place until October 19th. I take no responsibility for an earlier advance.[59]

The wider German offensive began on 17 October and in the face of this vast force many partisan units simply melted away. Soviet attacks on the east border proved to be insufficient in face of fierce resistance by the 1.Panzer Army to relieve the pressure on the rebels, or influence the course of the fighting. 18.SS-Panzergrenadier Division's advance was reluctantly postponed until 19 October.[60]

At this time the rebel-held area had been compressed into a zone of approximately 4,000 square miles and was being increasingly hemmed in by powerful German forces. Panzer Division 'Tatra' and SS-Kampfgruppe Schill attacked from the east towards Zvolen in the south and Banska Bystrica in the centre. SS-Brigade 'Dirlewanger' pressed in from the direction of Ružomberok in the northwest, while SS-Kampfgruppe Wittenmeyer, drawn from 14.SS-Grenadier Division 'Galicien', approached Brezno from the north. 18.SS-Panzergrenadier Division aimed for a link-up with Sturm Regiment 1 AOK around the city of Telgart once it had started its advance from the south.[61]

18.SS- Panzergrenadier Division lined up for its incursion in three separate mobile columns.

The left-hand column pushed off from the Losonc area and consisted of II. and III./SS-Panzergrenadier Regiment 39, its I.Battalion remaining behind as being unfit for combat through low personnel numbers, insufficient training and poor standard of equipment. Attached to the regiment in support were 1./SS-Panzer Abteilung 18 along with the Abteilung staff and II./SS-Artillery Regiment 18 consisting of two batteries of light field howitzers.

The central group formed around the town of Rimas Zombat and was comprised of the existing units of SS-Pz.Aufkl.Abt.18. This reconnaissance battalion had a staff and supply element, 2. and 3.Companies mounted in Schwimmwagen amphibious vehicles, a heavy company with support weapons and 4.Company that was made up of recruits that would be trained 'on the job'. This group was reinforced by 3./SS-Panzer Abteilung 18.

The right-hand group was made up of three battalions from SS-Panzergrenadier Regiment 40 with the addition of 2./SS-Panzer Abteilung 18 and two batteries from II./SS-Artillery Regiment 18.[62]

On 19 October 18.SS-Panzergrenadier Division attacked northwards over the Hungarian border in a previously passive sector of the rebel perimeter, defended by 2. and 3.Tactical Groups. The southern front had been stripped of manpower and equipment to meet more pressing situations further north. SS-Panzergrenadier Regiment 40 which attacked on the right wing of the divisional front made good progress against limited opposition. Thrusting northwestwards the regiment seized Muráň, ten miles inside Slovakia, on 20 September, which unhinged the whole Vernár-Telgárt defensive line. Slovak command ordered counterattacks but too few troops were available and with the front collapsing Telgárt had to be abandoned in the face of a two-pronged attack from elements of SS-Panzergrenadier Regiment 40 and a battalion of 86.Infantry Division which formed part of the Sturm Regiment 1 AOK advancing from the north. Much vital heavy equipment had to be left behind as the Slovaks retreated on foot into the mountains to create a new line of defence. The loss of Telgárt was a heavy blow for morale.[63]

The division's reinforced reconnaissance unit also launched its offensive on 19 October, crossing the border at Rimas Zombat and advancing on a converging line with SS-Panzergrenadier Regiment 40 up the deep, narrow Rimava Valley. It made rapid progress for the initial six miles, advancing to the southern edge of the town of Rimavska Baha, but was halted by the determined defence of a roadblock that proved to be immensely difficult to circumvent.[64] After three days of hold ups and inconclusive attacks SS-Hauptsturmführer Sonne managed to by-pass Rimavská Baňa and linked up with troops from SS-Panzergrenadier Regiment 40 in Tisovec on 22 October before the 2.Czechoslovak Parachute Brigade, which was marching to recapture the town, could intervene.[65]

SS-Panzergrenadier Regiment 39 on the left had been ordered to hold back its attack until the centre and right wing of the division had made progress and drawn off the Slovak's reserves from their line of advance. This strategy may have had some merit, as when the regiment advanced on 21 October it met little resistance and to everyone's surprise managed to occupy the Podkrivan-Detva area two days later.[66]

Following this success, SS-Panzergrenadier Regiment 39 launched an assault towards Zvolen with a spearhead of two motorised companies supported by four assault guns and the few remaining outposts of 3.Tactical Group were in no position to put up much of a defence.[67] By then the heart was going out of the rebels and the end of the uprising was in sight.

While SS-Panzergrenadier Regiment 39 pushed on to the northwest in the direction of Zvolen, the unified companies of SS-Panzergrenadier Regiment 40 and SS-Pz.Aufkl.Abt.18 advanced from Tisovec to meet up with Kampfgruppe Wittenmeyer, which was making steady progress southwards past Maluzina towards the city of Brezno, the rebellion was faltering fast, but pockets of resistance were still encountered.[68]

The commander of SS-Pz.Aufkl.Abt.18, SS-Hauptsturmführer Sonne recalled his unit's entry into Brezno:

> The lead platoon and lead company drove quickly through Brezno. Only at the western outskirts of the city was there resistance. We received heavy fire at the bend of the road, especially from a super-heavy machine gun...We could only advance by crawling. The bullets flew just above our heads. It seemed like a fairly long time before the first Sturmgeschütz finally came to the front and went into position. Shortly after that, there was a sharp bang and the Sturmgeschütz was in flames. An anti-tank rifle had set a gasoline container on the Sturmgeschütz on fire. Only the arrival of a tracked 2cm Flak gun liberated us.[69]

On 26 October, SS-Kampfgruppe Schill occupied Zvolen without a fight and pushed on towards Banska Bystrica, which the 18.SS-Panzergrenadier Division was advancing on from the east. Despite a stout defence by 2.Czechoslovak Parachute Brigade, Panzer Division 'Tatra' threatened to cut off their line of retreat and the decision was made to abandon the capital of the uprising on 27 October.[70]

With their forces scattered and ammunition exhausted, all that the remaining Slovak forces could achieve were delaying actions to enable as many rebels as possible to retreat into the mountains. The roads from Banska Bystrica towards the north, the only ones still clear of German forces, were crammed with soldiers and civilians looking for a safe haven, harried as they went by German aircraft.[71]

The collapse of organised resistance in Slovakia was very swift and the Germans were able to claim a substantial victory. General Viest, the commander of the Czechoslovak National Army and member of the émigré government in London and his chief of staff were captured, alongside an estimated 15,000 insurgents. More than 4,000 of their comrades lay dead on the battlefield. Initial after-action estimates put the amount of war materiel captured at two armoured trains, 267 aircraft, 104 tanks, 309 guns and the entire logistics apparatus of the uprising.[72]

A victory parade was held in Banska Bystrica on 30 October 1944 by Slovak President Tiso to express his gratitude to General Hofle and the units of Wehrmacht and Waffen-SS involved in freeing his country from the Communist threat. The command staffs of 18.SS-Panzergrenadier Division and Kampfgruppe Schäfer both participated in the parade even while some of their units were still carrying out mopping up operations.[73]

The uprising had failed to open the gates of Slovakia to the Red Army. It did not significantly affect transport and communications to the Carpathian front and the drawing off of large numbers of combat troops to put down the insurrection did not occur. Axworthy states that the 'uprising in central Slovakia was contained by ad hoc SS and army forces mostly unfit for frontline combat'[74] and this certainly proved to be the case as far as 18.SS-Panzergrenadier Division was concerned. While committed to advancing on the narrow fronts through the steep, confining valleys allowed by the mountainous terrain, the division could allow its most seasoned troops to lead the way while the untrained, untested bulk of the division could trail along in relative safety in their wake. This strategy worked well against an unconventional force of limited mobility and strictly limited armoured resources but was in no way an adequate preparation for meeting the victorious Red Army tank armadas on the open plains of Hungary.

6

HUNGARY

While Army Group North Ukraine had been tenaciously defending the Carpathian Passes throughout August and September to deny the Red Army access to the flat lands of central Europe, on its southern flank Army Group South Ukraine had been overtaken by a disaster of monumental proportions. Army Group South Ukraine represented the southernmost portion of the German defensive line on the Eastern Front and was comprised of the German 6. and 8.Armies and Romanian 3. and 4.Armies. The sudden defection of Romania to the Allied cause had left great gaping holes in the frontlines of both 6. and 8.Armies in western Ukraine through which the tank armies of 2. and 3.Ukrainian Fronts had poured relatively unopposed. 8.Army on the northern flank was able to retreat in a north-westerly direction and gained some protection from the broken-up terrain of the foothills of the southern Carpathians, but there was no hope for the slow moving infantry divisions of 6.Army, which was virtually annihilated for a second time in under two years. Only its command staff and some of its more mobile elements were able to outrun the Soviet advance and conduct a limited defence of eastern Hungary.

Reinforced by several panzer formations, and with the Hungarian Army proving much more willing to fight against the Romanians rather than the Russians, Army Group South Ukraine (renamed Army Group South on 23 September now that Ukraine had been irretrievably lost) managed to block the onrushing Soviet forces and even inflicted some local reverses at Arad and Debrecen, which wore down the Russian's armoured strength significantly. However, resources were too stretched to mount a proper defence of the country and by mid-October the Germans had been forced back to the line of the Tisza River, where they consolidated their positions as best they could and scraped together every available division for the defence of Budapest.

It had been the Russians' intention to take the city of Budapest 'on the march'; in other words, to capture it as part of their general advance rather than dedicate time and resources to planning and conducting a specific set-piece operation. The delay imposed by the scratch units of the German 6.Army and their Hungarian counterparts robbed the Red Army of its element of surprise and committed it to a two-month-long battle of encirclement that culminated in costly street fighting through the streets of the Hungarian capital.[1]

In early November the bulk of the Soviet forces employed in Hungary came under the control of Marshal Malinovski's 2.Ukrainian Front, which after weeks of fighting across the Hungarian Plain was relatively weak, especially when compared with the Fronts lining up to advance on Berlin to the north. 2.Ukrainian Front's cutting edge was based around two Cavalry-Mechanised Groups comprised of the 4. 5. and 6.Guards Cavalry Corps and the 18. and 23.Tank Corps. Large parts of these units had been encircled in the area of Nyiregyheza to the north of Debrecen and the ensuing breakout had saved a large proportion of their manpower at the expense of most of their vehicles and heavy equipment. During the same period, the 6.Guards Tank Army had expended much of its strength seizing the Szolnok Bridgehead across the Tisza River, which necessitated its move to the rear to refit.

Malinovski's tank and self-propelled gun strength throughout November and early December averaged around 700 vehicles, the Soviet Fronts fighting on the direct line of approach to Berlin getting priority for armour replacements. German tank figures reported to OKH by Army Group South were roughly 500 of all types and in all conditions, including those undergoing maintenance and rebuilds.[2] Under these circumstances 2.Ukrainian Front was robbed of the tactical flexibility provided by overwhelming armoured might that Soviet formations had come to rely upon over the last year of combat, rendering it a blunt instrument with little option but to try and batter its way head-on through the German defences, relying on weight of numbers alone to carry forward the advance.

A new operation was planned to begin on 10 November and envisioned the Soviet forces breaking through the German defences in the Cegled-Szolnok area and advancing across the eastern edge of Budapest via the city of Hatvan before sweeping westwards, following the Danube Bend and encircling the capital from the north.[3]

German intelligence had quickly identified the movement of Russian reinforcements into the proposed breakthrough area and German 6.Army began to filter in new units of their own to bolster their defences as the threat to the Hungarian capital unfolded. Army Group South ordered the German Commander in Slovakia to release the 18.SS-Panzergrenadier Division to 6.Army's control on 2 November (la TgbNr. 4298/44 g.Kdos), where it was incorporated into General of Panzer Troops Friedrich Kirchner's LVII.Panzer Corps, which at this date already consisted of three other severely understrength units: 13.Panzer Division, 4.SS-Panzergrenadier Division 'Polizei' and 46.Infantry Division, which were defending a thirty-mile-long frontline.[4]

Units of 18.SS-Panzergrenadier Division began moving into their assigned positions on 6–7 November. SS-Panzergrenadier Regiment 40 went into the line to the south of the town of Ujszäsz on the west bank of the Zagyva River with SS-Pz.Aufkl.Abt.18 on its right flank, creating a link with 46.Infantry Division to the south of Tapio Györgye. II. and III.Battalions of SS-Panzergrenadier Regiment 39 were assigned to defensive positions to the south of Jaszladany with the first companies arriving on the night of 6–7 November and others following throughout the next day. SS-Panzergrenadier Regiment 39 plugged a gap with 4.SS-Panzergrenadier Division to its left, which assumed command of the regiment on 7 November, presumably because it was separated from the rest of the division by the Zagyva River. Later that afternoon I.Battalion arrived at the front and was squeezed in between the other two battalions.[5]

II./SS-Artillery Regiment 18 was attached to 4.SS-Panzergrenadier Division and during the night of 9–10 November this Abteilung joined SS-Artillery Regiment 4 in firing positions to the west and southwest of the town of Janoshida, where it was connected to regimental headquarters by telephone.[6]

The new positions were created in a wide, open and completely flat landscape that was extremely unfavourable from a defensive standpoint and constant rain sapped the spirits of the soldiers as they marched towards the front.[7] The recruits were further disheartened to find that nothing had been done to fortify the line. The arriving companies discovered that there were not even foxholes or slit trenches to mark the positions. To compound these issues, the ground was heavily waterlogged making the deployment of the division's heavy weapons and assault guns in close support impossible.

Russian army intelligence quickly identified that it was being confronted with a new unit and gave the grenadiers of 18.SS-Panzergrenadier Division no opportunity to substantially strengthen their positions. At 09.00 on 8 November the Russians opened up a fierce barrage with artillery and mortar fire, strengthened by direct anti-tank fire against identifiable strongpoints. This softening up was swiftly followed by powerful infantry attacks against the dividing lines between 9, 10 and 11 companies of III./SS-Panzergrenadier Regiment 39.[8]

Totally unused to the violence of warfare against such a powerful opponent, 10.Company's morale quickly collapsed and the grenadiers fled their positions, taking their weapons with them. This backwards movement was witnessed by the men of 11.Company on their right wing, who quickly followed suit as Russian infantry began to infiltrate into 10.Company positions and outflank them.

Officers and NCOs were abandoned, their orders ignored, and even threats made at gunpoint had no effect as the panic-stricken men sought to escape. Total disaster was only averted by the NCOs and a handful of veterans who kept their heads and managed to seal off the first penetration points with concentrated machine gun fire. Subsequently, 9.Company came under direct attack while trying to conduct an evasive manoeuvre and its men also fell back in disarray. I.Battalion was routed in much the same way as III.Battalion and its men had to be driven back to their trenches by pistol shots. It took hours to round up the scattered and shell-shocked men and form them into some sort of temporary defence.[9]

The divisional staff's statements about the unpreparedness of their men had proved to be all too true and given their lack of training and poor standard of equipment, their inadequate performance was to be expected. It should have come as no surprise that the soldiers chose to flee rather face the T-34s that crushed their comrades in their foxholes with impunity. However, the commander of German Army Group South chose to blame them for the debacle. General Friessner's report to General Guderian, Hitler's Inspector General of Panzer Troops, was particularly contemptuous: 'In the 4th SS Police Panzergrenadier Division some commanders have shot themselves because their man had run away. The 18th SS Panzergrenadier Division has been a total failure.'

The daily war diary of Army Group South's operations was equally damning in its judgement of the division:

> 18.SS-Panzergrenadier Division ... consists of ethnic Germans living in Hungary. They cross over to the enemy, their combat value is like a Hungarian Division... Strength c.18,000, 1 rifle per 18 men.
>
> (HL KBT Hgr. Süd 896/b, report of 11 November 1944).[10]

SS-Panzergrenadier Regiment 39 compiled a report of its losses in its first day of action in Hungary which amounted to eleven killed, 137 wounded and 122 missing. The regiment believed that at least half of the missing men had been killed during the Russian penetration of the defensive positions while others were murdered by them after capture.

On the following day the positions of SS-Panzergrenadier Regiment 40 and SS-Pz.Aufkl.Abt.18 around Ujszäsz and Täpio Györgye became the focal point of the Russian assault. The battalions of SS Panzergrenadier Regiment 40 reacted in the same way to massed infantry and tank attack as SS-Panzergrenadier Regiment 39 had done on the previous day, but again the German cadres held the line throughout 9 and 10 November. Records in the November attachments of the War Diary of the German Army Group South recorded that localised counterattacks found the savagely mutilated bodies of surrendered SS soldiers amongst the wreckage of their old positions.[11]

On 11 November the Soviet forces began their large-scale offensive to break through the Cegléd-Szolnok front with the Russian attack being spearheaded by 2. and 4.Guards Mechanised Corps from 7.Guards Tank Army reinforced by General Pliev's hastily reconstituted 4. and 6.Guards Cavalry Corps and 23.Tank Corps with an overall tank strength of around 300 vehicles of all types.[12] 4.SS-Panzergrenadier Division and 18.SS-Panzergrenadier Division bore the brunt of the attack.[13] At exactly 6.30am an extremely heavy artillery barrage broke across the entire front held by LVII.Panzer Corps, reinforced by concentrated bombing and strafing carried out by ground attack aircraft. An hour later the frontline positions were stormed by three Russian Corps. In less than two hours the leading Russian tanks had broken through to the artillery positions several miles behind the fighting line and the gunners were forced to target marauding T-34s at almost point-blank range over open sights. As Russian tanks penetrated their positions a desperate tank battle developed to their flank and rear on the approaches to Jászpáti and Jászbereny.[14] To give an impression of the fighting that day we have the diary entry of Rottenführer Lunkenheimer; a gun commander in the 14. (2cm Flak) Company of SS-Panzergrenadier Regiment 40:

> We are replacing parts of the 4th SS Division and are instructed that when we move into position that it is necessary to dig foxholes strong enough to be steamrollered by tanks. When it grew light (11/11/44) [the silence was shattered by] a hurricane of fire... Gradually the enemy artillery fire slackens and moves rearwards. Behind and on the railway line from Ujszäsz to Nagykäta, our 88mm guns begin firing. And then the machine guns start to tack. More and more machine guns and rifles fall into the concert from hell. Russian infantry and armour attack. In dense lines they push forward slowly. And already the first soldiers run back from our ranks – the Russians shoot wildly behind them. Then our Infantry Regiment 40 draws back to the embankment north of Täpio Szele.
>
> The heavy, soggy soil makes everything very heavy going. Ustuf. [SS-Untersturmführer] Kohn [who came to 14/40 from the infantry] is wounded. Our 88s provide a powerful buffer between us and them. The main wedge Russian advance pushes on to the approaches to Täpio Györgye. The situation is pretty desperate. The infantry have given in ... weapons, equipment and ammunition boxes lying around in the terrain.[15]

The 88mm guns seem to have belonged to Troop 'Schwenke' of SS-Flak.Abteilung 4 which was positioned on the outskirts of Täpio Györgye and destroyed several Russian tanks on that day, although parts of SS-Flak.Abt.18 were also operating in this part of Hungary.[16]

The artillery of I./SS-Artillery Regiment 4 covered the sector of the front to the south of Täpio Györgye held by SS-Panzergrenadier

Regiment 40. SS-Unterscharführer Schäfer of 2.Battery describes the scene at first light on 11 November: 'I count 46 Russian tanks that have driven up in a semi-circle. Russian infantry are pouring [in] from left and right... Only now do I notice that there is no infantry in front of us.'[17]

At this crucial moment the artillery battery was unable to defend itself because of a critical lack of artillery ammunition caused by Russian air attacks and the poor state of the roads, which prevented proper resupply. As their infantry screen melted away, the artillery was forced to retreat.[18]

As the front collapsed south of Jäszbereny, the retreat of the motorized parts of the German forces took place on the only viable road from Ujszász through Jänoshida and Jäsztelek. After the road passed through Jäszbereny the thickness of the mud in the surrounding countryside prevented any off-road movement at all, and it was at precisely this point that the Russians attacked with all of their strength, throwing the whole German retreat into confusion.

During the late afternoon of 11 November SS-Pz.Aufkl.Abt.18 moved to a blocking position just outside of Jänoshida to protect the flow of the wheeled and tracked vehicles moving along the road to the north. By this time darkness had fallen and the Russians were increasingly harassing the long column of jammed-up rear echelon vehicles with artillery and mortar fire, which preceded the arrival of packs of tanks.[19]

Leading the offensive were the T-34 tanks of 23.Tank Corps, which continued to grind their way northwards towards Hatvan on their broad tracks that seemed impervious to the waterlogged conditions, closely supported by the highly mobile infantry of 4. and 6. Guards Cavalry Corps.[20] The fighting was fierce with the Red Army seemingly gaining ground everywhere along the front. However, while the extensive use of cavalry regiments allowed the Russians great tactical flexibility, they were horribly vulnerable in modern warfare as Doctor Röhrs, medical officer of SS-Pz.Aufkl.Abt.18 observed: 'We found ourselves in the middle of a space that was so fiercely fought over during the day. A whole Russian cavalry brigade bled to death here ... our few men managed to do it!'[21] Successes for the embattled 18.SS-Panzergrenadier Division were nevertheless few and far between.

By November 13, LVII.Panzer Corps had been pushed back 10-15 miles to the north and on the same day Russian mobile forces attacked the improvised positions between the 18.SS-Panzergrenadier Division and the neighbouring 46.Infantry Division where they again managed to breach the defences and force a further retreat.[22] The Red Army's main thrust had initially targeted the understrength 354.Infantry Division that held the line on the right of 18.SS-Panzergrenadier Division, but the Russians were quick to exploit the evident weakness displayed by the Hungarian SS recruits and the front could not be held in spite of more reinforcements from 46.Infantry Division being brought up.

Under the circumstances LVII.Panzer Corps had little option but to split up 18.SS-Panzergrenadier Division into a joint deployment with 4.SS-Panzergrenadier Division, twinning 8. and 39.SS-Panzergrenadier Regiments and 7. and 40.SS-Panzergrenadier Regiments respectively. The frontline was also pulled back from the southwest to the west of Jaszbereny.[23] 4.SS-Panzergrenadier Division, now with the attendant 18.SS-Panzergrenadier Division in tow, was tasked with defending the town of Jaszbereny and to add some backbone to the defence 23.Panzer Division was ordered to dispatch an armoured taskforce in support. Kampfgruppe Fischer, named after Hauptmann (later Major) Fischer, commander of II./Panzer Regiment 23, initially consisted of 10 Panthers from that battalion and 4./Panzer Aufklärungs Abteilung 23. It would provide invaluable cover to the two battered and shaky SS-Divisions.[24]

However, while the panzers were able to prevent the front from disintegrating completely, they had their limitations. Heavy losses in both men and materials combined with combat weariness were rapidly eroding the combat effectiveness of all units, but particularly the infantry, soaked and freezing in their open field positions. The armoured units faced their own set of problems with the sodden landscape being totally unsuitable for cross-country manoeuvring, while the few remaining supply routes were subjected to constant harassing artillery fire.[25]

Recognising the signs of disintegration amongst some of the troops under its command, 6.Army sent out the code word for individual units to start the retreat towards the 'Karola' position on the night of 14 November. The 'Karola' position was one of three fortified battle lines that had been designed to protect Budapest from invasion from the east. Their construction had been ordered by the German Army Supreme Command (OKH) on 21 September 1944 and the defences were built by construction battalions and impressed civilian labourers, many of them Jews from Budapest.

The position angled slightly north of east following the foothills of the Cserhát, Mátra and Zemplén Hills and blocked the neck of low-lying ground between Budapest and the Matra Mountains that was the 'traditional' invasion route into Slovakia. The Margit Line had been constructed between Budapest and Lake Balaton in the southwest to prevent an outflanking attack from the direction of Yugoslavia, and the Attila Line consisted of three concentric semi-circular positions to the east of Budapest to foil a direct approach to the city. To judge from the fieldworks of the Attila Line, the 'Karola' position would have consisted of 'earth bunkers, anti-tank ditches, occasional barbed-wire entanglements and minefields'.[26]

The order to retreat to the prepared positions in the north was also the signal to abandon Jaszbereny. Doctor Röhrs recorded that:

> ... at dawn we enter the hard-fought Jaszberény... Two field hospitals, two divisional headquarters, and the baggage train of two divisions rolled wildly out of the town, which had just been reached by the Russian tank advance. Had it not been for the dense fog, which made all visibility impossible for the Russian airmen, and had it not been for our adjutant, with a few quickly assembled guns—8.8 and anti-tank guns—to shoot down so many tanks that the rest preferred to turn away, it would have resulted in a catastrophe. That morning I realized where we were wrong. We have too many rear services and far too few combat units... Signals men are already taking down the telephone wires around town. Pioneers set explosive charges on the old stone bridge over the Zagyva in the middle of the city.[27]

The rear services evacuating Jäszbereny were forced to negotiate the narrow streets of the old city leading to the bottleneck at the Zagyya Bridge. The colossal traffic jam of retreating supply trains and headquarters staff quickly became unmanageable and the whole area jammed up with personnel and vehicles of every description. Confusion and panic reigned as Russian heavy artillery targeted the approaches, causing heavy casualties and wrecking much irreplaceable equipment.

As the evacuation of Jäszbereny got underway the Russians renewed their efforts to take the city and cut off the retreating columns. While to the west of the city the Russian formations largely halted at the Zagyva River, allowing the infantry of 4. and 18.SS-Panzergrenadier Divisions to slip away to the north, they were more determined to the east as they tried to establish an effective blocking position. Russian armour broke through the blocking positions established by Kampfgruppe Bradel from 1.Panzer Division, which consisted of I./Panzer Grenadier Regiment 113 alongside a mixed company of 15-20 Pzkfw. V Panther tanks from I./1.Panzer Regiment supported by self-propelled artillery and combat engineers. The Kampfgruppe was forced to retreat northwards from Jäszdosa, a village four miles northeast of Jäszbereny, but managed to partially restore the situation in the area of Jäszdrokszälläs by destroying nine of the eighteen leading tanks, which allowed the escape routes towards Hort and Hatvan to the northwest to remain open.[28]

It was here that some of the more mobile elements of the 18.SS-Panzergrenadier also fought short, sharp engagements in an attempt to fend off the leading Soviet units. For example, the Knight's Cross citation for SS-Obersturmführer Doctor Hans Lipinski recorded that he personally destroyed two T-34s on 15 November while in combat with his battery of 88mm guns from SS-Flak Abt.18, covering the retreat from Jäszbereny.[29] However, these actions could only delay the Red Army advance. By 15 November the Soviets had advanced about 25 miles, albeit against heavier than expected resistance, and by the night of 15–16 November Jäszbereny had been abandoned and the divisions of LVII.Panzer Corps had been forced back into the section of the 'Karola' position that ran roughly east to west on a line to the south of the Aszod-Hatvan-Hort road.[30]

For the wet and weary troops their retreat to the 'Karola' position was spurred on by the vision of a refuge where they could hunker down for the winter in warm bunkers, the Red Army kept at bay behind strong defences, and most of the infantry were in position by the evening of 16 November. Unfortunately for the luckless German infantry, the fortifications of the 'Karola' line proved to be barely adequate and considerable efforts had to be made to strengthen the defences, including laying minefields across the most obvious approaches.[31]

Following the poor performance of the 18.SS-Panzergrenadier Division during its initial actions in Hungary and its subordination to the 4.SS- Panzergrenadier Division, the divisional headquarters had very little influence over the movement and employment of most of its units but, finding a breathing space with their withdrawal into the 'Karola' position, the headquarters staff of 18.SS-Panzergrenadier Division were able to regain control of some of their forces and re-organise their battered battalions. Its two infantry regiments went into position to the south and east of the city of Hatvan, which was an important communications hub, while 4.SS-Panzergrenadier Division occupied a section of the frontline around Csany to their left. The divisional command post of 18 SS-Panzergrenadier Division was established in Apc behind the centre of the division's main position.[32] Given the obvious unreliability of its infantry units, more combat reserves of 1.Panzer Division were employed in support of the SS Grenadiers. These consisted of several batteries from Panzer Artillery Regiment 73 and Pzkfw. IVs from II./1.Panzer Regiment, which protected the junction between 4. and 18.SS-Panzergrenadier Division and helped to fight off Soviet attacks against Gyöpara and Apc.[33]

Additional firepower was also provided by a Kampfgruppe of twelve Tiger II tanks and a platoon of Wirbelwind Flakpanzers (tanks mounted with anti-aircraft guns) from schwere Panzer Abteilung 503 under the command of Leutnant Richard Freiherr von Rosen, which was deployed to Hatvan in mid-November and for operational purposes came under the command of 1.Panzer Division.[34]

18.SS-Panzergrenadier Division's defensive sector encompassed the Österreicher TN, an extensive country estate which was one of a number established by the German *Technisches Nothilfe* organisation for technical training purposes. The main road from Jäszbereny to the north ran through here and there was a key traffic junction which allowed access into, and around, the city of Hatvan. II./SS-Panzergrenadier Regiment 40 went in a wide semicircle in front of the Österreicher TN position during the evening of 17 November with a platoon of 2cm Flak Vierling quadruple-barrelled anti-aircraft guns from 14./SS-Panzergrenadier Regiment 40 firing in the ground support role. Rottenführer Lunkenheimer wrote in his diary:

> The very next morning the Russians marched towards us, with tanks and hauled Pak. We let them, unsuspecting, get to within 300 metres and then opened up on them suddenly with our three 2cm cannon fire. The effect was devastating. The Russians fled away or were taken by our weapons. Their horses ran

> wild through the area. But after the scare the Russians, under courageous leadership, found the strength to fight back and two tanks took our guns under fire. But we quickly changed our position to behind the large buildings of the estate, and after a while the Russians withdrew. In the following days, there was enemy pressure, and the positions changed hands several times.[35]

Kampfgruppe Fischer from 23.Panzer Division also continued to support LVII Panzer Corps, covering 18.SS-Panzergrenadier Division in their defensive actions east of Hatvan at the Osterreicher TN, although this was not always as effective as it could have been. Concentrations of Soviet infantry and armour tried to infiltrate the position undercover of thick fog and in the ensuing tank battle the disorientated Panzers blundered into the Russian anti-tank screen, which promptly knocked out two tanks, forcing the kampfgruppe to withdraw to regroup.[36]

At this time SS-Pz.Aufkl.Abt.18 was subordinated to the SS-Panzergrenadier Regiment.40 and positioned in the vineyards in the hills between Pusztamonostor and Hatvan, but as early as 18 November it was clear that the defensive line had been breached in numerous places and that Russian tanks were operating freely in the rear areas. SS-Hauptsturmführer Sonne, commander of SS-Pz.Aufkl. Abt.18 recalled:

> Riepe's battalion (I/ 40) went into position on the left of my Aufkl. Abt. Because there was disagreement on the boundaries between our units, I went to Riepe's command post the next morning, which was housed in a spacious manor house. Suddenly three T-34s emerged from the morning mist. A T-34 and an assault gun stood opposite while the two other T-34s drove around the manor house and fired into it. But then it was probable that the T-34s became uneasy and they rattled off in the direction from which they came.[37]

46.Infantry Division on the right flank of 18.SS-Panzergrenadier Division had fallen back on the town of Aszod to the west of Hatvan, but even as they arrived the Soviets were pushing through a gap in the line supposedly covered by 18.SS-Panzergrenadier Division and the threat of them being outflanked was only cleared up by the intervention of a Kampfgruppe from 1.Panzer Division.[38]

By 20 November the Red Army had reached the 'Karola' line along its whole length and in places had breached it, but the Russians temporarily paused their advance to replenish their combat units and strengthen their logistical base in preparation for their next large-scale offensive, due to begin on 5 December.[39] However, small probing attacks and extensive patrolling wore away at the German and Hungarian defences, keeping the defenders guessing about their next point of attack while searching out weak points in their dispositions. Even as these probing attacks continued, Malinovski brought up the 7.Guards Army to the south of Hatvan in order to spearhead the new offensive.[40]

Between 23 and 24 November there were extensive attacks on the defensive line along the Hort-Hatvan road and on Hatvan itself, which were initially repulsed leaving 32 Russian tanks destroyed. In response, the Russians increased their attacks against Hatvan from the southeast with all of their available strength and managed to break through in the area of Esced to the Esced-Scüci road, which exposed the lines of communication to the 4.SS-Panzergrenadier Division and forced the evacuation of the sections of the 'Karola' position held by both 4. and 18.SS-Panzergrenadier Divisions.[41] Lunkenheimer recorded the last battle for his unit's position in his diary:

> 24/11/1944: During the night the first snow has fallen. It is wet, cold weather. And the T-34s roll forward again. Our assault guns shoot, and the T-34s turn back. An hour later enemy infantry comes with the cry of 'Urrä' roaring down the slope. Our 2cm shreds their ranks. In the evening, the Russians force their way into our positions. And again we counterattack with the assault guns. The old main line of defence is again occupied, but the assault guns go back. Then comes our order to retreat, too. When darkness falls, we leave the positions carefully and gather further back. The infantry is moved back in trucks.[42]

The divisional staffs had already accepted that the much vaunted 'Karola' position could not be held and, almost immediately after their arrival had prepared plans for a retreat to a new position. On 25 November, the 4. and 18.SS-Panzergrenadier Divisions occupied a new defensive line between the towns of Kartal, Heréd and Ecséd. Fortunately for the two divisions, the tempo of the Russian attacks slackened as they re-organised their forces and brought up supplies for their assault to take Budapest.

Under 18.SS-Panzergrenadier Division's new deployment, SS-Panzergrenadier Regiment 40 was positioned around Hered with SS-Pz.Aufkl.Abt.18, temporarily commanded by SS-Hauptsturmführer Von Fehrentheil, on its right wing, II.Battalion, commanded by SS-Hauptsturmführer Herbert Teufel, in the middle and I.Battalion, led by SS-Sturmbannführer Riepe, on the left. SS-Panzergrenadier Regiment 39 went into the line on the left of SS-Panzergrenadier Regiment 40 on both sides of Ecsed, although after the pounding that it had taken in its first few days of combat I.Battalion was disbanded, the remnant being integrated into III.Battalion.[43]

Meanwhile, Marshal Tolbukhin's 3rd Ukrainian Front had steadily advanced from northern Serbia throughout November and established bridgeheads on the western banks of the Danube to the south of Budapest. On 26 November powerful forces broke out of these bridgeheads and stormed the city of Pecs as a prelude to sweeping north-westwards as the southern pincer of the giant encirclement.[44] In response to this threat the Germans started to transfer the bulk of their armoured forces from the Hatvan front. The first to leave was LVII.Panzer Corps headquarters, followed by the 1. and 23.Panzer Divisions.[45]

On 27 November, 18.SS-Panzergrenadier Division took over the sector of 46.Infantry Division, the unit covering their right flank, which had been decimated during the fighting in Hungary and was withdrawn to refit behind the front. With the forced withdrawal of the two panzer divisions, the 46.Infantry Division was immediately re-inserted into the frontline on 18.SS-Panzergrenadier Division's left wing to cover the reassignment of 1.Panzer Division from the Apc area to the north of Hatvan.[46]

Between 28–29 November, 23.Panzer Division pulled out of its positions with its infantry, artillery, pioneer and anti-tank units, handing over their sections of the front to 18.SS-Panzergrenadier Division, which left its depleted units badly overstretched. 24.Panzer Division was also earmarked for withdrawal to the south of Budapest, but common sense prevailed at the last moment, and it remained as the only viable mobile reserve in the north.[47]

On 27 November, 4. and 18.SS-Panzergrenadier Divisions had come under the command of the IV.Panzer Corps, which had only been established on 10 October 1944 and was itself in the process of being reclassified as Panzer Corps *Feldherrnhalle*, (an SA honour title) under the command of General of Panzer Troops Ulrich Kleeman. The intention had been for the Corps command to direct the operations of the re-constituted 13.Panzer Division and Panzer Division *Feldherrnhalle*, which would be an upgraded version of the Panzergrenadier division of the same name. However, the rapidly unfolding disaster around Budapest quickly overtook these plans and Kleeman's newly designated Corps was assigned elements of six other divisions; 1.Panzer Division, 46. 76. and 357.Infantry Divisions and 4. and 18.SS-Panzergranadier Divisions, all of which were significantly understrength. 1.Panzer division was already departing for another sector and 357.Infantry Division was soon to be transferred to 6.Army. Despite the name change, many official documents (and most post-war texts) would still refer to the unit as IV Panzer Corps until the Corps reached its intended organisational state in March 1945.[48]

Interestingly, an order dated 27 November 1944 authorised all Panzer Corps personnel to wear the distinctive brown '*Feldherrnhalle*' cuff band and SA kampfrune on their epaulettes,[49] which must have been incomprehensible to men like Trabandt, Schäfer and Petersen who been in the SS prior to the 'Night of the Long Knives' and undoubtedly had a hand in bringing the SA down.

By the beginning of December the 18.SS-Panzergrenadier Division had been bled white and the German High Command considered it to have 'no significant combat value'. It had been reduced to the strength of a few Kampfgruppe and it had intended to pull the Division out of the front line for a re-fit. The process of stripping it of its remaining assault guns, artillery assets and vehicles for redistributed to the 4.SS-Panzergrenadier Division had already started when the Soviet offensive began on 5 December.[50]

This assault was the largest operation undertaken by the Red Army in Hungary to date. The rifle divisions of the 7.Guards Army reinforced by the 30.Guards Rifle Corps struck on a narrow sector defended by the 18.SS-Panzergrenadier Division and Lieutenant General Rintelin's 357.Infantry Division at the boundary of the German 6. and 8.Armies.[51]

Major i.G. Wind recalled:

> ... many of the Hungarian SS men did not fight when the Soviets had attacked but had thrown away their weapons and surrendered

> at the sight of the T-34s. Our German SS men had fought bravely, and then, by delaying actions, fought their way back... This news was just a confirmation [that the] Russian attack had focused on our division, because they knew our weaknesses.[52]

The weakness of the seam between 6. and 8.Armies was appreciated by IV.Panzer Corps headquarters and an attempt was made to remedy the situation. When 4.SS-Panzer-Jäger Abteilung arrived at the front on 3 December it was posted to a reserve position behind 357.Infantry Division and 18.SS-Panzergrenadier Division as a precautionary measure instead of being sent to its parent unit.[53] But this foresight was to no avail. The two German divisions were assailed by nine rifle divisions, one tank corps, two mechanised corps and two cavalry corps. Following a violent artillery barrage, the Russians began their ground offensive with a massed infantry attack supported by ground attack aircraft dropping fragmentation bombs and supported by around 70 tanks. The attack was launched over the more rural terrain on either side of the city of Hatvan and quickly achieved a deep penetration of the German frontline. Exploitation was carried out by General Kravchenko's newly reconstituted 6.Guards Tank Army, its 5.Guards Tank Corps and 9.Guards Mechanised Corps having been refitted with 350 tanks and self-propelled guns, while following in its wake to guard its exposed eastern flank was Pliev's Cavalry Mechanised Group consisting of the 4.Guards Mechanised Corps and 4. and 6.Guards Cavalry Corps.[54]

After some initial patchy opposition, the advance gained momentum and the villages of Kartel and Hered on IV Panzer Corps' right wing were quickly lost while on the left flank Rozsaszentmarton and Szucsi were captured. The swift collapse resulted in one of 18.SS-Panzergrenadier Division's artillery detachments, probably IV Abteilung, being overrun.[55]

As the German front crumbled and 18.SS-Panzergrenadier Division and 357.Infantry Division were forced apart, Russian tanks poured through the gap in a north-westerly direction. 18.SS-Panzergrenadier Divisional headquarters found itself in the eye of the storm with little contact with most of its sub-units and the reports that it was receiving being universally bad; of chaos everywhere and of their infantry fleeing from the frontline without putting up a fight. The headquarters staff had little option but to retreat northwards with as much of its precious communications equipment as they could salvage.

An example of the total collapse that had taken place in some areas is demonstrated by the situation in which II./SS-Artillery Regiment 18 found itself on the evening of the first day of the offensive. Although positioned just south of the village of Hehalom, about six miles behind the front at the start of the day, its shocked gun crews were suddenly confronted with a column of ten T-34s right in front of their gun lines. The artillerymen defended their position tenaciously, firing their 10.5cm howitzers point blank at the tanks over open sights while the abteilung commander, believed to have been SS-Hauptsturmführer Köhler, commandeered all available infantry to protect his guns against the inevitable infantry attack to come. Eventually the tanks turned away, allowing the abteilung to retreat in good order.[56]

Confusion reigned in the breakthrough area as sub-units from several different German divisions became mixed with Hungarian home guard units and civilian refugees, all trying to flee north before Russian tanks attacked around the exposed flank and cut off their retreat. The roads became hopelessly congested with most vehicles being confined to the paved highways, as the ground around was too boggy to drive over. Many roads were completely blocked by abandoned equipment and burnt-out vehicles. Telephone cables were ripped up as armoured vehicles tried to make the most of their better cross-country capabilities, which exacerbated the communications problems, while supplies could no longer be brought forward in sufficient quantities.

The broad tracks of the Russian T-34s carried them forwards, regardless of the state of the ground, and the attack continued at a furious pace. Palotas was captured on 7 December, deep in the rear of 18.SS-Panzergrenadier Division's positions of only two days previously.[57]

In spite of this chaotic situation, or possibly in ignorance of it, IV.Panzer Corps (now under 8.Army control) made the decision to move the bulk of 46.Infantry Division from its already dangerously undermanned eastern wing to cover its increasingly exposed western flank.[58] In the hilly country to the north of Hatvan, all movement, but particularly that of heavy artillery, became hugely difficult. During the night march to the north of the village of Apc, III./Artillery Regiment 114 of 46.Infantry Division found the churned dirt track that it was negotiating blocked by a 12-ton Sdkfz 8 half tracked artillery tractor belonging to SS-Artillery Regiment 18 bogged down on a steep slope, and by a Tiger tank, presumably from schwere Panzer Abteilung (Heavy Tank Battalion) 503, immobilised through a broken track. This incident not only highlights the intermingling of different units in a small area but also the near impossibility of recovering immobilised heavy equipment under such circumstances.[59]

By 7 December, the frontline of 18.SS-Panzergrenadier Division had been peeled back to the northeast and its battalions were scattered in a string of small towns to the north of Hatvan facing a Russian force that was now attacking from the southwest.

II. and III. Battalions of SS- Panzergrenadier Regiment 39 were holding positions around Szurdokpüspöki, 5 km south of the small town of Pásztó with the 4th SS-Panzergrenadier Division to their left and the SS-Panzergrenadier Regiment 40 on the right. SS-Panzergrenadier Regiment 40 controlled three battered infantry battalions and the understrength SS-Pz.Aufkl.Abt.18, which had been reduced to two companies. These units were dug in around the villages of Csécse, Buják, Ecseg and Kozárd.

As Army Group Pliev steamrollered north, IV.Panzer Corps recognised the danger to its thinly held western flank and freed up whatever forces it could scrape together to cover it and the town of Szécsény, situated 25 km east of Balassagyarmat on the Slovak-Hungarian border, which became the key point of the new and tenuous German defensive line that was being created. A major supply road ran through the town and it covered the retreat routes of both IV.Panzer Corps and XXIX.Army Corps. 18.SS-Panzergrenadier Division was made responsible for the defence of this area.

Desperate to pull units out of the line to cover Szécsény, 18.SS-Panzergrenadier Division ordered I./SS-Panzergrenadier Regiment 40 under SS-Sturmbannführer Riepe to defend the town. Riepe had already received orders to transfer to Szécsény when his battalion's positions around Kozárd and Alsótold to its rear came under powerful enemy attack, which effectively cut the road to Szécsény.[60] The Russian attack on Kozard and Alsótold was launched on 7 December and amidst fierce fighting it was only through the personal intervention of SS-Obersturmbannführer Schäfer that Alsótold was held and the threat to the headquarters of the 4.SS-Panzergrenadier Division which had been recently established there averted. The headquarters took the opportunity to move to

Pásztó, leaving III./SS-Panzergrenadier Regiment 40 and SS-Pz.Aufkl. Abt.18 to bear the brunt of the defence on the Csécse-Buják front.[61]

I./SS-Panzergrenadier Regiment 40 had been extricated from the line further south and was moving into a semi-circular defensive position in front of Szécsény facing west. SS-Feld Ersatz Bataillon 18 (the division's training and replacements battalion) had been based in Szécsény until recently before being pulled back into Slovakia and, in addition to their training programme, had developed the town for all-round defence, which was to prove immensely useful almost immediately. The divisional command post was established in the town centre in a house near the church.[62] With reinforcements arriving for Kampfgruppe Riepe in the north and Kampfgruppe Schäfer deployed on the right wing of the 4.SS-Panzergrenadier Division next to SS-Panzergrenadier Regiment.7, the extremities of the IV.Panzer Corps' flank cover were secured; but there remained a gap about eight miles wide between the two, which was only covered by a string of outposts established by the partly motorised but understrength Aufkl.Abt.46.[63]

The Russians had their sights set on capturing Szécsény and determined on a frontal attack of overwhelming force to get the job done. Army Group Pliev captured the town of Balassagyarmat on 9 December and with a minimum of regrouping was poised to strike eastwards towards Szécsény and into the rear of 8.Army. Pliyev must have assumed that the German army was routed in his sector, as he confidently ordered 4.Guards Mechanised Corps to capture Szécsény on the evening of 9 December before rolling on to take Losonc on the following morning. 36.Guards Tank Brigade led the assault with the detached tank regiments from each of the two mechanised brigade within the corps in support. 14.Guards Mechanised Brigade advanced to its left, covering the northern flank of the armour wedge while 15.Guards Mechanised Brigade came up in support on the southern wing.[64]

Unaware of the armoured avalanche bearing down upon them, Riepe's men were relieved to find prepared positions waiting for them; trench lines and earthen bunkers situated about three miles to the west and southwest of Szécsény, anchored on the villages of Hugyan and Varsány. However, SS-Sturmbannführer Riepe had barely settled into his new quarters when he was violently disturbed by the sharp crack of tank cannons and the unmistakable clatter of T-34 tracks. Outside he found the defensive positions abandoned and his troops fleeing into the night. With the assistance of Hauptmann Karl Heinz Dierks, commander of II./Infantry Regiment 42 (46.Infantry Division) whose battalion had also been rushed to Szécsény in the nick of time, Riepe got a grip on the situation and rounded up the panicked troops, forming them into a new line of resistance. The first enemy tanks were destroyed and the rest turned back, restoring the situation for the moment.[65]

15.Guards Mechanised Corps managed to occupy some high ground approximately one and a half miles west of the town but could advance no further in the face of concentrated artillery and machine gun fire. With their ambitious timetable already behind schedule, the Soviets resumed their attack at dawn the next morning, 10 December.[66]

The after-action report of Major i.G. Wind, *1.Generalstabsoffizier* of the 18.SS-Panzergrenadier Division gives a vivid account of the action that followed:

> The Divisional command post was in a house near the church in Szécsény. Our greatly shrunken companies were sited around the town at a distance of about five kilometres. The Artillery Regiment was in position to the east of the village. To the west and southwest the roads leading to the town were covered by 88s of our Flak Abteilung. At 07:00 on 10/12/1944 the commander of the battalion, which was deployed on both sides of the road to Balassagyarmat, called and told me that a column of T-34s had just rolled past the house in whose cellar he had his headquarters, and headed towards Szécsény. In a short time they would probably be in Szécsény. There was just enough time to alert the anti-aircraft battery, but their boss had already heard the tanks rolling down the road and had alerted his battery.
>
> An 88 was about 500 metres north of the road and about 800 metres in front of the town in a very well-chosen firing position. The Russians suspected that the road was mined and drove in a fan to the left into the open fields and into a ravine. The flak crew held their nerve and only fired their first shot after the first T-34 had moved out of the ravine towards Szécsény. As the next T-34 came into the open an 88mm shell slammed into the tank hull and it was soon ablaze. Twelve burning enemy tanks adorned the field and the others tried to escape quickly. The attack was repulsed.[67]

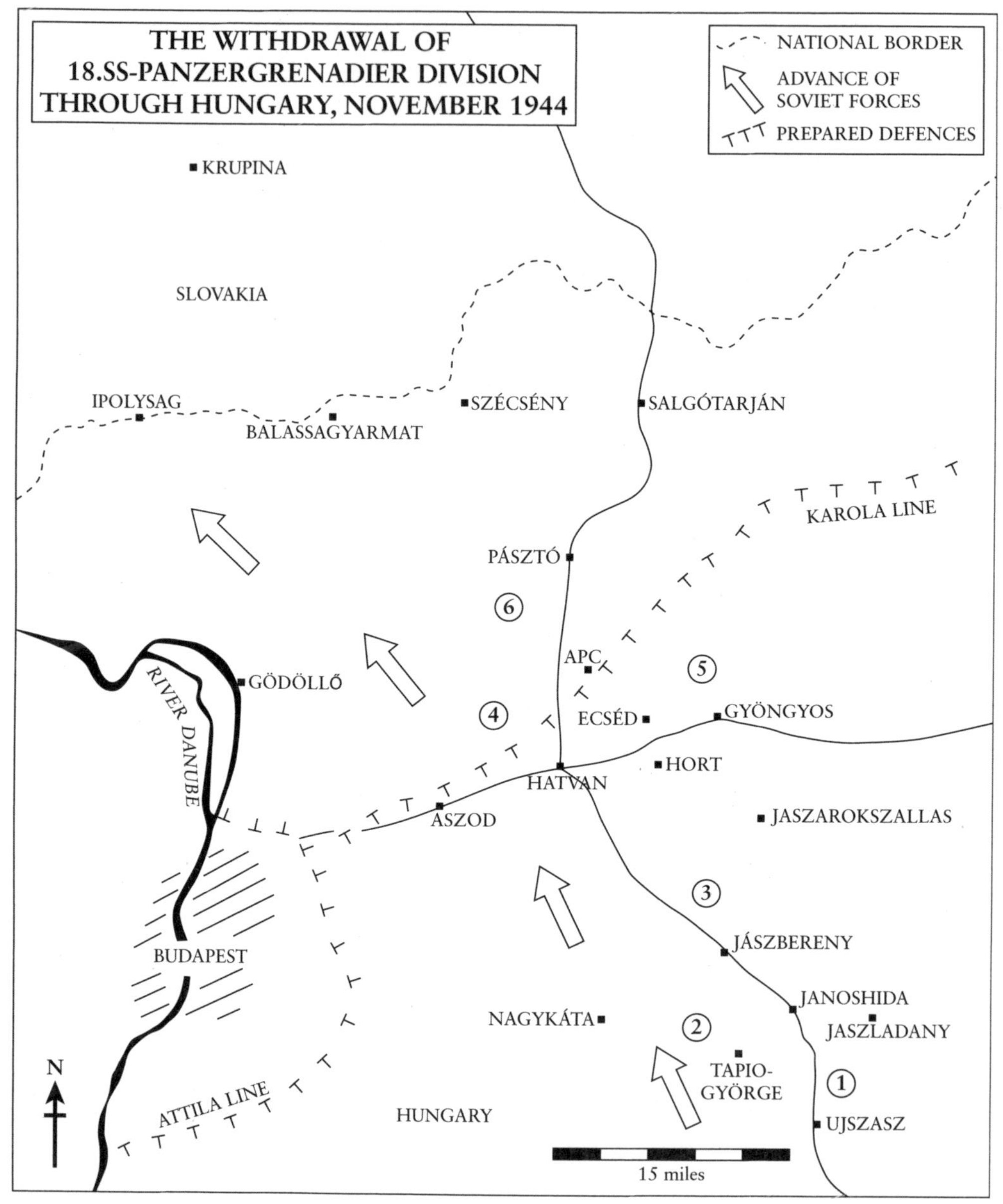

Hungary Map Notes

1 18.SS-Panzergrenadier Division was assigned to General Kirchner's LVII Panzer Corps, which at this date consisted of 13.Panzer Division, 4.SS-Panzergrenadier Division 'Polizei' and 46.Infantry Division, defending a thirty-mile-long frontline. Units took up position on 6–7 November, SS-Panzergrenadier Regiment 40 placed

to the south of Ujszäsz with SS-Pz.Aufkl.Abt.18 on its right flank, creating a link with 46.Infantry Division. II. and III.Battalions of SS-Panzergrenadier Regiment 39 were assigned to defensive positions to the south of Jaszladany.

2 Russian army intelligence quickly identified the insertion of a new unit into the line ahead of them and on 8 and 9 November launched powerful infantry attacks against 18.SS-Panzergrenadier Division positions, which it was hard pressed to resist.

3 On 11 November the Soviet large-scale offensive began against the Cegléd-Szolnok front, their attack spearheaded by 7.Guards Tank Army reinforced by Army Group Pliev. LVII Panzer Corps was forced back towards Jäszbereny, but the town could not be held. By the night of 15–16 November Jäszbereny had been abandoned and LVII Panzer Corps had withdrawn into the 'Karola' Position to the south of the Aszod-Hatvan-Hort road.

4 By 20 November the Red Army had reached the 'Karola' line and in places had breached it. Their concentrated attacks evicted the defenders in less than three days.

5 On 25 November, the 4. and 18.SS-Panzergrenadier Divisions occupied a new defensive line between the towns of Kartal, Heréd and Ecséd while the Russians temporarily paused major operations to replenish their strength in preparation for their next large-scale offensive.

6 As of 27 November, 4. and 18.SS-Panzergrenadier Divisions came under the command of the IV Panzer Corps.

The 88mm guns belonged to 1./SS-Flak Abteilung 18 under the command of SS-Obersturmführer of Reserves Doctor Hans Lipinski. During the attack some of Lipinski's men began to waver and at one point looked ready to abandon their positions, but he rallied his men and personally destroyed six T-34s in less than an hour. Regaining their confidence, the gunners shot up another six or seven tanks (accounts vary) and prevented a breakthrough by at least twenty-two Russian tanks into the flank of IV.Panzer Corps. For this action Lipinski was awarded the Knight's Cross on 2 January 1945. During the defence of Szécsény, 1./SS-Flak Abteilung 18 was to account for twenty-four Russian tanks destroyed. One was knocked out at close range by SS-Unterscharführer Armbruster with a panzerfaust.[68]

The 88mm guns of 1./SS-Flak Abteilung 18 maintained the weapon's reputation as an effective tank killer and their crews had positioned them with skill for maximum effect, but as a weapon intended for anti-aircraft defence it was heavy, unwieldy and vulnerable when confronting a highly mobile opponent. Given the weight of Soviet armour arrayed against them, the garrison of Szécsény required tank support to mount a truly viable defence. However, 8.Army lacked any significant armoured reserves and was therefore forced to make a difficult choice. It split up 24.Panzer Division, its single remaining armoured asset, which at this point was largely concentrated on the Ipolysag front, and parcelled out its armoured units to help corset the defences of its weakened divisions. Trying to pre-empt the unreliability of the Hungarian SS infantrymen, II./Panzer Grenadier Regiment 26, reinforced by a company of tanks from 24.Panzer Division, was ordered to the Szécsény sector on 10 December.[69]

The arrival of the panzer grenadiers coincided with a brief lull in the fighting while Army Group Pliev brought up fresh assault units and IV Panzer Corps tried to scrape together a more meaningful defence. Fortunately for the Germans, the terrain around Szécsény was very favourable from a defensive point of view. The town was situated at the edge of a line of hills rolling away to the east, allowing the defenders unobstructed observation of the countryside as far as Balassagyarmat; the ground over which 4.Guards Mechanised Corps had to advance.[70] Added to this was the wretched state of the road network and boggy nature of the ground around it, which caused huge logistical problems for the attackers with even their artillery pieces having to be manhandled forward in conditions reminiscent of the winter fighting during the First World War.

The brief lull in the fighting ended on 12 December when, following an intense artillery barrage, 4.Guards Mechanised Corps now reinforced with troops from the 4. and 6.Guards Cavalry Corps mounted a general attack on Szécsény in successive waves from the west and southwest with infantry and thirty tanks. The attack was supported by machine guns, mortars, and engineers. Regardless of the hardware employed, the attackers suffered heavy losses for no gains.

Despite the initial success of the defensive battle, SS-Sturmbannführer Riepe recognised the fragility of his men's morale and led his makeshift garrison with a firm hand. Wherever the Russians achieved a penetration, Riepe personally led counterattacks with boldness and was able to recover the old frontline positions on each occasion.[71] However, his limited resources were insufficient to prevent a separate Soviet thrust from occupying Rimóc and Nagylóc just a few miles to the south of his perimeter.[72]

The Russians were quick to capitalise on this success and intended to further isolate the garrison. German radio monitoring units identified five Soviet cavalry regiments massing around Rimóc, indicating a new assault was imminent. This attack developed during 13 December with ground attack aircraft and armoured vehicles in support, but again the assaults were repeatedly driven off. German reconnaissance identified Soviet armoured forces with approximately 30 tanks assembling in the Kaprasi-redo, a wooded area less than two miles to the west of Szécsény, and the defenders were able to concentrate artillery fire on the area which broke up these forces, destroying three tanks and damaging five more.

Events on the ground were mirrored by action in the air, as on 14 December the weather cleared sufficiently for the combined German and Hungarian Air Forces to fly a total of 260 sorties against the Soviet supply trains identified between Ipolysag and Szécsény, during which fifty horse-drawn wagons and motor vehicles were destroyed and seventeen Soviet aircraft shot down.[73]

The Russians attacked Szécsény again and again. Infantry attacks were met with withering machine gun and mortar fire and were finally driven off at bayonet point. The few tanks and anti-tank guns available to the defenders met the Soviet armoured wedges head on and when these failed, infantry stalked the T-34s and lend lease Sherman tanks with Panzerfauste, mines, and improvised explosive charges. Frustrated by the lack of progress, Pliev reinforced his spearhead units with elements of the 72.Guards Rifle Division and again committed tanks to the assault. The 15.Guards Mechanised Brigade supported by 15 tanks of the 36.Guards Tank Brigade broke into the German defences at Hermina Farm, less than a mile to the southwest of Szécsény. With artillery support and ground attack aircraft making strafing runs over the town centre to drive the defenders back, they had occupied fifteen houses on the southwest edge of town by 16.00 hours on 15 December. Infantry from 1.Guards Motorised Battalion penetrated into the German trench line, killing and capturing a large number of the defenders before the breach was sealed in close-quarter fighting. Simultaneously, the 14.Guards Mechanised Brigade was involved in an attack a half a mile to the north of the town. The Germans launched an immediate counterattack with infantry, assault guns and armoured personnel carriers against both arms of the pincer and drove them back, the 15.Guards being forced to abandon the houses that they had occupied.[74]

In the early hours of 16 December, the Russians again managed to penetrate through the thinned out German ranks, making a breakthrough with 300-400 men and nine tanks into the southwest sector of Szeczeny. With his defences in danger of being rolled up from the south, Riepe pulled every available man from less vulnerable parts of the line and, although heavily outnumbered, launched a surprise counterattack that inflicted heavy losses on the Russian infantry and destroyed six of their tanks, pushing them out of the town and back to their start line. For leading this assault and for his conduct throughout the defence of Szeczeny, SS-Sturmbannführer Julius Riepe was awarded the Knight's Cross on 13 January 1945.[75]

After this latest failure, the Soviets regrouped their cavalry forces and adjusted their line of attack to outflank Szécsény to the east. Here they broke through the weak line south of Nagylóc and units of the 6.Guards Cavalry Corps captured Nagybárkány and Kisbárkány while the spearhead Cavalry Division of the 4.Guards Mechanized Corps reached Hollókő that evening. Soviet units occupied Pásztó late on 16 December and during the following morning launched a strong attack from that direction against Szécsény with massed infantry and tanks which broke into the town. The infantry was ejected in a series of short, sharp counterattacks and four tanks were destroyed, but the afternoon saw repeated Soviet attacks with battalion-sized forces from the west and south, which again were fought off.[76] In desperate hand-to-hand fighting the infantrymen of II./Infantry Regiment 42 distinguished themselves alongside Riepe's grenadiers and for his resolute leadership their commander, Hauptmann Karl Heinz Dierks, was also rewarded with the Knight's Cross on the same day as Riepe.[77]

By this stage of the battle the defence of Szeczeny was becoming, at least on the German side, an infantryman's war. IV.Panzer Corps' already limited armoured reserves had been decimated since the beginning of the December offensive and by mid-December it was reporting that 46.Infantry Division could only field three operational Stug III assault guns, 18.SS-Panzergrenadier Division had five serviceable Jagdpanzer IV (probably Stug IV), 4.SS-Panzergrenadier Division had thirteen remaining armoured fighting vehicles of all types and 24.Panzer Division only had four combat-worthy Panzer IVs, although it had a dozen more in various states of disrepair in its forward workshops. These resources were spread across the whole Corps' front, never allowing a concentration for a significant counterthrust. The armour was therefore largely reduced to an infantry support role. Overall direction of the fighting north of Ipolysag was transferred to 18.SS-Panzergrenadier Division on 16 December from 24.Panzer Division, which was being moved to shore up the defences further south, and a new divisional command post was established in Krupina (Korpona) in Slovakia.[78]

On the same day, the majority of Pliev's mechanised forces were ordered to disengage from the fighting around Szécsény and were redirected for more mobile operations in the Ipolysag Corridor, being replaced by 53.Army and elements of 27.Army. For a whole week these Armies launched infantry assaults in battalion strength against Szécsény from the west, southwest and south, which stretched the defences to breaking point but never breached the line, every attack driven off with heavy casualties.[79]

However, the bulk of 18.SS-Panzergrenadier Division further south was in danger of being overrun. On the evening of 12 December, SS-Panzergrenadier Regiment 40 had been forced to continue its retreat to the north and gave up its positions around Ecseg and Csécse. SS-Rottenführer Luckenheimer wrote in his diary:

> 13 December 1944: We fought the approaching Russians with our 2cm *Flak*. The HKL [Main Line of Resistance, i.e. frontline] ran along a brook. Once again, the Russians used their super heavy mortars and then their Infantry. *Kompanie* Dombeck abandoned its position. The Russians pursued. Our counterattack, led by *Oberscharfü*hrer Botz, bogged down, but the penetration was cordoned off. And then our own mortars entered the fray; and they shoot well.
> 14 December: A renewed counterattack does not get us back our section of trench lost on the previous day. To the contrary: the mess got worse and once the Russians occupied the village of Buják, the order to withdraw came during the evening. New position in an open field. Adjacent to the left of us is the 4 *SS-Polizei-Panzer-Grenadier-Division*. During the night the Russians drove with bright headlights along the road from Csécse toward Ecseg.[80]

The remnants of SS-Hauptsturmführer Wagner's SS-Pz.Aufkl.Abt.18 were surrounded in Ecseg on 14 December and following desperate

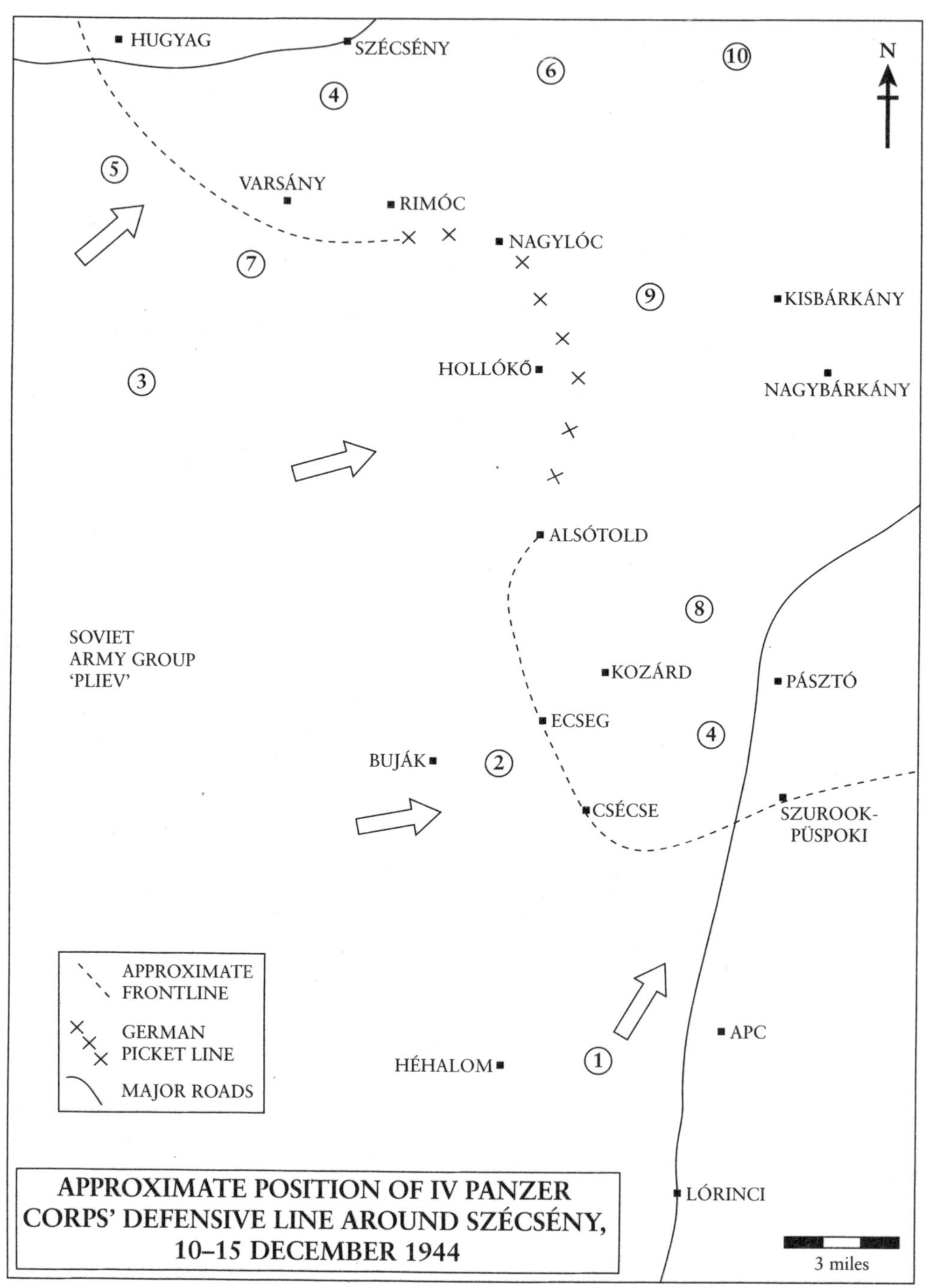
HUGYAG
SZÉCSÉNY
N
VARSÁNY
RIMÓC
NAGYLÓC
KISBÁRKÁNY
HOLLÓKŐ
NAGYBÁRKÁNY
ALSÓTOLD
SOVIET
ARMY GROUP
'PLIEV'
KOZÁRD
PÁSZTÓ
ECSEG
BUJÁK
CSÉCSE
SZUROOK-
PÜSPOKI
APPROXIMATE
FRONTLINE
GERMAN
PICKET LINE
MAJOR ROADS
APC
HÉHALOM
LÓRINCI
APPROXIMATE POSITION OF IV PANZER
CORPS' DEFENSIVE LINE AROUND SZÉCSÉNY,
10–15 DECEMBER 1944
3 miles

Szécsény Sector Map Notes

1 The Soviet offensive began on 5 December and 7.Guards Army smashed the lines between 357.Infantry Division and 18.SS-Panzergrenadier Division, which was also the junction between the German 6. and 8.Armies. The two divisions were forced apart and Russian tanks poured through the gap in a north-westerly direction.

2 By 7 December the frontline of 18.SS-Panzergrenadier Division had been peeled back to the northeast and its battalions were scattered around the villages of Csécse, Buják, Ecseg and Kozárd to the north of Hatvan, facing a Russian force that was now attacking from the southwest.

3 Army Group Pliyev followed up 7.Guards Army's breakthrough that threatened IV Panzer Corps' thinly held western flank, forcing it to hurriedly organise a covering force to hold the strategically important town of Szécsény, which covered its line of retreat.

4 18.SS-Panzergrenadier Division was put in charge of the defence of Szécsény and ordered I./SS-Panzergrenadier Regiment 40 to defend the town while III./SS-Panzergrenadier Regiment 40 and SS-Pz.Aufkl.Abt.18 held the southern flank on the Csécse-Buják front. II. and III. Battalions of SS-Panzergrenadier Regiment 39 were assigned positions around Szurdokpüspöki,

5 General Pliyev ordered 4.Guards Mechanised Corps to capture Szécsény on 9 December and strike eastwards into the rear of 8.Army.

6 Trying to pre-empt the unreliability of the Hungarian SS infantrymen, II./Panzer Grenadier Regiment 26, reinforced by a company of tanks from 24.Panzer Division, was ordered to the Szécsény sector on 10 December.

7 Repeated attacks by 14. and 15.Guards Mechanised Brigade supported by 36.Guards Tank Brigade, from 10–14 December failed to capture the town, although the garrison was stretched to breaking point.

8 On 12 December, SS-Panzergrenadier Regiment 40 had been forced to give up its positions around Ecseg and Csécse and continue its retreat to the north. SS-Pz.Aufkl. Abt.18 were surrounded in Ecseg on 14 December and following desperate resistance they broke out that night and retreated to Kozárd which they were also unable to hold. This precipitated a retreat into the Slovak mountains.

9 On 15 December the Soviets regrouped their cavalry forces and adjusted their line of attack in an effort to outflank Szécsény to the east. They broke through the picket line south of Nagylóc and units of the 6.Guards Cavalry Corps captured Nagybárkány and Kisbárkány while the 4.Guards Mechanized Corps reached Hollókő that evening. Soviet units also occupied Pásztó late on 16 December.

10 Although effectively cut off from their parent units, the mixed force of SS and Army infantry and armour held Szécsény for another week, allowing the bulk of IV Panzer Corps to retreat into Slovakia.

resistance they broke out that night and retreated to Kozárd. The next day they took over the defence of Kozárd from SS-Panzergrenadier Regiment 40. Casualties within the Abteilung mounted rapidly and both the commander of the Heavy Company, SS-Hauptsturmführer Fehrentheil, and SS-Untersturmführer Zipser in command of 2.Company, were wounded. The weakened Kampfgruppe Schäfer found itself overextended and couldn't withstand the pressure of the Russian onslaught. The Soviets broke through on the left wing, cutting contact with SS-Panzergrenadier Regiment 7[81] resulting in the loss of Alsótold to the Russians. On the night of 15–16 December Kozárd was abandoned, the retreating reconnaissance troops walking out through the snow to the northeast.

The Russians were quick to follow up and launched cavalry attacks from the Kozárd area against the string of outposts linking the two 18.SS-Panzergrenadier Division Kampfgruppen. These attacks bypassed Kampfgruppe Riepe's positions in Szécsény, breaking the line at its weakest point further south.[82] By this point SS-Pz.Aufkl.Abt.18 had been reduced to a combat strength of eighteen men and the shrunken battalions of SS-Panzergrenadier Regiment 40 were not in much better shape. By the night of 19–20 December, their position had become untenable and the remainder of Kampfgruppe Schäfer retreated into Slovakia.

It was clear that the whole line held by IV.Panzer Corps was becoming indefensible, but on 18 December German reconnaissance confirmed that the bulk of the Soviet forces facing the Corps were redeploying for the anticipated thrust into Slovakia, towards Bratislava and Vienna. This movement combined with the steady withdrawal of the Corps to the north into the Matra Mountains gradually eased the danger to the Corps' deep western flank. While spoiling attacks continued until the end of the year, the last mention of Szecseny appears in official reports on 28 December 1944 when the town was finally abandoned.[83]

Reorganisation

By the first day of 1945 all combat elements of 18.SS-Panzergrenadier Division had been withdrawn from the front and ordered to regroup in the Banská **Štiavnica** (Schemnitz) area of Slovakia. On 2 January, the division ceased to be under the control of 4.SS-Panzergrenadier Division as it became clear that the focus of the fighting had shifted away from the mountainous region of the Slovak-Hungarian border. This order had a sting in the tail: I./SS-Panzergrenadier Regiment 40, which had fought so hard at Szecseny, was retained by the 'Polizei' Division and eventually officially incorporated into it, although SS-Sturmbannführer Riepe and a small command staff were allowed to return to reform the battalion within SS-Panzergrenadier Regiment 40.

4.SS-Panzergrenadier Division also received the few remaining armoured vehicles and heavy weapons from 18.SS-Panzergrenadier

Division, which according to the war diary of Army Group South (BA: RH 19 V/56) amounted to four heavy anti-tank guns, three Sturmgeschütz assault guns, two Hetzer tank destroyers and one heavy battery, believed to be the 88mm battery from SS-Flak Abt.18. It is likely that the Hetzers already belonged to SS-Panzer-Jäger Abteilung 4 which was deployed with 18.SS at the beginning of December.[84]

Units of 18.SS-Panzergrenadier Division had begun to be pulled back from the fighting front in Hungary as early as the beginning of December, SS-Feld-Ersatz-Bataillon 18 under SS-Hauptsturmführer Paul Liebermann going ahead to Kremnica (Kremnitz) in central Slovakia to prepare for the arrival of the rest of the division, while continuing an intensive training programme. Here it took charge of small groups of recruits sent from SS-Ausbildungs and Ersatz-Bataillonen (SS-Training and Replacement Battalions) in Breslau and Hamburg who were to be assimilated into the division.[85]

As the war entered its final year, Germany's remaining manpower resources largely consisted of recruits who were totally untrained and largely unsuitable for an infantry role as they lacked both weapons training and combat experience. Some were in poor health. Many were redundant Luftwaffe ground crew personnel, and highly trained aircrew grounded through a lack of both aircraft and fuel were also used to pad out infantry units. The severely truncated Kriegsmarine also provided excess staff and reclassifications of civilian workers roles produced a haul of men from professions that had previously been exempt from conscription.[86] It was thought that these drafts of Reich Germans would make the division more 'Germanic' and therefore more efficient in battle; but using airmen in an infantry role was to create its own particular problems.

I./SS-Panzer-Grenadier Regiment 39, which had been wretchedly ill-prepared for action, was the first combat unit to be transferred to the Kremnica area on 10 December, the other two battalions of that regiment following in the middle of December. The shattered remnants of SS-Pz-Aufkl.Abt.18 were moved to Deutsch-Proben (Nitrianske Pravno) on 21 December where its reconstitution was supervised by SS-Hauptsturmführer Wagner. Only part of SS-Panzer-Abteilung 18 had seen action in Hungary, as there had been insufficient vehicles to equip either the staff or 1.Company. The remains of the unit were reunited in the Kremnitz area at the end of December under their new commander, SS-Hauptsturmführer Wunsch.

Both SS-Artillery Regiment 18 and SS-Flak Abteilung 18 had been savaged in battle in Hungary, with only IV. Abteilung from the artillery regiment arriving in Kremnitz, and these units were largely unarmed after handing over most of their guns and prime movers to 4.SS-Panzergrenadier Division. With few replacement guns forthcoming, most of the crews were integrated into the shrunken infantry regiments, although I./SS-Artillery Regiment 18 and 1./SS-Flak Abteilung 18 were partially reconstituted later. Only the support services including SS-Sanitäts Abteilung 18 and SS-Nachrichten Abteilung 18 seem to have been able to retreat into Slovakia largely intact. Elements of SS-Panzergrenadier Regiment 40 were the last to be withdrawn from Hungary with Il. and III./ SS- Panzergrenadier Regiment 40 occupying a blocking position in the mountains south of Schemnitz until the end of December 1944.[87]

However, even in their new rest area, sections of the division were called upon to defend their billets and lines of communication against partisan attacks. These actions were so serious that even the war diary of Army Group South commented on it on 31 December 1944: 'Civilians and gangs joined the fighting in the rear of our own troops.'[88]

Relocation to Kremnitz allowed the divisional staff to take stock of what remained of the division, and it was clear that it was in no condition at that time to take part in further operations. A report on the state of division compiled by Army Group South and dated 18 January 1945 was particularly scathing about its condition:

> Combat value IV. Consists of ethnic Germans from Hungary. Not up to crisis situations. Still only remnant units on hand. Command not strict enough. The Reichsführer has already ordered its officers replaced.[89]

This replacement of officers appears to have referred to the transfer of SS-Oberführer Trabandt during Christmas 1944 who left to become the commandant of *SS-PanzerGrenadier-Schule 'Kienschlag'* but it is unclear whether his move was prompted by illness or for leadership failures during the Hungarian campaign.[90] He was replaced by SS-Gruppenführer Josef Fitzthum. The three regimental commanders and most of the battalion commanders within the division remained until the end of the war and, as noted above, even when Riepe's battalion was removed from the division, he was sent back to the division to raise a new one.

There is some confusion around the official dates of when Fitzthum (written as Vitzthum in some sources) and subsequently Georg Bochman took command. Ultimately, Fitzthum arrived at the division in the last week of December 1944 and Bochmann was in command by the end of the second week of January 1945. Josef Fitzthum was an Austrian by birth who had been chief of police in Vienna before the war. He had joined the Waffen-SS in 1940 and was given command of a unit in the SS-Totenkopfverbände.

He was assigned combat duties following the invasion of Russia and took command of the SS-Legion 'Flandern' in the savage fighting to reduce the Volkhov pocket following the severe wounding and repatriation of its original commander in April 1942. This was followed by a command role within the SS-Legion 'Niederlande' on the Leningrad Front under the overall of control of 2.SS-Infantry Brigade (mot). Estes notes that Fitzthum 'displayed some skill in handling foreign troops'.

Between April 1942 and May 1943, he was stationed in the Netherlands where he oversaw the establishment of the Voluntary Associations of the Waffen-SS, which was essentially a recruitment and administration role. After Italy's defection to the Allied cause in September 1943, SS-Brigadeführer und Generalmajor der Waffen-SS und Polizei Fitzthum was sent to Albania in October 1943 as part of the German military's efforts to fill the vacuum in the Balkans left by the departing Italian forces.

He was made chief political advisor and personal representative of the Reichsfuhrer SS in Albania and reporting directly to Himmler himself, largely due to his Austrian heritage as the Albanians had a long affinity with the Austro-Hungarian Empire that the Germans appreciated and exploited with unusual perceptiveness.[91] Outwardly, Fitzthum's main task was to rebuild the Albanian police force, but as he had been appointed without a specific command he had licence to act as he saw fit. It was his idea to raise an Albanian Legion within the ranks of the Waffen-SS as the Austrians had done during the First World War, and he involved himself in the recruitment and training of the Albanian mountain division, 21.Waffen-Gebirgs-Division der SS 'Skanderbeg'.[92]

In August 1944 he was promoted to SS Gruppenführer und Generalleutnant der Waffen-SS and granted very broad powers. By the time the Germans evacuated Albania in October 1944, Fitzthum was probably the most powerful man in the entire country. After his return to Germany he was posted to 18.SS-Panzergrenadier

Division as its new commander following SS-Oberführer Trabandt's departure.[93] According to the notes of Major i.G. Wind:

> Vitzthum [Fitzthum] arrived on the first day of Christmas... [He] had me brief him on the combat strength, organization and equipment of 18.SS-Division. At that point he decided not to take over his command but go to Himmler and get him to provide replacements and equipment. Vitzthum had a fatal accident on his return from Himmler, who at that time was in Vienna.[94]

Reports indicate that his car crashed on an icy road near Wiener Neudorf. He was buried in Vienna.[95] Despite his success whilst leading 'Germanic' volunteers earlier in the war. Fitzthum may not have been an ideal commanding officer. It was recorded that Fitzthum had disliked working with the Albanian authorities and Albanians generally, being impatient, overbearing and bullying with a penchant for brutality.[96] The Ukrainian volunteers of 14.SS-Grenadier Division had suffered under their commanding officer SS-Brigadeführer, Fritz Freitag, who had treated them with nothing but contempt, and it is possible that Fitzthum may have had a similar attitude to his Hungarian Volksdeutsche recruits.

In the interim, SS-Standartenführer Heinrich Petersen, commander of SS-Panzergrenadier Regiment 39 and the senior of the regimental officers, took temporary command of the division, overseeing its reconstruction while awaiting Fitzthum's replacement. That officer was SS-Oberführer Georg Bochmann – an entirely different breed of soldier to Josef Fitzthum. Prior to being transferred to command the 18.SS-Panzergrenadier Division Bochmann had displayed a knack for leadership of all types of unit, for which he had been highly decorated. He had spent his entire military career in the SS, most of it fighting on the Eastern Front.

He was a relatively early recruit into the SS-Totenkopfverbände when he enlisted in April 1934. Promoted to the rank of SS-Untersturmführer, he was posted to SS-Totenkopf-Standarte 1 'Oberbayern' stationed at Dachau concentration camp,[97] where he was serving when the SS 'Totenkopf' Division was officially formed there on 16 October 1939.[98] Bochmann fought with that division as a company commander through the French campaign of 1940 and rose to command SS-Totenkopf-Panzerjäger-Abteilung, the division's battalion-sized anti-tank unit, with the rank of SS-Sturmbannführer following the invasion of Russia.[99]

Bochmann was awarded the Knight's Cross for successfully leading 'SS-Kampfgruppe Bochmann', a mixed force of infantrymen, reconnaissance troops and assault guns that led the breakout of II Army Corps across the Lovat River during the savage fighting to escape from the Demyansk pocket in April 1942. In September 1942, having suffered almost eighty per cent casualties, the 'Totenkopf' Division was withdrawn to France for refitting as 3.SS-Panzergrenadier Division 'Totenkopf'. Bochmann was given command of the newly designated SS-Panzergrenadier Regiment 5 'Thule', which he led through the heavy defensive fighting around Kharkov in the spring of 1943 as the Red Army surged westwards in the wake of their triumph at Stalingrad. As a result of his leadership he received the Oak-Leaves to his Knight's Cross from Hitler personally and was rewarded with command of SS-Panzer Regiment 3 in time for the Kursk offensive; arguably the largest tank battle of all time.

Following the heavy and irreplaceable losses at Kursk, the German military's entire eastern front went into the long retreat westwards which even units like the newly upgraded 3.SS-Panzer Division could not halt. The division was ground down in costly rear-guard actions and local counterattacks until it was forced back to the Polish border in the summer of 1944. At this point Bochmann left the 'Totenkopf' Division and temporarily commanded SS-Panzer Regiment 9 in the 'Hohenstaufen' Division, where he remained until January 1945.[100]

On 5 January 1945, 18.SS-Panzergrenadier divisional staff received the order to move to the Marburg-Cilli area in Lower Styria, which was thought to be an area far enough away from the main fighting front to provide a respite for the troops while providing protection for local garrisons against the increasing partisan threat. Unfortunately for the division, the deteriorating situation in Army Group Centre's area of operations necessitated their immediate transfer to Silesia and their proposed move was cancelled. On 1 February 1945, SS-Standartenführer Bochmann received the order to move the freshest of his fighting units immediately to a staging area around Mährisch-Ostrau where they would come under the command of 1.Panzer Army to counter the Soviet breakout from the Vistula bridgeheads, which was posing a serious threat to the Silesia industrial region.[101] Undermanned and lacking almost all of its heavy weapons, 18.SS-Panzergrenadier Division was being sent to confront a major Russian attack with the absolute minimum of resources.

7

SILESIA

After its tremendous territorial gains of the summer and autumn of 1944 the Red Army's advance had finally run out of steam on the east bank of the Vistula River, but two projecting bridgeheads, at Magnuszew to the north of Warsaw and Baranov to the south, provided ideal jumping-off points for the next, and as STAVKA hoped, final push towards Berlin.

On 7 January 1945 Marshal Konev's 1.Ukrainian Front had burst out of the Baranov Bridgehead with five armies and two tank armies in a steel armada that exceeded one thousand tanks and self-propelled guns. The three divisions of XXXXVIII.Panzer Corps manning the German frontline were shattered and the supporting XXIV.Panzer Corps was overrun. The main thrust of Konev's advance was directly west, on the shortest route to Berlin, which employed the bulk of his mechanised forces. However, Stavka was acutely aware of the importance of Upper Silesian coal and steel production to the Nazi war effort and Konev was ordered to deploy some of his infantry and second echelon units to take Krakow and the industrial areas of Upper Silesia, which would have the added benefit of covering his exposed southern flank.

Within two weeks the Russians had crossed the Reich border east of Oppeln, which allowed their armies to take advantage of the good road network, the tank units averaging twenty to thirty miles a day and the infantry armies eighteen miles. By 22 January, the left flank of 1.Ukrainian Front had reached the river Oder and over the next three days the scattered German forces were unable to prevent Konev's armies occupying a 140-mile stretch of the river between Cosel and Glogau and crossing it in a number of places.[1]

Most of the German 17.Army, commanded by General Friedrich Schulz, was facing the Soviet advance in Upper Silesia and like every other major German formation, all of its divisions were dangerously understrength. Faced with overwhelming odds and with his army in danger of being surrounded in a flanking manoeuvre from the north, Schulz was nevertheless pinned to his positions by a 'Führer Order' demanding that Upper Silesia must be held regardless of the cost. With the destruction of 17.Army looking like a certainty, the commander of Army Group Centre, the ardent Nazi Generaloberst Ferdinand Schörner, ordered the evacuation, and therefore abandonment, of the whole industrial area and pulled the army back to the Ratibor (Raciborz)-Cosel line. This retreat not only saved an army, it also freed up divisions to cover the approaches to the Mährisch Ostrau industrial region on the borders of Silesia and Moravia.[2]

Further south, units of 4.Ukrainian Front had been thwarted in their advance by dogged German defence in the mountainous Beskides region of the Slovak frontier. The outcome of this determined opposition was that the 4.Ukrainian Front attempted to shift the weight of its attack northwards to the gap of relatively flat land between the mountains and the Vistula River in Upper Silesia. The frozen landscape ensured that the numerous ponds and rivers were passable to infantry, and again, the excellent highways were ideal for tanks.

In attempting to create a defensive front to counter this new and unexpected two-pronged attack the LIX.Army Corps was subordinated to 1.Panzer Army on 29 January. It defended a stretch of frontline between Bielitz (Bielsko) and Pless (Pleß or Pszczyna) on the upper Vistula. In the north and south the front held, but troops from 4.Ukrainian Front seized a bridge over the river between the two towns that carried the railway line from Oswiecim (Auschwitz) to Mährisch Ostrau (Ostrava), severely disrupting the movement of both reinforcements and supplies.[3]

Having escaped from the trap in Upper Silesia, the battered divisions of 17.Army were moved north into Lower Silesia and 1.Panzer Army shifted its already overstretched units to cover their vacated positions on the Ratibor-Cosel front.[4] This movement coincided with a switch in strategy by 4.Ukrainian Front, which had been attempting to make a breakthrough on a broad front with too limited resources to achieve much success. Appreciating its mistake, the Front command concentrated its forces for an assault in the Pless area with a view to exploiting any penetration in the direction of Schwarzwasser and Mährisch-Ostrau. A further advantage to this axis of attack was the lack of any natural obstacles to hinder the armoured spearhead.[5]

By this stage of the war the importance of the Mährisch Ostrau industrial region to the war economy of the Reich could not be overstated. For example, the eastern district of Karwien shipped 16,000 tons of coal and coke to the Reich, the equivalent of twelve trainloads each of sixty wagons, every single day until the end of the war.[6] Mährisch Ostrau was also a centre for ammunition production and local distilleries made alcohol for use as fuel in place of petrol. The whole area was considered so vital to the war effort in the last few months of the war that German troops were forbidden to enter in uniform so as not to provoke the Red Air Force into attacking it.[7]

On 10 February, 4.Ukrainian Front launched a major attack at the junction between XI.Army Corps and LIX.Army Corps which achieved a significant breakthrough and threw the Germans back to Schwarzwasser,[8] but to either side of the penetration area the battered German divisions clung on in their foxholes and trenches. Subsidiary attacks to either side of Ratibor and to the north west of Pless by 1.Ukrainian Front, hoping to draw off some of the German defenders from these areas, also failed to breach the frontline.

It was in the face of these attacks that 18.SS-Panzergrenadier Division was sent directly from its reconstitution area in Slovakia to reinforce XI Army Corps and, alongside 371.Infantry Division, arrived just in time to help contain a Russian attack from the Leobschütz bridgehead launched by units also under the command of 1.Ukrainian Front.[9] However, the loss of both Pless and Bielitz in the opening stages of the attack allowed the leading Russian elements to quickly push further to the west. By nightfall on 11 February, the Russian armoured spearhead had reached the villages of Rychold and Pilgrimdorf and was already advancing deeper into the Schwarzwasser region.

Army Group Centre had already deployed the bulk of the 18.SS-Panzergrenadier Division to the north between Cosel and Ratibor in the area around Gross Neukirch, but as the crisis in the Schwarzwasser area developed it was clear that a powerful armoured group was required to restore the situation. The newly activated

SS-Panzerjäger Abteilung 18 (SS-Pz.Jäg.Abt.18) and SS-Pionier Battalion 18 (SS-Pi.Btl.18) were placed under the command of the LIX.Corps, part of General Heinrici's 1.Panzer Army, which had no other reserves available.[10]

The SS-Pz.Jäg.Abt.18 was led by a combat veteran, SS-Sturmbannführer Neubert, SS-Pi.Btl.18 was under the command of SS-Sturmbannführer Fink, a former Luftwaffe officer with neither combat nor engineering experience. Accompanying the pioneer battalion were the missing pioneer companies from SS-Panzergrenadier Regiments 39 and 40 along with the pioneer element of SS-Pz.Aufkl. Abt.18, which had all been trained together at the Radotin and Ober Chernowitz training grounds near Prague.

SS.Pi.Btl.18 consisted of a battalion staff, three pioneer companies and a light bridge column, all of which were destined to be used as infantry, despite having spent almost a year in training for their specialised roles. The Panzerjäger Abteilung initially arrived in Mährisch-Ostrau without any heavy equipment and had been prepared to receive Hetzer tank destroyers. However, on 6 February the unit received twenty Stug IVs armed with 75mm anti-tank guns and eight Sturm Haubitzen equipped with 105mm howitzers, directly from the Alkett Works in Berlin, which were divided equally between 1. and 2.Companies. With deployment to the front imminent, this left virtually no time for the men to familiarise themselves with their new weapons.[11] SS-Untersturmführer Rebstock of the 1./SS-Pi.Btl.18. saw the new guns: 'From Freistadt we marched to Seibersdorf… On the way we met brand new assault guns – you smell the paint heated by the engines – some of which were already stopped on the roadside due to engine failure.'[12]

During this period a significant number of German armoured vehicles began to experience mechanical defects and breakdowns. For example, a suspiciously large proportion of brand new Jagdpanzer IV, delivered to 20.Panzer Division directly from the Reichswerke Hermann Göring in Linz suffered from technical defects that rendered them useless long before their employment on the battlefield. Inspections carried out by the Panzer Regiment discovered 'empty [oil] tanks and other troubles'. Steel wool had been stuffed into the carburettors. Oil pipes and other things too had been broken, 'all of which were clear signs of sabotage committed by forced labourers during the manufacturing process'.[13]

The vehicular problems were not confined to the Panzerjägers. As the perennial shortage of motor vehicles made itself felt throughout the division, SS-Pi.Btl.18 was ordered to hand over the majority of its trucks to the divisional transport column, which were traded in for horse-drawn wagons, only the battalion's officers and staff were allocated a handful of cars and motorcycles.

SS-Standardenfuhrer Bochmann briefed SS-Sturmbannführers Neubert and Fink on the situation on 11 February and ordered them to combine their units into a Kampfgruppe led by SS-Sturmbannführer Neubert, the more experienced of the two officers. Kampfgruppe Neubert was to counterattack a Russian regiment which had broken through the German lines at Pless and was advancing on Mährisch-Ostrau. From the outset Kampfgruppe Neubert suffered from a lack of coordination between the two units and there was considerable confusion in the instructions given to the company and platoon commanders. Individual members of both SS-Pi.Btl.18 and SS-Pz.Jäg. Abt.18 were oblivious to the fact that they had been combined into a single unit.

On the night of 11 February, SS-Kampfgruppe Neubert was alerted for an immediately departure towards Freistadt to block and throw back enemy units that had penetrated beyond the town of Schwarzwasser and had just taken the village of Pilgrimsdorf. SS-Sturmbannführer Fink informed his company commanders that the enemy was advancing in unknown strength and that while German troops from 75.Infantry Division held a solid front to the north of Pilgrimsdorf, there was no continuous frontline to the south where a connection with 544.Volksgrenadier Division should have been.

Kampfgruppe Neubert was ordered to advance from the town of Freistadt, retake Pilgrimsdorf and re-establish a link between the two flank divisions. At dawn on 12 February the sapper companies deployed for the attack, supported by 1./SS.Pz.Jäg. Abt.18 under SS-Obersturmführer Zeise and succeeded in not only retaking Pilgrimsdorf but also continuing on to liberate Mühlfeld and Schwarzwald before establishing contact with the 75.Infantry Division. The Russian infantry units put up a fight before being driven off by fire from the supporting assault guns and the commander of the 2./SS.Pi.Btl.18, SS-Obersturmführer Witzmann and one of his platoon commanders, SS-Untersturmführer Habernoll, were killed during the attack at the head of their men.

On 13 February, SS Pi.Btl.18 had established a two-mile-wide frontline on either side of the small town of Schwarzwald and the Soviet advance had stalled for the moment. The next morning 2. and 3.Companies were charged with recapturing the village of Rychold, just over a mile to the east of their position. The action was set for 11.20 and parts of the SS-Artillery Regiment 18 were used to support the attack. The assault began as planned with the pioneers again supported by assault guns, but the approach to the village was difficult with open pastures being cut up by barbed wire stock fences and drainage ditches. To make matters worse, several inches of wet snow had made the going very heavy and the Russians were strongly entrenched in and around the village and amply supplied with heavy support weapons.

As the advance crawled forwards heavy mortar fire hit the pioneers who, having little or no combat experience, took to their heels and ran for the safety of their own lines, oblivious to the orders of their officers and NCOs. With 2.Company completely routed and no sign of 3.Company, SS-Sturmbannführer Fink threw in his reserve platoon under SS-Untersturmführer Rebstock to continue the attack. However, a hidden Russian anti-tank gun knocked out the reserve platoon's supporting assault gun and a breakdown in communications meant that they were unable to call in artillery support of their own. The advance floundered on for another few hundred metres, but when Rebstock was wounded the attack broke down.[14]

On 16 February, while the Soviets were attempting their first breakout from the Cosel bridgehead, the Red Army launched another attack against the German defences in the Schwarzwasser area. Attacks, penetrations, and counterattacks continued until the Soviets succeeded in breaching the line in the sector of the 253.Infantry Division, the right-hand neighbour of 544.Volksgrenadier division, to the south of Schwarzwasser, which was only partially sealed off with difficulty. To stabilise the situation between Saybusch and Skotschau the entire 3.Gebirgs Division had to be redeployed on the south wing of the LIX.Corps. A message from the Army Group to the OKH dated 17 February emphasised the seriousness of the situation: 'At the 1.Panzer Army Continuation of enemy attacks, especially near Schwarzwasser... The attacks can be expected to continue. The 1. Panzer Army and Army Group can no longer supply reserves of any large size.'[15]

However, by the timely shifting of forces from one crisis point to the next the battered German defences held and, although local attacks continued, by 22 February the focus of the fighting had shifted elsewhere and the Mährisch-Ostrau industrial area had been preserved intact.[16]

Between 30 January and 21 February the Soviet offensive had been thwarted for a westward advance of only twelve miles.[17] Kampfgruppe Neubert remained on the defensive in the area around Rychild and Pilgrimsdorf until the end February. The Russians made localized attacks without seriously challenging the position, although patrols and harassing artillery fire took a steady toll on both men and equipment. When the Kampfgruppe returned to the division southwest of Cosel, SS-Pz.Jäg.Abt.18 was ordered to hand over its few remaining assault guns to SS-Panzer Abteilung 18, but the attrition rate had been so great over the last two weeks of combat that they only had eight or ten vehicles remaining, following which the Panzer Abteilung totalled only sixteen assault guns of all types. SS.Pz.Jäg.Abt.18 did not receive any more Sturmgeschütz before the end of the war and its personnel were redeployed as infantry.[18]

The Cosel Bridgehead

Meanwhile, the main force of 18.SS-Panzergrenadier Division was settling into its new positions covering the Soviet bridgehead between Ratibor and Cosel. This bridgehead was a protruding bulge on the west bank of the Oder some seventeen miles long and six miles wide. 18.SS-Panzergrenadier Division was responsible for a front of around eight to ten miles in length at the centre of the bulge, flanked to the north by 344.Infantry Division and with 371.Infantry Division to the south. General Niehoff, commander of 371.Infantry Division at this time before being made commandant of besieged Breslau, had part of the 18.SS-Panzergrenadier Division under his command.[19]

The unit in question was SS-Pz.Aufkl.Abt.18 which spearheaded the 18.SS-Panzergrenadier Division's move from to the Ratibor-Cosel front. It arrived around 8 February and was subordinated to 371.Infantry Division until the arrival of the main body of the division. It was assigned a particularly exposed section of frontline in the Gross Neukirch-Holderfelde area to defend.[20] When the rest of the division arrived at the front it was severely undermanned.

It reported a strength of 13,000 personnel, which was at least 5,000 below authorised troop levels, with more than 1,000 men serving with Kampfgruppe Neubert. Its entire artillery regiment only possessed twelve light and two heavy field howitzers and its transport assets amounted to 800 trucks, 359 cars, 204 motorcycles and forty-three artillery prime movers, while, as stated above, the thirty-one assault guns and howitzers operated by SS-Pz.Jäg.Abt.18 were fighting as a separate unit under a different corps command.[21] 18.SS-Panzergrenadier Division's most potent anti-tank weapons were concentrated in a single battery of 88mm anti-aircraft guns from SS-Flak.Abt.18 attached to SS-Panzergrenadier Regiment 40.[22]

SS-Pz.Aufkl.Abt.18 remained in its original positions, which became the southern portion of the divisional front around the particularly exposed villages of Gross Neukirch and Schwerfelde and formed a small salient into the Russian bridgehead. To their north and west were the newly reconstituted I. and original II./SS-Panzergrenadier Regiment 40 entrenched between Klein Ellguth and Klein Nimsdorf and II. and III./SS-Panzergrenadier Regiment 39 held their assigned positions on either side of the village of Langlieben on the northern shoulder of the bridgehead bulge.[23]

The Gross Neukirch sector was constantly harassed by Russian small unit incursions and brief barrages of artillery fire. Doctor Röhrs, trying to find a suitable position for his dressing station, found nothing but chaos. He had been ordered to relieve the medical staff of an infantry battalion from 371.Infantry Division whose sector they were taking over, but the army doctor had not yet received permission to leave. The chateau where his dressing station was to be established was under sporadic shell fire and its courtyard was littered with burning military vehicles.

Röhrs found that he could do little to help many of the severely wounded being brought back from the main fighting line and had to resort to bandaging the less serious cases from the back of his staff car. Casualties mounted steadily and not all were caused by enemy action. The reconnaissance units newly arrived and long-awaited pioneer platoon blundered into a minefield that had been laid by a German army unit but left unmarked, and they suffered many losses including the death of their commander, SS-Untersturmführer Mödinger.

Gross Neukirch turned out to be Doctor Röhrs last operational posting as he himself fell victim to heavy mortar fire while trying to cross a road intersection in the town. Seriously wounded in the head, Röhrs lost his right eye and was evacuated back to the Reich.[24]

The 18.SS-Panzergrenadier Division and 371.Infantry Division had only just been taken under the command by XI.Corps, commanded by General von Bunau, when the Russian 59. and 60.Armies of 1.Ukrainian Front broke out from the bridgehead on 16 February and launched a heavy attack towards Leobschütz with the aim of cutting communications to the frontline.[25]

The attack was launched in the early hours with an hour's concentrated artillery barrage backed by strafing runs and pinpoint bombing from ground attack aircraft. Early attacks concentrated on the junction between SS-Pz.Aufkl.Abt.18 and Infantry Regiment 671 from 371.Infantry Division which covered its southern flank. The army unit was compelled to withdraw from the Rittersdorf area, back about half a mile to new positions along Reichstrasse 118 which ran north out of Ratibor.[26]

Oberscharführer Dollnig was in position with 2./SS-Pz.Aufkl.Abt.18 on the high ground east of Gross Neukirch when the attack began:

> After approximately two hours the hurricane of fire moved to the rear and Russian infantry charged in great masses towards out position. Many of us had been killed or wounded. Our position looked as if it had been dug up and turned over. Everywhere, there was mud and dirt. Our defensive fire that had started with rifles and machineguns was becoming weaker. The 'Hurrah!' of Russians ... everywhere detonations from hand grenades ... hand-to-hand combat!
>
> Gruppe Gerharder on the left wing of my platoon was completely overrun. Unterscharführer Gerharder and his men defended to the last ... and fell. The same thing happened to Unterscharführer Nußbaumer's sMG Zug positioned to the right of my Zug. There were no more orders during this chaotic situation. Each Gruppe, and even each individual, had to act on his own initiative. I fired and fired with my submachine gun but it appeared that ever more Russians showed up.[27]

During the evening of 16 February Gross Neukirch had to be abandoned and the surviving members of SS-Pz.Aufkl.Abt.18 fell back towards the village of Klein Ellguth immediately to the west, in the sector of SS-Panzergrenadier Regiment.40. The adjacent village of Puhlau became another focal point of the defence which SS-Sturmbannführer Teufel, commanding II./SS-regiment 40, alongside officers and men from the battalion staff fortified for all-round defence and established as a rallying point for retreating men. Heavy casualties were sustained by all units but, with the exception of the exposed position at Gross Neukirch, the 18.SS-Panzergrenadier Division held its ground for the remainder of that day.[28]

By 17 February the Russians had employed five rifle divisions and one tank brigade along a six-mile-wide front in an attempt to push through with sheer weight of numbers. The 1.Panzer Army newspaper reported the loss of Gross Neukirch and Soviet advances towards the west but went on to describe the defensive fighting. The Soviets 'after only small territorial gains and taking high, bloody casualties from accurate fire of our artillery, encountered bitter resistance from the SS Grenadiers fighting in this position'.[29]

With Gross Neukirch in their hands the Russians brought up significant reinforcements and continued their breakthrough attempt on 17 February. Wave after wave of infantry, supported by heavy artillery and mortar fire, broke against the positions of SS-Panzergrenadier Regiments 39 and 40. The First World War field fortifications around Annahof to the east of Puhlau and the village itself, defended by sections of SS-Panzergrenadier Regiment 39, were overrun. 1./SS-Panzergrenadier Regiment 39 launched a frontal assault to recapture Puhlau and after the village had been retaken the extent of the devastation was evident: 'The village looked terrible. All the houses were shot up; dead, torn-apart Russians and Germans and dead animals lay everywhere. Russian shells exploded among them.'[30]

Once again, the losses were high and an indication of the savagery of the fighting was that SS-Untersturmführer Malkemus of the Flak Company was obliged to take over command of the decimated III. Battalion because it had lost all of its other officers. It was nonetheless able to hold onto its retaken positions.

Meanwhile, to the south SS-Panzergrenadier Regiment 40 was also forced to abandon Klein Ellguth with heavy mortar fire causing heavy losses amongst the retreating troops. The village was situated on a hill overlooking the entire 18.SS-Panzergrenadier Division sector and was therefore a key strategic prize for both sides and had to be quickly retaken, but an immediate counterattack was bloodily repulsed by small arms fire from Russian soldiers at the edge of the village. [31]

However, despite their substantial material superiority, by 18 February the Russian offensive was losing momentum, allowing both SS-Panzergrenadier Regiment 40 and the two battalions of Infantry Regiment 671 to put in some spirited counterattacks which retook some of the outlying villages to the west of Gross Neukirch. A combined attack on Schwerfelde was aided by men of the local Volkssturm battalion and succeeded in forcing out the Russian infantry,[32] but it was Klein Ellguth that became the most hotly contested village over the next few days. An intensive barrage would herald a new attack by either side for its possession. Recaptured by the Germans on 19 February, where twenty-four officer candidates from SS-Panzergrenadier Regiment 40 were killed, the village was lost again with heavy casualties being incurred, including the wounding of SS-Sturmbannführer Teufel.

The Russians felt strong enough to sally out of Klein Ellguth on 20 February, assaulting SS-Panzergrenadier Regiment 40's main defensive line to the west of the village. The weather was cold and wet, the countryside a sea of mud and the fighting quickly degenerated into murderous close-quarters combat with bayonets and spades as weapons failed to fire in the filthy conditions. The Russian forces proved to be too strong, and the SS men were forced to temporarily abandon their positions. The battle ebbed and flowed as far as Schneidenburg, where SS-Panzergrenadier Regiment 40 had its command post, a surprise Russian attack causing a disruption in communications with subordinate units, but the situation was quickly restored and a new frontline was established. The village of Klein Ellguth was eventually retaken in a surprise attack on the night of 21-22 February by 15.(Pi.)/SS-Panzergrenadier Regiment 40, led by SS-Untersturmführer Merker, the Russians being totally routed for the loss of one dead and four wounded.[33]

Ultimately, although the Russians had advanced over a mile at the centre of their bridgehead, these determined counterattacks had reduced their gains to such an extent that General Von Bunau commanding XI Corps proclaimed that the action had been a 'complete defensive success'.[34]

As the German forces regained lost territory, they discovered evidence of atrocities committed by the Red Army. General Hermann Niehoff reported that in the village of Klein Ellguth some of his soldiers (even though it was actually a unit from 18.SS-Panzergrenadier Division that had actually retaken the village) had discovered the 'terribly mutilated corpses' of murdered soldiers of the 18.SS-Panzergrenadier Division alongside the desecrated corpse of a young girl. The manor of Count Matuschka in Gross Neukirch had been plundered and devastated in an indescribable way.[35]

The Soviets were forced to call a halt to the offensive of their 59. and 60.Armies on 19–20 February due to the exceedingly high casualties and lack of reserves. It was clear that they had underestimated the defensive power of the two German divisions that they were facing, and a pause was required to bring up fresh forces and to replenish their ammunition supplies.[36]

Counterattack, Early March 1945

After the savagery of the fighting during the Soviet breakout attempt, the division was grateful for breathing space with which to rejuvenate its shattered units with fresh replacements. However, SS-Standartenführer Bochmann was distinctly unimpressed with the calibre of recruits that were being sent to his decimated division. In a top-secret document, he wrote:

> ... after five years of war the quality of our infantryman and grenadier has sharply fallen in comparison with what we had when we had only begun to fight. This may be explained by the fact that the infantryman goes to take up his position not being as well trained as before and, on the other hand, what is more important to root out, is that the infantryman has completely lost faith in himself and his weaponry in connection with the numerous defeats and related withdrawals. In the most recent fighting these shortcomings have revealed themselves with particular vividness.[37]

As to equipment, everything that was required for the division to function as a credible military unit was in short supply. By the beginning of March, the logistical situation was becoming untenable. The near constant bombing of the few remaining industrial facilities, combined with a lack of both rail and motor transport and the interdiction of the communications network by the Allied air forces had reduced the flow of armaments to the frontlines to a trickle. The lack of shells and cartridges for light and heavy field howitzers had become so critical that Bochmann was forced to issue Order No.35/45 on 6 March which laid down under what conditions this type of ammunition could be used. The order stated that the howitzers could only fire 'for supporting an attack by forces up to a battalion and more in strength and, in exceptional cases, for repelling enemy attacks of more than a company in strength'. To disguise this shortage, the order stipulated that other heavy weapons whose ammunition did not present such pressing supply problems should be fired instead.[38]

Following the stabilisation of the frontline there was growing evidence that the Russians were massing troops and equipment for another offensive. Prisoner interrogations confirmed that an operation to break through to the Leobschütz area was being prepared. XI.Corps planned a pre-emptive strike which was hoped would compress, if not eliminate, the bridgehead and severely disrupt the Russian preparations by targeting their assembly areas and supply dumps.[39]

The plan called for a pincer movement across the base of the bridgehead along the line of the Oder River. 18.SS-Panzergrenadier Division would attack, unaided, from the north, while 371. Infantry Division and 97.Jäger Division attacked form the south, supported by a Sturmgeschütz Brigade (battalion-sized at best) and a company of Hetzer tank destroyers. Hopefully the two columns would link up somewhere in the middle of the bridgehead area.

At a planning conference Major i.G. Wind had suggested that the Corps' armoured assets should be combined under the command of SS-Standartenführer Bochmann, who was an experienced panzer commander, and a thrust be attempted from west to east aimed directly at the Oder crossing points. This plan was vetoed by General von Bunau who, as an infantryman of the 'old school', preferred a more conventional approach.[40]

SS-Panzergrenadier Regiment 40 led the assault on the morning of 8 March, supported by the assault guns of SS-Panzer Abteilung18, although the expected covering artillery barrage never materialised. The grenadiers jumped off from the now destroyed village of Langlieben and fought their way southwards with SS-Panzergrenadier Regiment 40, advancing on the left, taking the village of Mühlengrund and

SS-Panzergrenadier Regiment 39 capturing Rosengrund along the Cosel-Ratibor railway line against determined Russian opposition. The Soviets had built solid field fortifications throughout the bridgehead and laid extensive minefields, especially on the approaches to the Oder bridge at Friedenau, the destruction of which was one of 18.SS-Panzergrenadier Division's objectives.

To penetrate as far as Friedenau, SS-Panzergrenadier Regiment 40 had to take Hill 176, which dominated that area of the bridgehead. With support from the assault guns the SS grenadiers stormed up the slope and took the hilltop at bayonet point, but their victory was fleeting as the Russians concentrated all of their available artillery and blasted them from the summit. Possession of Hill 176 was clearly vital to the overall success of the German plan and XI.Corps ordered a renewed attack on 9 March with the same results as the previous day.

In the south, the attack had started more promisingly with the anticipated artillery barrage hammering along the whole width of the front. III./Ski Jäger Regiment 1, which was attached to 97.Jäger Division for the operation, stormed the village of Eichendorffmühl in the face of tenacious Russian resistance and the advance proceeded with only 'moderate' losses. However, as the point units tried to break into the settlement of Herzoglich-Ellguth they were hit by a massive artillery barrage quickly followed up by a strong armoured counterattack. The casualty list was enormous and included almost every officer from the Ski Jäger battalion. The southernmost portion of the attack had been comprehensively blocked.

To their left, 371.Infantry Division attacked in a north-easterly direction towards Gross Neukirch, overrunning the forward Russian defence zone around the division's former positions at Langenfeld, but their attack ran up against the heavily fortified area around Gross Neukirch and concentrated artillery fire again broke up the attack. Both southern attacking wedges had pushed forwards less than two miles.[41]

In the 18.SS-Panzergrenadier Division's sector, the assault companies had sustained horrendous casualties by this time to no advantage, as any advance they attempted was met with overwhelming firepower. Therefore, when the XI.Corps command demanded that the offensive against Hill 176 be resumed on 10 March, SS-Standartenführer Bochmann refused. His refusal was passed up the chain of command until Generaloberst Ferdinand Schörner stormed into divisional

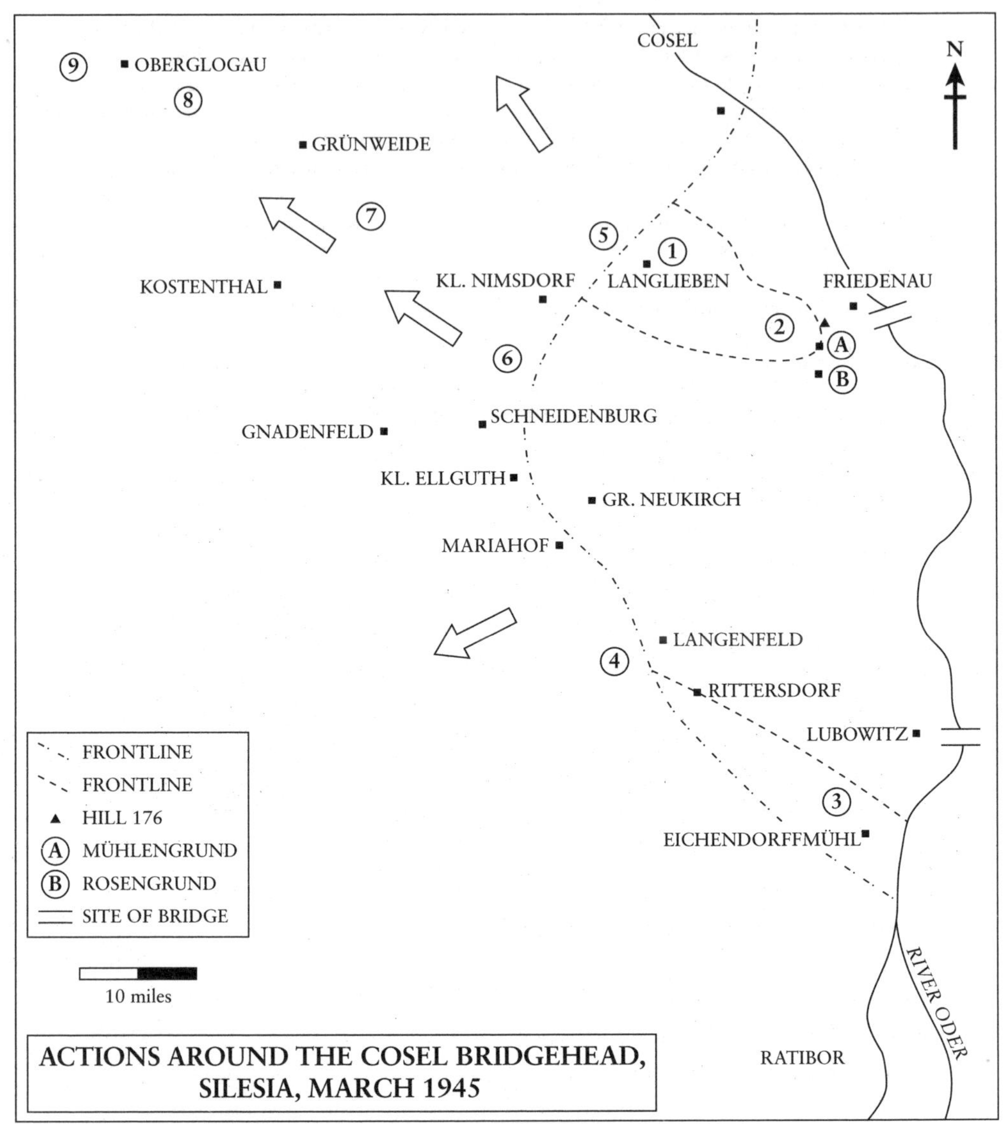

Silesia Map Notes

German counterattack

1 At dawn on 8 March 18.SS-Panzergrenadier Division jumped off from Langlieben with SS-Panzergrenadier Regiment 40 advancing southwards on the left to take the village of Mühlengrund and SS-Panzergrenadier Regiment 39 capturing Rosengrund on the right. The division's ultimate objective was the Oder bridge at Friedenau, but had to be preceded by an assault on Hill 176, which dominated that area of the bridgehead. With support from SS-Panzer Abteilung 18 the SS grenadiers took

the hilltop at bayonet point but concentrated Russian artillery fire forced them to retreat. XI Corps ordered a renewed attack on 9 March, which also failed.

2 In the south, I./Ski Jäger Regiment 1 attached to 97.Jäger Division stormed the village of Eichendorffmühl in the face of tenacious resistance but could advance no further.

3 At the outermost face of the bridgehead bulge, 371.Infantry Division attacked in a north easterly direction and recaptured the division's former positions at Langenfeld, but their attack ran up against the heavily fortified area around Groß Neukirch and concentrated artillery fire broke up the attack. Both southern attacking wedges had pushed forwards less than two miles.

4 On the morning of 11 March, the counterattack was abandoned and 18.SS-Panzergrenadier Division was pulled back to its jumping-off positions.

Russian Breakout

5 At 06.30 on 16 March a devastating artillery barrage preceded the attack of the Soviet 59. and 60.Armies, which broke through on a seven-mile-wide front. A concentrated Soviet armoured thrust smashed into the junction between 18.SS-Panzergrenadier Division and 371.Infantry Division to its right and by the afternoon of 16 March Russian tanks had broken through Infantry Regiment 671 and SS-Pz.Aufkl.Abt.18, which had been maintaining contact with 371.Infantry Division around Klein Ellguth.

6 On the same day 18.SS-Panzergrenadier Division retreated through Kreuzlinden reaching Grünweide by evening. 17 March: the division defended Grünweide but Kosenthal was abandoned. 18 March: the retreat continued through Friedersdorf. At this point the division was in contact with scattered units of Ski-Jäger battalion, 344.Infantry Division and 254.Infantry Division.

7 On that day 18.SS-Panzergrenadier Division ordered all of its sub-units that it was in contact with to assemble in Oberglogau.

8 On the morning of 19 March 18.SS-Panzergrenadier Division and 344.Infantry Division found themselves surrounded in an area around the town of Oberglogau. Lieutenant General Jollasse was placed in command of all encircled troops.

headquarters to demand the resumption of the attack. When presented with the facts even he saw the futility of another attempt. This moment marked the end of the German operation. The southern pincer had been equally unsuccessful in overcoming the Russian defences and clearly any sort of link-up was now impossible. All that day the German riflemen crouched in their sodden fox holes and fought off increasingly aggressive Russian attacks until on the morning of 11 March common sense prevailed and the troops were pulled back to their jumping-off positions, hounded all the way by Russian artillery fire.[42]

The attack by XI.Corps was a costly failure. It had barely deflected the Red Army from its own offensive preparations and had been extremely costly in both men and material. As the grenadiers bailed out their waterlogged trenches and pillboxes at night, they could clearly see the endless columns of Russian trucks bringing reinforcements into the bridgehead. The vehicles travelled with headlights full on, safe in the knowledge that neither the Luftwaffe nor German artillery were able to interfere with them.[43]

Encirclement, Mid-March 1945

The Soviet preoccupation with their breakout from the Ratibor-Cosel bridgehead stemmed from a larger strategic concern. As the Soviet forces advanced further into Reich territory during the spring of 1945, 1.Ukrainian Front was becoming increasing alarmed by the potential threat that was being posed by its laggard left wing. The fact that these forces had been unable to overcome the Oder defences between Oppeln and Ratibor had left the southern flank of the Front's central forces dangerously exposed and resulted in a delay in the final assault on Berlin while the threat of the Oppeln Bulge was neutralised.[44]

Their plan was for a two-pronged attack with one attacking column, consisting of 21. and 5.Guards Armies, thrusting south from Grottkau and the other, comprised of 59. and 60.Armies, advancing directly west from the Cosel area with both the arms of the pincer advancing roughly 30 miles and aiming to meet up at Neustadt. This was to be a classic battle of encirclement in the best Blitzkrieg tradition, which, if all went to plan, would not only eliminate the Oppeln Bulge but also remove at least five German divisions from the order of battle.[45]

In the Cosel area the impending disaster began to unfold at 06.30 on the morning of 16 March with a devastating artillery barrage that lasted eighty minutes and flattened the forward German fieldworks, allowing the point units of the 59. and 60. Armies to break through on a seven-mile-wide front. The initial assault captured the strongpoints of Eichungen, Langlieben, Klein Nimsdorf, Ridgund and Schneidenburg, all of which were in 18.SS-Panzergrenadier Division's defensive zone.[46]

The concentrated ferocity of the barrage had convinced the command staff of 18.SS-Panzergrenadier Division that the expected Russian offensive was finally underway in earnest, but Soviet reconnaissance had accurately identified the location of their headquarters which was subjected to a particularly brutal hammering. All communications with their forward units were cut and the staff had no idea how the defence was coping until streams of panic-stricken grenadiers appeared out of the thick morning fog, having abandoned their positions. As the T-34s of the Soviet armoured spearhead rolled over the flattened trenches, contact with 344.Infantry Division covering the northern flank was lost.

It quickly became clear that 18.SS-Panzergrenadier Division was suffering the full force of the Soviet offensive and while some SS grenadiers fought back when and where they could, the division was no longer in control of events and was soon in full retreat. Russian sources reported that they had to fight off at least ten separate counterattacks varying in strength from a company up to a battalion and supported to a greater or lesser degree by tanks and assault guns.[47] But in the central breakthrough zone SS-Panzer Abteilung 18, with its few remaining assault guns, had been ordered by XI.Corps to redeploy to Neustadt and had left the divisional zone that very morning.[48]

While fighting along the entire divisional front continued, a concentrated Soviet armoured thrust smashed into the junction between 18.SS-Panzergrenadier Division and its neighbour to the south, the 371. Infantry Division, and by the afternoon of 16 March Russian tanks had broken through Infantry Regiment 671.[49] SS-Pz.Aufkl.Abt.18 had been maintaining contact with 371.Infantry Division around Klein Ellguth and the armoured attack broke up the unit, forcing the bulk of it to break contact with its own division and retreat to the southwest out of the rapidly forming encirclement. The reconnaissance unit was directed to Leobschütz, where 18.SS-Panzergrenadier Division's rear services were based, and was only able to rejoin the division much later. The 18.*Schwere Granatwerfer Battailon* (this unit was the 18.Heavy Mortar Battalion equipped with 12cm mortars that formed part of the 1.*Ski Jäger* Division) that was acting as a fire brigade for the hotspots in this sector had been sent to reinforce the right flank of 18.SS-Panzergrenadier Division, but Soviet armour got there first. The 18.Heavy Mortar Battalion also had no option but to pull out to the southwest with the remnant of 371.Infantry Division to avoid encirclement.[50]

To the north of Cosel, in the Krappitz area, the north flank of 344.Infantry Division was hit by another Russian assault. Although not of the strength or intensity of the firestorm that had overtaken 18.SS-Panzergrenadier Division, it was powerful enough to sever contact with *Korpsgruppe Schlesien*, formerly LVI.Panzer Corps and part of 17.Army, which was in danger of being overrun itself. Forced to withdraw to the southwest, of 344.Infantry Division battalions forced their way through the Russian rifle regiments that were following up in the wake of their armour, and reconnected with 18.SS-Panzergrenadier Division as both units contracted into the pocket forming around the town of Oberglogau.[51]

As the SS units were pushed north-westwards every available man was called upon to fight. The divisional Ic, SS-Hauptsturmführer Stüber recorded:

> 16 March 1945: Withdrawal and retreat to Kreuzlinden. Hand-to-hand fighting near the division command post. By evening in Grünweide.
>
> 17 March: Battle for Grünweide. Division command post in Friedersdorf. Kosenthal was abandoned...
>
> 18 March: Division command post in Repsch... Found the command post of a Ski-Jäger-Battalion in a wood... In contact with Ski-Jäger and 344.Infanterie-Division as well as 254. Infanterie-Division.
>
> 19 March: On my way to Willenau to establish a division command post. Shortly after arrival the Russians enter the village. The Ic clerk Kristen and Untersturmführer Lanneau of the Nachrichten-Abteilung [Signals Detachment] are killed during the street fighting. Back to Repsch.[52]

On 18 March, 18.SS-Panzergrenadier Division ordered all of its sub-units that it was in contact with to assemble in Oberglogau. Many of the SS recruits who had been unwilling to fight in the first place and who were now disorientated and terrified by the disaster that was overtaking their division took the first opportunity to surrender; an action for which many paid with their lives. It is reported that in the village of Kosenthal, approximately four miles west of Langlieben, the Red Army carried out a mass shooting of captured SS men and this is very unlikely to have been the only incident of this kind.[53]

The Russian breakout of the Cosel bridgehead was not without cost, however. The German forces had had several weeks to improve their defences, which they had spent strengthening trench systems, building earthen pillboxes and bunkers, erecting barbed wire obstacles, and extensively mining all obvious approach routes. Single houses were turned into strong points while hamlets and small villages in the frontline zone were transformed into fortresses linked by communications trenches and with interlocking fields of fire. Additionally, while ammunition for field guns may have been in short supply, Panzerfauste, the German handheld, rocket-propelled anti-tank missile, were readily available and deadly to all Soviet armour at close range. As a result, the Russian spearhead units incurred very heavy casualties: 7.Guards Mechanised Corps lost a quarter of its tanks, 31.Tank Corps lost a third.[54] It should be noted that such heavy casualties at this late stage of the war, when Allied victory was assured, were particularly hard to take and only served to provoke the Soviet troops to carry out many acts of mindless vengeance.

The fragmented remains of 18.SS-Panzergrenadier Division were constricted into a pocket around the town of Oberglogau alongside 344.Infantry Division, commanded by Lieutenant General Jollasse, who was placed in command of all encircled troops. On the morning of 19 March, the two divisions found themselves surrounded. Radio contact was established with XXIV Panzer Corps Headquarters, but as Schörner had commanded not a step back, they hesitated to give the withdrawal order.[55]

As the situation worsened, Jollasse and Bochmann met to discuss a breakout. The intention was to strike in a west-south-west direction for Deutsch-Rasselwitz, close to where the two encircling Soviet pincer arms had met, which was therefore assumed to be a relatively weak point.[56] A precondition of the success of the breakout was that the village of Deutsch-Müllmen on Reichstrasse 115 at the western edge of the encirclement, had to be held at all costs. Bochmann took personal control of the defence with his SS-*Panzergrenadiers,* supported by a handful of assault guns from *Stug Abteilung* 344 commanded by Hauptmann Lederer. Bitter fighting raged all day, and the village was razed, but despite extremely heavy casualties they held off every attack.[57]

On the northwestern edge of the pocket, to the north of the village of Willenau, the fighting was equally intense, but the grenadiers were slowly pushed back into an ever-smaller area. The pocket had become so constricted that the long-range artillery could engage the advancing

Russians in a direct fire role over open sights.[58] At 15.00 on 19 March, General Jollasse authorised the breakout on his own initiative to commence at 17.00. Anything that could slow down the evacuation was to be left behind. Vehicles without fuel and broken-down carts were shoved into ditches and set on fire, along with official documents.[59]

The 10.5cm howitzers of I./SS-Artillery Regiment 18 and the heavy battery of 15cm guns of IV./SS-Artillery Regiment 18 were destroyed along with their towing tractors, as there was neither the fuel to move them or ammunition to make the effort worthwhile. The last 88mm guns from I./SS-Flak.Abt.18 were also rendered useless and abandoned in their positions.[60]

As the troops struggled across the muddy, pathless countryside towards Deutsch-Rasselwitz and what they hoped was freedom, the 'Bush Telegraph' spread the word amongst the civilian population trapped in the *Kessel* that a breakout attempt was underway. Hauptmann Vogt, Operations Officer of 344.Infantry Division, remembered:

> ... the troops were interspersed with many refugees. Old people, some of them women with prams, in the gathering dusk, among the attacking infantry units, were seeking their way to freedom over fields which provided no cover... It was terrible to see the mutilated bodies of women and children hit by mortars, to hear the loud screams of the wounded, and to know the deadly fear and indescribable misery of these people.[61]

This was the last chance for the men of 18.SS-Panzergrenadier Division and 344.Infantry Division as they were no longer strong enough to hold a coherent front. Desperation at their own situation and the plight of the civilians drove the soldiers on with a fierce determination. The mass of men from the two divisions simply stormed the thin Soviet frontline in and around Deutsch-Rasselwitz. The town itself was a shambles of wrecked vehicles, gutted tanks and the strewn baggage of the divisions that had retreated through it previously. The Russians had dug in with tanks and artillery around the railway station, which was attacked by the light of burning buildings, under constant artillery and mortar fire.[62]

A wedge of assault guns from *Stug Abteilung* 344 began the attack, but Russian infantry occupying the houses on the edge of the town met them with a fusillade of captured *panzerfauste*. With the assault floundering, SS-Standartenführer Bochmann, who was following close behind the lead unit in his command half-track, rapidly organised combat teams to clear the houses with hand grenades and provide close support for the armoured vehicles. By around 22.00 the railway station and southern part of the village had been cleared.[63]

For the next two hours, exhausted, disorientated troops filtered through the burning town. Just as the survivors thought that they had escaped the net, the road carried them to the river Hotzenplotz, a mile to the southwest of the town, where disaster struck. The only bridge over the river had been demolished by German army engineers who had retreated over it previously. Soldiers and civilians alike spread out to find a crossing point, but the banks were marshy and under constant enemy artillery fire. Eventually, a ford was found, and the desperate mass of humanity surged towards it.

The ground was just too soft to take even tracked vehicles, which became hopelessly bogged down in the fields leading down to the crossing. As General Jollasse recounts: 'Many vehicles, guns and the last assault guns were stuck in the attempt to cross the Hotzenplotz. It all had to be blown up and abandoned.' However, most of the remaining personnel of both divisions were saved and by midnight the main body of the escaping troops had reached the village of Hotzenplotz and the safety of the new German frontline.[64]

The following day *Korpsgruppe Schliesen*, which consisted of the remnants of the Estonian 20.SS-Grenadier Division and 168.Infantry division which had also been reduced to a Kampfgruppe, broke out of the Falkenberg pocket and managed to regain the German lines, although again at an extremely heavy cost in both men and material, including the commanding officer of the Estonian 20. SS-Grenadier Division, SS-Brigadeführer Franz Augsberger, who was killed leading his men.[65]

The Russians hailed the eradication of the Oppeln Bulge as a great victory, claiming 30,000 German officers and men killed and almost 15,000 captured. The Red Army also estimated that it had captured or destroyed fifty-seven tanks, 464 artillery pieces and more than 3,000 motor vehicles.[66] Even accounting for exaggeration, the battle of encirclement had certainly crippled four frontline divisions with the losses in both men and equipment being largely irreplaceable by this date. It is probably true that this was a more serious loss than the territory that had had to be given up.

18.SS-Panzergrenadier Division was initially regrouped around Hotzenplotz and acted as rear-guard for 344.Infantry Division and the fragments of other units that had managed to escape from the Oberglogau pocket. 344.Infantry Division gathered in the Arnsdorf-Hennersdorf area where they were visited by Colonel-General Schörner, who congratulated General Jollasse on the success of the breakout – without commenting on the fact that he had expressly forbidden it. Schörner then inexplicably chose to condemn Bochmann for going against his orders and although he sanctioned the award of Swords to Bochmann's Knight's Cross with Oak Leaves on 25 March for his personal bravery in leading his men throughout February and March, he had him relieved of his command just two days later. Hitler personally presented Bochmann with his Swords and rewarded him with command of 17.SS-Panzergrenadier Division 'Gotz von Berlichingen' which fought out the war on the Western Front.[67]

On 26 March the divisional headquarters were transferred to the Karlsbrunn area where they were to oversee the reconstitution of shattered units. SS-Standartenführer Petersen took over command of the division following Bochmann's departure. SS.Pz.Aufkl.Abt.18, never the division's strongest unit, had returned to it from Leobschütz several days previously and the remains of II./SS-Panzergrenadier Regiment 40 were positioned around the town; but the whereabouts of the rest of the regiment's units at this time remains uncertain.

I. and II./SS-Panzergrenadier Regiment 39 were despatched to the Böhmen-Mähren SS troop training grounds, where amongst other recruits they received 200 volunteers from the Panzer Grenadier Division 'Feldherrnhalle'. These were the only SA recruits that the division ever received, although the original premise of the 'Horst Wessel' Division had been to man it entirely with SA volunteers. According to an anecdotal report, these 200 men were issued with the SA kampfrune collar patch, although much doubt has been cast on the authenticity of the few photos showing the collar patch being worn. The two battalions were combined into a single unit under the command of SS-Sturmbannführer Prochaska and a new 13.(IG) Company was established, although it only possessed two infantry guns and a handful of 8cm mortars.

SS.Pz.Jäg.Abt.18 and SS.Flak.Abt.18 were both disbanded and their personnel distributed between the remaining battalions of the two grenadier regiments, while the utterly decimated SS.Pi.Btl.18 was padded out with rear area personnel and made into an alarm unit of about company strength.

The artillery regiment had lost all of its guns with the exception of 9.Battery that had been detached by XI Corps after the division's transfer from Slovakia and so had not been involved in the Cosel bridgehead meltdown. Alongside this only 1. and 2.Batteries were re-equipped with light field howitzers while, again, its excess personnel were transferred to the infantry.

At this time III./SS-Panzergrenadier Regiment 39 was detached from the division and fought as Kampfgruppe Schumacher in the Ratibor area, where it eventually drew in parts of several other units, and SS-Pz.Abt.18 was still deployed away from the division in the Neustadt area.[68]

On 15 March, with the Soviets 21. and 5.Guards Armies attacking south from Grottgau and with 59. and 60.Armies poised for a breakout from the Cosel area,[69] the two companies of SS-Pz.Abt.18, under SS-Hauptsturmführer Wunsch, were rapidly relocated to the Neustadt area on the orders of XI.Corps as Neustadt had been pinpointed as the likely meeting point of the two Russian pincer arms and therefore the position where the strongest forces should be sent to prevent this. As was often the case for German military planning in 1945, there were simply not enough troops or tanks to prevent the encirclement. However, in an unexpectedly successful night raid, SS-Obersturmführer Christiansen's 1./SS-Pz.Abt.18 was able to penetrate into the surrounded town of Neustadt on the night of 20–21 March and escort out Oberst Kramer and the town's garrison. Following this action, the Abteilung remained around the village of Gräflich Wiese two miles to the west of Neustadt, providing defensive fire support for infantry from Parachute Panzer Division 'Hermann Göring'.[70]

There were indications that a new Russian offensive to capture Ratibor was imminent. 18.SS-Panzergrenadier Division was charged with providing a regimental-sized battlegroup to help to defend the city, to be led by SS-Sturmbannführer Schumacher who at that time was commander of III./SS-Regiment 39. He was provided with a decidedly mixed force drawn from the least fragmented units of the divisions. Three battalions were mustered, although it is unlikely that any of these contained more than a couple of hundred men each.

'Battalion Grill' was commanded by SS-Hauptsturmführer Grill, formerly the Adjutant of SS-Panzergrenadier Regiment 40, whose force was based around troops from that regiment. 'Battalion Dittmann' was largely drawn from SS-Panzergrenadier Regiment 39, although it also contained pioneers and displaced flak crews. SS-Hauptsturmführer Dittmann had served with the divisional headquarters prior to this. 'Battalion Reutzel', under SS-Hauptsturmführer Reutzel of 14.(Flak)SS-Panzergrenadier Regiment 39, was formed from a mixed company of SS-Panzergrenadier Regiment 39 and assorted divisional troops.

Battalions Dittmann and Reutzel took up entrenched positions to the west of Ratibor facing the Russian salient to the north, while Battalion Grill was to fight in the city itself. 9./SS-Artillery Regiment 18 covered the fieldworks from gun positions to the west of the city. Several reconstituted units were sent as reinforcements just prior to the Russian offensive, notably the alarm company formed from SS-Pi. Btl.18 and three companies from SS-Feld Ersatz Bataillon 18 (FEB), led by SS-Hauptsturmführer Liebermann. SS-FEB 18 was sent to join Battalion Reutzel.[71]

The Russians were determined to take Ratibor as quickly as possible and claim to have been reluctant to sacrifice a large number of men in the process. Therefore, they brought their superior weight of arms to bear against its German defenders. The Red Air Force flew over 2,000 bombing sorties against the town itself in the two days prior to the attack and brought up the 25.Artillery Breakthrough Division to add its firepower to the 17.Artillery Breakthrough Division, which was already in position.[72]

The Russian attack commenced on 28 March with an overwhelming artillery barrage on the first line of field fortifications, followed up with powerful armoured attack and by mid-morning the forward positions to the west of Ratibor were overrun. In the sector to the west of Battalion Reutzel, 97.Jäger Division was forced out of the villages of Preussisch-Krawarn and Gross-Peterwitz by heavy Russian infantry attacks, supported by tanks. The commander of 204.Jäger Regiment, Oberst Leo Exler, was killed during the bitter fighting.[73]

SS-Hauptsturmführer Reutzel was given the task of recapturing Gross-Peterwitz and he employed the newly arrived FEB 18 for the mission. 1.Company set out from Schammerau and the 2.Company marched from Janken in the early hours of the morning for the attack. The situation was confused as it was unclear exactly where the enemy's position was. Support from heavy weapons was non-existent and the telephone connection to Reutzel's command post was destroyed.

The attacking force had to cross the branch line from Katscher to Groß-Peterwitz and a large, open space in front of the town. With no cover, the attacking companies received heavy fire from mortars, anti-tank guns and infantry weapons and substantial losses were incurred, including SS-Untersturmführer Neumann, commander of 1.Company, who was brought back wounded. Nevertheless, the companies broke into Gross-Peterwitz and by noon three-quarters of the town was in German hands. However, a mass of Russian tanks intervened in the battle and the attackers were forced out again by weight of numbers.

While re- crossing the open area and the railway embankment the companies again suffered significant losses and the dead and wounded could not be recovered. The attack cost the battalion fifty per cent of its strength and after the survivors had been rallied it was found that they could no longer contact Reutzel or his staff. The remnants of the battalion retreated to the village of Janken and established it for all-round defence. By the morning of 30 March, the remains of SS-FEB 18 were virtually surrounded and were forced to break out with the order 'Every man for himself!'[74] According to the records of the tracing service of the German Red Cross: 'There was heavy house and street fighting in the villages of Schammerau and Janken with substantial losses, where an SS-Kampfgruppe was surrounded and completely destroyed.'

The assumption is that this battlegroup was the balance of Battalion Reutzel as it totally disappeared from all divisional records after this date.[75]

By 31 March, all of the Soviet artillery that could be brought to bear was concentrating on eliminating the defences on the outskirts of the town and Russian aviation units were targeting identified artillery and mortar positions around the clock. After substantial softening up, 15.Guards Corps and 106.Rifle Corps, strongly supported by tanks, stormed the city.[76]

Even with the front collapsing to its rear, the defences in and immediately around Ratibor held. On 30 March 14.(Flak) SS-Panzergrenadier Regiment 40 was sent into the city to support the infantry of Battalion Grill during the street fighting. SS-Rottenführer Lunkenheimer was chosen to make up part of a six-man crew for a captured Russian *Ratsch-Boom*, a 76.2mm high velocity field gun:

> Once the Russians started their attack we intervened with our *Ratsch-Boom* in the defensive battle. Two of our Sturmgeschütze, in a good ambush position on the northern outskirts of Ratibor, destroyed eight Russian tanks. The fighting then shifted gradually into the centre of the town. With our *Ratsch-Boom,* we moved as a pathetic little group from one street corner to the other and fired. The street fighting became ever more violent.[77]

By the end of 31 March, the city of Ratibor was in flames. Desperate street fighting was still going on in the southern suburbs and SS-Artz Doctor Ernst Kurz, medical officer of SS-Panzergrenadier Regiment 40 now attached to SS-Kampfgruppe Schumacher, remembered that SS-grenadiers were still putting up a fight around the burning Church of the Sacred Heart on the morning of Easter Sunday, 1 April.[78]

After the fall of Ratibor the two remaining battalions of SS-Kampfgruppe Schumacher fell back in the direction of Mährisch-Ostrau, twenty-five miles to the south. By 14 April the Kampfgruppe was sandwiched between 97.Jäger Division on the left and 371. Infantry Division, which was hard up against the Oder River on the right. These three units manned a front facing northwest along the line of the Troppau-Ratibor railway. 18.SS-Panzergrenadier Division continued to feed company-sized units into the battlegroup as they became available, but the quality of most of these replacements was very low.

The Russian advance could sometimes be temporarily halted but was ultimately unstoppable. It remained the case where a few battle-hardened veterans with machine guns would hold the front while the recruits took to their heels. Casualties, particularly from artillery and mortar fire, mounted rapidly and were no longer replaced. Actions that had previously been carried out by battalions were now assigned to company-sized units to achieve. The Kampfgruppe, now under the command of 371.Infantry Division, retreated southwards through a succession of Czech fortified positions that had marked the pre-war border zone, but the Russians were always too strong and too mobile for them to attempt a meaningful defence and their positions were constantly outflanked. The Kampfgruppe made a stand in an old chain of bunkers in the Boorwald on 21 April and immediately began to strengthen the defences with wire entanglements and new trench lines, but their efforts were in vain as the Russians had already broken through to the village of Haatsch and were advancing remorselessly into their rear.

Surrounded again, the grenadiers slipped through the net and retreated to the approaches of Mährisch-Ostrau where Battalions Dittmann and Grill put up determined resistance for Petershofen (Petřkovice) alongside 671.Infantry Regiment, but there was no holding the Soviet onslaught and the town had to be abandoned.[79] By 30 April the city was surrounded and the Kampfgruppe began to disintegrate. Grill's Battalion was assigned to hold the Oder bridge in the north outskirts of the city, but Grill failed to undertake any measures to defend it. Eventually, an army pioneer unit blew it up, but by then Grill and his unit had disappeared.

Battalion Dittmann and the remnants of 371.Infantry Division retreated southwards again on 1 May, but there was nowhere to go. The severely weakened units were attacked from all sides by both Russians and groups of marauding Czech partisans and were dispersed. Individual elements managed to work their way through to the American lines, but most of the troops ended up in Russian captivity.[80] Dittmann and Schumacher managed to evade the massacre of the majority of SS men who fell into Czech hands and finally surrendered to the Russians in Tabor on 15 May.[81]

Further to the north and west, the Russians had continued their attacks following their successes at Ratibor and Neustadt, and by the end of April had steadily pushed 17.Army and 1.Panzer Army back to the Oderberg-Troppau-Jägerndorf line. The fighting in this area had been savage, despite the obviously hopeless situation for the German military, as they tried to ensure the evacuation of the German population into the former Austrian Silesian areas of Troppau and Jägerndorf. Both sides fought for every hill, village, and yard of ground until the Germans were forced to withdraw and re-grouped at a new line of defence.[82]

While SS-Kampfgruppe Schmacher was involved in its fighting retreat from Ratibor, the rest of the division was assigned to 17.Army reserve and relocated to the Hirschberg area. It had been bled white and by 31 March 18.SS-Panzergrenadier Division was reporting a total strength of just 5,212 men of all ranks, significantly less than half of its strength at the beginning of the defence of Silesia. It was now judged to be no longer combat effective due to a lack of equipment[83] although, inexplicably, SS.Pz. Aufkl.Abt.18 was issued with armoured cars for the first time, which were used to provide a protective screen for the deployment of the rest of the division.[84] 18.SS-Panzergrenadier Division found itself under the command of General von Mellenthin's VIII.Army Corps, with the shredded remnant of the Estonian 20.SS-Grenadier Division on its right flank, on the left LVII.Panzer Corps belonging to 4.Panzer Army.[85]

SS-Panzergrenadier Regiment 40, reduced to two battalions of two rifle companies each, with a scattering of support weapons, took up positions to the north of the divisional area towards Zobten (Sobótka) while II./SS-Panzergrenadier Regiment 39 was positioned around Hirschberg itself and SS.Pz.Aufkl.Abt.18 took over the southern flank. As mentioned previously, the division's support units had been broken up and reallocated to infantry companies or were employed in the construction of field fortifications, but SS.Pz. Abt.18 returned to divisional control at the beginning of April, as did SS-FEB 18.[86]

They were opposed by Polish troops of 1.Ukrainian Front but most of its forces and all of its attention was focused on the battle for Berlin on its right wing far to the north, and the Polish forces made no attempts at a serious advance in this area before the end of the war. On 7 May, as news of the capitulation filtered down from higher commands, SS-Standartenführer Petersen received the order from VIII.Army Corps to break away from the frontline and move westwards to the demarcation line between the Soviet and American forces.[87]

18.SS-Panzergrenadier Division's war was not over everywhere. 2./ SS-Pz.Abt.18, still separated from divisional command, had one more action to fight. Throughout March 17.Army had made every effort to amass sufficient armoured forces to relieve the city of Breslau that had been besieged since mid-February, but each time a concentration was begun a crisis arose at another sector of the front, which required the Panzers to be sent to deal with it.[88]

By the first days of May the last armoured resources had been assembled and, while it was considered optimistic that a penetration would be achieved, it was hoped that a powerful armoured thrust would at least draw off some of the encircling Soviet troops and allow the defenders of Breslau a brief respite. The troops moved into their assembly areas between 3–5 May and the garrison was informed of the rescue attempt. However, this effort came too late and after an epic defence General Niehoff, the garrison commander, surrendered the city on 5 May, despite direct orders from Generalfeldmarschall Schörner forbidding this course of action.

At this point a relief attack became pointless, but with the surrender of the city the Soviet high command immediately released substantial forces from the encircling troops to continue the advance to the west. To forestall this new Russian offensive the assembled German forces attacked.[89]

On 28 April the last eight combat-worthy Sturmgeschütz had been combined into SS-Kampfgruppe Dirks, under SS-Obersturmführer Dirks, and redeployed to the area southwest of Breslau to join the assembly of armour for a last attempt to relieve the besieged city.[90] The attack was launched in the early hours of the morning of 6 May and after an exceptionally heavy artillery bombardment, infantry from SS-Grenadier Regiment 79 of 31.SS-Grenadier Division stormed the town of Zobten as a precursor to the advance on Breslau.[91]

One of the units that the Russians had involved in the advance was 72.Infantry Division, which was attacking into Zobten from the opposite direction when its point units found themselves trapped in the town by the unexpected assault of SS-Grenadier Regiment 79, which overran both flanks of the town and hit the Russians from the rear.[92]

As the German infantry streamed forwards, the armoured SS-Kampfgruppe began its own attack from its assembly area southwest of Zobten. SS-Oberscharführer Schilb gave this account:

> On 3 May 1945 departure from Schweidnitz to Zobten. After short preparation in the area north-east of Zobten, in the morning hours of 5 May [actually 6 May] 1945 the attack began together with infantry of the 100th Jäger Division. On the right of SS-Kampfgruppe Dirks, Hetzers from an Army Abteilung were attacking.
>
> After only about 400 metres the first Hetzers were on fire. I couldn't see where the defensive fire was coming from. As I later found out, it must have been Stalin tanks lying in wait in

> a good position. It thus became clear that the Soviets had made the ring of encirclement around Breslau extremely strong and that from the beginning our attack was doomed to failure. In the meantime, we had good cover due to a rise in the ground and our Kampfgruppe had no casualties. The attack was broken off and we rolled at top speed back to where we started and a little later back to Schweidnitz again.[93]

The anti-tank fire that broke the armoured attack was witnessed by Lieutenant Moniushko, who was a battery commander in the 9.'Leningrad' Artillery Regiment of Russian 72.Infantry Division. Having barely escaped from Zobten when it was overrun by SS-Grenadier Regiment 79, he was acting as forward artillery observer for an advancing infantry unit:

> On the southern edge of Vorst Nonnen Busch forest, about 3 km from Freiburg we became witnesses of, and to some degree participants in the last serious combat engagement. [When we] reached the line of the forest's edge, a line of German assault guns started to advance towards us ascending a gentle slope from the edge of Freiburg.[94]

However, unseen by the approaching assault guns, the Russians had a battery of SU-152s in a hull-down position right on the German axis of attack.[95] The SU-152 was a Soviet low-slung, heavy assault gun mounting a 152mm cannon in a thickly armoured box built on a KV-1 tank chassis. Its gun could penetrate the armour of even the heaviest German tanks of the war and the relatively light weight Hetzers and Sturmgeschütz stood no chance in a duel with them.[96]

> The slaughter began in several minutes. Six-inch shells of our self-propelled guns literally tore the German boxes to pieces, but their return fire could not pierce the front armour of the SU-152s. [The day] ended in ten smoky fires across the entire field.[97]

The remaining assault guns of SS-Pz.Abt.18 were able to extricate themselves from the worthless and abortive attack on Zobten but found themselves swept away in the chaos of retreating units trying to fight their way across the Elbe and avoid Soviet captivity. SS-Oberscharführer Schilb recounts the last days of SS-Kampfgruppe Dirks:

> We rolled to a new deployment on 7 May. There apparently was no front. We moved around as in peacetime and had no idea where the enemy was. Suddenly, our column received flanking fire and Unterscharführer Krug was wounded in his Sturmgeschütz. Under mutually protecting fire, the column was able to cross the sector that the enemy had under fire and were then able to drop Lothar Krug off at a first aid station. Our column soon found itself in a stream of German soldiers heading west.[98]

Kampfgruppe Dirks had had no contact with SS-Panzer-Abteilung 18 since the end of April and SS-Obersturmführer Dirks was forced to act on his own initiative. Having learned of the capitulation from officers of 100.Jäger-Division his small unit joined the general withdrawal into Slovakia.[99]

Further south, as the bulk of the division disengaged from the frontline around Hirschberg, the units moved into the Reichenberg area in a relatively orderly manner, but from this point onwards their unit cohesion began to break down as troops and vehicles from many different units became intermixed. From Reichenberg, the men tried to reach the Elbe individually or in small groups. Many were captured by the Russians, wounded and exhausted, while others fell into the hands of the Czech insurgents, which often meant a brutal end for them.[100]

SS-Standartenführer Petersen and a small party of divisional headquarters troops decided to attempt to cross the Elbe at Melnik. While Petersen was scouting ahead in his personal vehicle with his driver and the commander of the headquarters escort company, SS-Hauptsturmführer Fritz Weibel, they were betrayed by a Czech civilian who was acting as their guide and found themselves surrounded by Russian troops. Petersen drew his pistol and shot two Russian officers as they approached the car, then shot himself. However, in the chaos that followed Weibel and the driver managed to escape back into the mass of retreating German units.[101]

SS-Sturmbannführer Teufel's I./SS-Regiment 40, acting as rear-guard for the division, quickly lost contact with its parent Regiment and splintered into numerous small groups in the Reichenberg area.

SS-Standartenführer Schäfer still had the regimental staff, some regimental ancillary units and II./SS-Panzergrenadier Regiment 40, led by SS-Sturmbannführer Prochaska, under his command when they crossed the Elbe at Kosteletz-Branders.

Schäfer led the remaining elements of his regiment south with the aim of reaching the American lines at Pilsen, but the Moldau River blocked his path. With the Russians pushing from the north and east and Czech insurgents gaining in strength and boldness all the time, Schäfer fanned out his men to search for a bridge that had avoided the attentions of the Allied air forces and they eventually found one at Davle, where the Sasau River flows into the Moldau. The column pushed on south-westwards, destroying their vehicles as they ran out of fuel and overloading the rest, determined to leave no one behind. Eventually the tattered column reached the town of Horovice where they were stopped by Czech militia and an American reconnaissance unit. Here they formally surrendered and were transported to an American camp at Pilsen as prisoners of war.[102]

SS-Rottenführer Krause was a motorcycle messenger in the 2./SS-Pi.Btl.18 and recorded the last days of his company:

> On 7 May the company was ordered to drive to Gablonz and wait there for further orders. We were just before Gablonz on 9 May. The company had already become separated. We were informed by an Oberleutnant from the Heer about the capitulation and that everybody had freedom of action. Only then did the words sink in that my Kompanie Chef, Untersturmführer Berger, had shouted to me from a passing tank: 'For God's sake Krause, take off!' It was the last time that I saw him and I realized that I no longer had to defend Germany, only myself.
>
> With one leap, I ended up in a burning Wehrmacht truck and dragged out a few laundry bags, which had, amongst other items, three pair of fatigue uniforms without any military markings. My B-Krad [Motorcycle and sidecar combination] crew, there were three of us, destroyed all SS emblems and put on the fatigues. That saved us from a dreadful death at the hands of the Czechs.
>
> Disguised Czechs in German uniforms directed us not to Gablonz but to Turnau. One tank from our unit was driving in front of us; the men sitting on top cursed us because we had

destroyed our weapons. They gave us a Panzerfaust. The chaos on the road was getting worse so we beckoned a boy to us to show us a better way. With him on the motorcycle, we made it to a brick factory in Turnau, where a large number of Germans had already been collected. We disappeared into that mass.

From some distance we could already see how the Czechs dragged SS comrades from approaching trucks, always six tied together, and then worked them over with sabres. Those who could still walk had to drag the other to a clay pit, where all were shot. The treatment was gruesome, and death was a release.[103]

CONCLUSION

The verdict of history is that almost all of the Waffen-SS Divisions raised in the last 18 months of the war were abject failures – with 18.SS-Freiwilligen-Panzergrenadier Division 'Horst Wessel' lumped into this group, when it is remembered at all. The most commonly cited reasons for the failure of these divisions are poor leadership from their commanding officers at every level, insufficient resources of all types to make each division an effective unit on the battlefield and a lack of motivation amongst the men recruited to fight in them. Each of these reasons has been used to explain away the ostensibly dismal performance of 18.SS-Panzergrenadier Division during the last year of fighting on the Eastern Front, but are they really merited? Can it be ranked alongside the mutinous 'Handschar' Division or a murderous rabble such as the 'Kaminski' Brigade?

It is a reasonable assumption that if soldiers flee from a battlefield then there has to be negligence in their leadership, and the suggestion has been made that a large proportion of the blame for the failure of 18.SS-Panzergrenadier Division was down to the calibre of the officers that led it. As Mitcham points out: 'The SS-Main Leadership Officer drew upon the established divisions for men of all ranks, to be used as cadres for the new divisions. Naturally the older divisions selected for transfer men they did not care to keep, or at least did not care if they lost.'[1]

This may be an oversimplification of what was a much wider problem. Given the appalling casualty rates amongst officers and NCOs, there was a constant shortage of competent leaders that forced the SS authorities to shorten their leadership training courses drastically and accept candidates that they would have rejected in better times. The attrition rate was so great that junior officers were given responsibilities normally well beyond their rank, with even senior NCOs sometimes having to step up to command roles. Additionally, unlike in other armies, the Wehrmacht did not routinely return wounded and convalescent soldiers from rear area hospitals to their original unit but either sent them to where the need was greatest or banded them together ad hoc into new formations. Therefore, it was probably as much pure luck as Machiavellian design that decided which officers were assigned to which unit, and how well prepared they were to lead it.

It is also difficult to ascertain what kind of reputation 18.SS-Panzergrenadier Division had within the SS itself prior to being committed to action and it is therefore impossible to judge whether the seasoned veterans that were posted to it relished the challenge of forging a new unit or saw the 'Horst Wessel' as another dilution of the elite status of the Waffen-SS and were resigned to the posting as a professional cul-de-sac. The impression left in the first-hand accounts of veterans (albeit from predominantly German rather Volksdeutsche servicemen) regarding the formation of the Division and its subsequent actions suggest that its battle-hardened and professional officers worked hard to make their units as efficient as possible and, with a few exceptions, were generally competent and reasonably well liked.

In November 1944 SS-Hauptsturmführer Sonne, the outgoing commander of the reconnaissance battalion, cared so much about his unit that he made a personal appeal to the Führer's headquarters in Berlin in a vain attempt to procure armoured cars for the missing 1.Company, even after he had been re-assigned to a training command outside of the division.

SS-Oberführer Bochmann had begun his career immersed in the brutality of the concentration camp system and had thrived in the 'Totenkopf' Division which had endured three long years of savage fighting on the Eastern Front. As a veteran of a division that, although it had never exceeded a strength of 20,000 men at any one time, had sustained over 50,000 battle casualties, it could be assumed that he was immune to the suffering of his fellow soldiers but, after taking command of the division, Bochmann disobeyed direct orders from superior officers on at least two occasions during the fighting in Silesia to spare the lives of his men.

Even SS-Gruppenführer Vitzthum, arriving at the division in the last days of 1944 fresh from a political appointment in Albania, was so appalled at the shattered state of the new command that he had inherited that he immediately hurried to Vienna to make a direct appeal to Himmler himself for urgent reinforcements for the division.

By 1944, relations between the Army and Waffen-SS were strained to say the least, especially following the attempt by army officers to assassinate Hitler on 20 July 1944, but Major i.G. Wind, a German army officer who had been seconded to Waffen-SS to act as the senior staff officer in the division, talked of 'our division' and 'my division', while seeming to have a good working relationship with both Trabandt and Bochmann.

This is in stark contrast to 14.SS-Waffen-Grenadier-Division 'Galicien', for example, which was commanded by SS-Brigadeführer Fritz Freitag, a former senior staff officer in 1.SS-Infantry Brigade (mot). Freitag was a difficult, overbearing commander who had nothing but contempt for the Ukrainian volunteers under his command and little patience with his staff. His relationship with his divisional Ia, Major Hieke, who was another army general staff placement, was so bad that it had a detrimental effect upon divisional operations, which only contributed to 14.SS-Waffen-Grenadier-Division's near annihilation in the 'Brody Pocket'.[2]

Alongside the established cadre of officers within the division, there seems to have been some efforts made by the SS-Hauptamt to ensure that leaders with frontline experience were posted to the division as replacements for officers who became casualties. SS-Standartenoberjunker Fritz Biegi had fought with the 'Germania' Regiment in Poland and France and continued his service with this unit when it had been integrated into the highly regarded 'Wiking' Division. He had won the Knights Cross on 16 June 1944 before being transferred into 18.SS-Panzergrenadier Division as an officer candidate. He served with divisional headquarters until he was killed on the night of 15–16 March 1945 in the Leobschütz area while delivering an order to the commander of SS-Panzergrenadier Regiment 39.[3]

Period photographs of regimental officers show them wearing the cuff bands of other elite divisions with which they had previously served, including the prestigious 'Adolf Hitler' title. SS-Untersturmführer

Doctor Biller who took command of 4./SS-Panzergrenadier Regiment 40 in February 1945 had fought with the SS-Leibstandarte 'Adolf Hitler' Division in Greece and Russia and had subsequently passed through SS officer training at the SS-Junkerschule Bad Tölz before being made a weapons instructor at the SS-Panzergrenadier Schule Kienschlag.[4] Men like Biegi and Billar who had served on the frontlines for much of the war and were well trained and highly decorated must have been a serious loss to the elite divisions from which they came. Their transfers undermine Mitcham's claim that other units were palmed off with unwanted men.

There is a report that Himmler demanded that all officers within the division should be replaced following the dismal performance of large parts of it during the campaign in Hungary, but ultimately only the divisional commander SS-Oberführer Trabandt left and that was to take up a new posting as head of the SS-Panzergrenadier Schule Kienschlag rather than being consigned to obscurity. It must be wondered whether Trabandt was removed by the Reichsführer, who remembered his previous disgrace and dismissal from the SS. It is also possible that the SS-Hauptamt could not find suitable replacements for so many frontline officers and simply ignored the order.

To a casual observer it might seem delusional for a country in Germany's position to keep trying to conjure up new and ideally ever more powerfully armed divisions as late in the war as the summer of 1944, when assailed on all fronts, its armies were in headlong retreat and its infrastructure was being smashed from the air. Logic would surely dictate that the Wehrmacht should concentrated upon replenishing the veteran units that it already possessed, rather than trying to magic up men and material to raise new armies.

However, despite the best efforts of the combined Allied air forces, Germany's war economy endured, and its output remained high. It produced more tanks and anti-tank guns during 1944 than in any other year of the war and although manpower reserves were stretched, they were by no means exhausted. The SS-Hauptamt, which always seemed to prefer quantity over quality, was able to tap into these assets and despite obvious shortcomings put considerable resources into equipping 18.SS-Panzergrenadier Division.

At the peak of its manpower resources in September 1944, the division had a bayonet strength of 10,063,[5] weak for a full division but still theoretically a force to be reckoned with and, while at least two-thirds of these were raw recruits, the other third were either combat veterans or highly trained specialists in radio communications, vehicle maintenance or gunnery.

Where the Allied air effort was more keenly felt was in the communications systems across both the Reich and occupied Europe. The strategic bombing campaign paid particular attention to railway junctions, bridges, viaducts, and canal locks resulted in huge bottlenecks in the distribution chain that were felt right up to the frontline. As the recruits began to congregate in the forming up areas assigned to 18.SS-Panzergrenadier Division, everything was in short supply, from the basic necessities such as uniforms, boots and rifles, to trucks, tanks and field guns.

Even when equipment did arrive, the division was constantly pillaged for its vehicles and heavy equipment in favour of more established units, which had a negative impact on both the division's state of training and strategic flexibility in the field. As stated earlier, 200 Schwimmwagen amphibious jeeps and 300 trucks were requisitioned from the division during its initial formation period and given to the 3.SS-Panzer Division 'Totenkopf', and following the fighting in Hungary the division's entire inventory of heavy weapons was released to 4.SS-Panzergrenadier Division 'Polizei'.

Measures had been taken to speed up armaments production and by 1944 the Wehrmacht's quartermasters had given up trying to supply actual tanks to Panzergrenadier divisions, preferring to issue assault guns to both army and Waffen-SS Panzer battalions within these units instead. Lacking a rotating gun turret, they were quicker, easier and cheaper to produce but left their crews at a distinct tactical disadvantage in an engagement, as of course the whole vehicle had to turn in order to aim the gun. Even this diminution in quality did not enable every panzer battalion to be fully equipped, and the first batch of assault guns destined for SS-Panzer Abteilung 18 was redistributed to the 12.SS-Panzer Division 'Hitlerjugend', which had been reduced to a burnt-out shell during the battle for Normandy.

Motorisation and a sufficiency of heavy weapons were, however, the exception rather than the rule for the German army throughout the war. The conflict had been fought on a shoestring since the very beginning, the Germans relying on superior tactical ability, communications, and camaraderie to win their battles. A paucity of equipment had never been considered as a serious hindrance to the

German Army's infantry divisions, the vast majority of which had marching into Russia with their horse-drawn artillery and baggage train raising dust in their wake. These divisions had travelled on foot all the way to Stalingrad and a few of them had marched all the way back again, too. Divisions like 46.Infantry Division had been amongst those units that had stormed the fortifications at Sevastapol, which at that time was the most heavily defended fortress in the world, while 83.Infantry division had fought off T-34s with rifles and grenades in temperatures of -50° Celsius during the winter of 1941. Admittedly, the performance of these divisions would have been greatly enhanced had they each been fully motorised and supplied with an armoured component, but equipment limitations were often overcome by strong unit cohesion and fighting spirit.

18.SS-Panzergrenadier Division was essentially a 'foreign' formation created from a body of 8,000 conscripted Volksdeutsche men predominantly from northern Hungary. John Keegan observed that 'The Volksdeutsche formed an important part of many of the better Waffen-SS divisions, though the few raised from that source alone were of mediocre quality.'[6] This comment should be qualified by the fact that many of the Volksdeutsche who ended up in the 'better' divisions would have been recruited from the earlier rounds of volunteers and any disgruntled groups of conscripts into these units would have been leavened by a strong cadre of motivated men.

The success or otherwise of units consisting of Volksdeutsche recruits certainly appears to have a direct correlation with Germany's fortunes during the war. 1.SS-Infantry-Brigade (mot) and 18.SS-Panzergrenadier Division Kampfgruppe fought as well as could be expected under the circumstances at Smolensk and in Galicia respectively, and both of these units were then largely manned by Volksdeutsche recruits. However, by the time recruiting for 18.SS-Panzergrenadier Division began in earnest amongst the Volksdeutsche populations in central Europe, it was clear that Germany was losing the war and incurring staggering numbers of casualties in the process, and that the recruits' homes were in imminent danger of being overrun by the Red Army. As many of the younger men had already either volunteered or been drafted earlier in the war, there was a high percentage of older, family men inducted into the division, who were obviously more conscious of what they had to lose than their younger, devil-may-care counterparts.

A further blow to the development of any esprit de corps was the aforementioned chronic lack of uniforms, personal weapons and training, which did not allow the recruits either to look or feel like proper soldiers. I./SS-Panzergrenadier Regiment 39 was particularly afflicted by each of these shortcomings and partly as a consequence, after October 1944, was consistently the worst performing unit in the entire division.

Following the considerable number of combat casualties that the division sustained during the fighting in Hungary, its ranks were filled out with surplus Luftwaffe and Kriegsmarine personnel who were largely Reichsdeutsche, which had the advantage of making the division more 'Germanic' for those who cared about such things – but did nothing for its combat efficiency. While it is true that some of these men possessed technical skills in radio communications or first aid knowledge, virtually none of them had experience of lying in a hole in an open field waiting to engage enemy tanks.

Taking after-action reports at face value, it would be easy to draw the conclusion that those units with a hard core of Reichsdeutsche men within them did outperform those that contained a higher percentage of Volksdeutsche personnel, but it should be remembered that there is a considerable lack of source material written by Volksdeutsche recruits themselves. Judging from written sources it would seem that the reconnaissance battalion, which was predominantly comprised of Reichsdeutsche recruits, was one of the steadiest and hardest fighting units in the division – but one of the few histories of the division from which much first-hand source material is derived was written by Wilhelm Tieke who served as a Reichsdeutsche NCO within that unit.

In purely military terms, it is clear that 18.SS-Panzergrenadier Division did not live up to the fighting reputations of the elite divisions that came before it, but from any study of Waffen-SS Divisions during the last years of the war it quickly becomes apparent that even before battlefield attrition is taken into consideration, there was no such thing as standardisation amongst units. Every division raised in the last eighteen months of the war had its own unique weaknesses that were not displayed in the earlier divisions and which do not seem to have been considered on the German High Command situation map.

Army Group South in particular went to some lengths to highlight the worthlessness of 18.SS-Panzergrenadier Division, to blame it for repeatedly undermining 6.Army's fighting retreat through Hungary and to emphasise the lack of motivation amongst the Volksdeutsche recruits to fight on the losing side at the cost of their lives, homes and families. This understandable unwillingness to sacrifice everything for a lost cause significantly diminished the combat effectiveness of the whole division. This was in stark contrast to the Estonian and Latvian Divisions which had tasted the bitterness of Soviet occupation and fought hard and well to prevent a repetition until their homelands were actually overrun. However, with this example aside, it was ludicrous to expect any division that was raised and equipped under such circumstances to perform anywhere near as well as the older, long-established divisions.

Appendix

WAFFEN-SS RANKS

Waffen-SS ranks and their equivalents used by the British Army in World War II.

It should be noted that these equivalents are approximate as Waffen-SS ranks were derived from political units rather than military ones.

Waffen-SS	British Army
SS-Grenadier / SS-Schütze / SS-Kanonier	Private / Rifleman / Gunner
SS-Sturmmann	Lance-Corporal
SS-Rottenführer	Corporal
SS-Unterscharführer	N/A
SS-Scharführer	Sergeant
SS-Oberscharführer	Sergeant Major
SS-Hauptscharführer	Regimental Sergeant Major
SS-Sturmscharführer	N/A
SS-Untersturmführer	Second Lieutenant
SS-Obersturmführer	Lieutenant
SS-Hauptsturmführer	Captain
SS-Sturmbannführer	Major
SS-Obersturmbannführer	Lieutenant Colonel
SS-Standartenführer	Colonel

Waffen-SS	British Army
SS-Oberführer	N/A
SS-Brigadeführer	Brigadier
SS-Gruppenführer	Major-General
SS-Obergruppenführer	Lieutenant-General
SS-Oberstgruppenführer	General

The ranks of SS-Oberjunker or SS-Standartenoberjunker were given to NCOs who were officer aspirants who were undergoing training as such.

ENDNOTES

Introduction

1. Lumans, 1993, p 212.
2. Weale, 2013, pp 301 - 305.

1 Horst Wessel and the SA

1. Lepage, 2016, p 164 www.scribd.com
2. Lepage, 2016, p 165 www.scribd.com
3. Lepage, 2016, pp 241, 246 www.scribd.com
4. Siemens, 2013, pp 21 - 25.
5. Siemens, 2013, pp 30, 41.
6. Siemens, 2013, pp 3 - 15.
7. Carradice, 2018, pp 13-14.
8. Carradice, 2018 pp 121 - 122.
9. Carradice, 2018, p 125.
10. Weale, 2010, p 88.
11. Oven, 2010, p 130.
12. Weale, 2010, p 89.
13. Höhne, 1972, p 88.
14. Höhne, 1972, p 88 - 89.
15. Weale, 2010, p 90 - 91.
16. Carradice, 2018 pp 127 - 128.
17. Oven, 2010, p 132.
18. Carradice, 2018 pp 120 - 121.
19. Höhne, 1972, p 99.
20. Weale, 2010, p 91.
21. Weale, 2010, pp 92 - 93.
22. Höhne, 1972, p 116.

23. Weale, 2013, p 93- 94.
24. Carradice, 2018 pp 198, 201.
25. Höhne, 1972, p 120.

2 *1.SS-Infantry Brigade (mot)*

1. Lumans, 1993, p 11.
2. Goldsworthy, 2018, p 33.
3. Höhne, 1969, p 418.
4. Bremm, 2018, pp 145.
5. Maclean, 1999, p 12.
6. Koehl, 1983, p 163 - 165.
7. Dorondo, 2012, pp 174 - 175.
8. Koehl, 1983, p 163 - 165.
9. Klietmann, 1965, p 307.
10. Schmitz et al, 2000, p 73.
11. Bremm, 2018, p 146.
12. Nafziger, 2001, p 37.
13. Stein, 1966, p 109.
14. Rode, 1947, in Goldsworthy, 2018, pp 55 - 56.
15. Klietmann, 1965, p 307.
16. Bremm, 2018, pp 145-146.
17. Maclean, 1999, p 12.
18. Bremm, 2018, pp 145 - 146.
19. Büchler, 1986, p 15.
20. Pontotillo, 2009, p 48.
21. Bremm, 2018, p 148.
22. Bremm, 2018, p 149.
23. Rudling, 2020, p 158.
24. Klietmann, 1965, p 307.
25. Bremm, 2018, p 152.
26. Pontotillo, 2009, p 48.
27. Büchler, 1986, p 15.
28. Pontotillo, 2009, pp 48 - 50.
29. Bremm, 2018 pp 151 -152.
30. Bremm, 2018 pp 152-153.
31. Nafziger, 2001, p 37.
32. Melnyk, 2002, p 64.
33. Bremm, 2018 pp 152 - 153.
34. Büchler, 1986, pp 15 - 17.
35. Baade et al, 1965, p 19.
36. Dacre in Klee, Dressen and Riess Eds. 1991, p xiii.
37. Marini, 2006, pp 49 - 51.

38. Carell, 1987, p 69.
39. Marini, 2006, pp 49 - 51.
40. Marini, 2006, pp 52 - 54.
41. Marini, 2006, pp 55 - 57.
42. Trang, 2000, p 30.
43. Büchler, 1986, pp 15 - 17.
44. Pontolillo, 2009, p 50.
45. Büchler, 1986, pp 15 - 17.
46. Michaelis, 2010, p 148.
47. Forczyk, 2006, p 85.
48. Baade et al, 1965, pp 84 - 87.
49. Michaelis, 1997, p 207.
50. Carell, 1987, p 176.
51. Nafziger, 2001, p 37.
52. Michaelis, 1997, p 207.
53. Tieke, 2015, p 292.
54. Tieke, 2015, p 292.
55. Stöber, Hans, 1984, p 368.
56. Michaelis, 2010, p 148.
57. Bremm, 2018, p 155.
58. Michaelis, 1997, p 206.
59. Bremm, 2018, p 155.
60. Michaelis, 2010, pp 148 - 150.
61. Melnyk, 2002, pp 9 - 10.
62. Melnyk, 2002, p 10.
63. Koehl, 1983, p 207.
64. Koehl, 1983, p 209.
65. Heer and Naumann Eds., 2000, p 97.
66. Heer and Naumann Eds., 2000, p 107.
67. Heer and Naumann Eds., 2000, p 111.
68. Michaelis, 2010, p 150.
69. Williamson, 1995, pp 62 - 63.
70. Heer and Naumann Eds., 2000, p 113.
71. Michaelis, 1996, p 210 - 211.
72. Heer and Naumann Eds., 2000, p 113.
73. Michaelis, 1996, p 211.
74. Baade et al, 1965, pp 175 - 178.
75. Baade et al, 1965, p 180.
76. Ziemke, 1968, pp 106 - 107.
77. Carell, 1994, pp 276 - 277.
78. Ziemke, 1968, p 108.
79. Carell, 1994, p 277.

80. Forczyk, 2020, p 49.
81. Kurowski, 1992, pp 202 - 203.
82. Kurowski, 1992, p 205.
83. Forczyk, 2020, pp 60 - 61.
84. Kurowski, 1992, p 217.
85. Tieke and Rebstock, 2000, p 193.
86. Forczyk, 2020, pp 60 - 61.
87. Tieke and Rebstock, 2000, p 193.
88. Bjerregaard and Larsen, 2017, p 175.
89. Kurowski, 1992, p 272.
90. Forczyk, 2020, pp 70.
91. Kurowski, 1992, p 190; Tieke and Rebstock, 2000 p 273.
92. Forczyk, 2020, pp 80.
93. Michaelis, 1996, pp 215, 217.
94. Michaelis, 1996, p 217.
95. Michaelis, 1996, p 223.
96. Forczyk, 2019, p 28.
97. Forczyk, 2016, pp 169 -170.
98. Forczyk, 2019, pp 50 - 54.
99. Forczyk, 2016, p 172.
100. Ziemke, 1968, p 159.
101. Forczyk, 2019, pp 55 - 65.
102. Mooney, 2012, p 204.
103. Michaelis, 1996, p 226.
104. Forczyk, 2019, p 68.
105. Mooney, 2012, p 204.
106. Forczyk, 2019, p 68.
107. Michaelis, 2010, p 156.
108. Tieke, 2015, p 308.
109. Forczyk, 2019, pp 69 - 71.
110. Mooney, 2012, pp 240 - 241.
111. Forczyk, 2019, pp 72 - 73.
112. Yerger, 1999, p 282.
113. Forczyk, 2019, p 81.
114. Mooney, 2012, pp 156.
115. Yeager, 1999, pp 280 - 284.
116. Yerger, 1999, p 282.
117. Mooney, 2012, pp 292 - 295.
118. Yerger, 1999, p 282.
119. Mooney, 2012, pp 156 -158.
120. Mooney, 2012, pp 205 - 206.
121. Forczyk, 2019, pp 80 - 82.

122. Yerger, 1999, pp 282 - 284.
123. Michaelis, 1996, p 228.
124. Michaelis, 2010, p 157.
125. Stöber, 1984, p 370.
126. Nafziger, 2001, pp 37, 118.
127. Yerger, 1999, pp 282 - 284.
128. Tieke, 2015, p 297.
129. Michaelis, 2010, p 157.

3 Expansion to Divisional Strength

1. Michaelis, 1996, p 233.
2. Mitcham, 2007, p 74.
3. Hinze, 2012, pp 331 - 332.
4. Michaelis, 1996, p 233
5. Mitcham, 2007, p 237.
6. Luck, 1989, p 263.
7. Schmitz et al, 2000, p 72.
8. Tieke and Rebstock, 2000, p 171.
9. Trang, 2000, p 206.
10. Nafziger, 2001, pp 117 - 118.
11. Michaelis, 1996, p 233.
12. Michaelis, 1996, pp 235 - 236.
13. Ziemke 1968, p 208.
14. Ziemke 1968, p 287.
15. Michaelis, 1997, p 233.
16. Pallud, 1983, p 2.
17. KTB of OKW, Vol.7, p 627 in Pallud, 1983, pp 3 - 4.
18. Tieke and Rebstock, 2000, p 12.
19. Pallud, 1983, pp 4.
20. Ziemke 1968, p 287.
21. Tieke, 2015, p 13.
22. Goldsworthy, 2018, p 33.
23. Lumans, 1993, p 224.
24. Lumans, 1993, p 224.
25. Zakić, 2014, p 321.
26. Lumans, 1993, p 10.
27. Goldsworthy, 2018, pp 34 - 35.
28. Goldsworthy, 2018, p 39.
29. Eby, 1998, pp 197 - 198.
30. Zakić, 2014, pp 321-322.
31. Lumans, 1993, p 215.

32. Lumans, 1993, pp 12 - 13.
33. Zakić, 2014, p 329.
34. Lumans, 1993, p 235
35. Lumans, 1993, p 223.
36. Lumans, 1993, pp 224 - 226.
37. Höhne, 1969, pp 417 - 418.
38. Siemens, 2017, pp 280 - 282.
39. Lumans, 1993, pp 224 - 226.
40. Ránki, 1984, p 243.
41. Ránki, 1984, p 244.
42. Ránki, 1984, p 245.
43. Ránki, 1984, p 245.
44. Ránki, 1984, p 247.
45. Ránki, 1984, p 247 - 248.
46. Michaelis, 2006, p 27.
47. Pencz, 2002, p 9.
48. Höhne, 1981, pp 436 - 437.
49. Höhne, 1981, p 438.
50. Höhne, 1981, p 439.
51. Röhrs, 2012 pp 29 - 31.
52. Pencz, 2002, p 11.
53. Pencz, 2002, p 33.
54. Tieke, 1977, pp 212 - 213.
55. Tieke, 1977, p 215.
56. Michaelis, 2010, p 161.
57. Forty, 2018, p 38
58. Forty, 2018, p 38.
59. Littlejohn, 1987, p 127.
60. Michaelis, 1996, p 236.
61. Pencz, 2002, pp 10-11.
62. Niepold, 1987, P.192.
63. Mitcham, 2007, P.55.

4 *Galicia*

1. Tieke, 1977, p 216.
2. Hinze, 2013, p 75.
3. Forbes, 2006, p 68.
4. Buttar, 2020, p 412.
5. Tieke and Rebstock, 2000, p 16.
6. Michaelis, 1996, p 238.
7. Tieke, 2015, p 20.

8. Michaelis, 1996, p 239.
9. Tieke, 1977, p 216.
10. Tieke and Rebstock, 2000, p 17.
11. Hinze, 2013, pp 75 - 76
12. Michaelis, 1996, p 239.
13. Hinze, 2013, p 75
14. Tieke, 2015, pp 22 - 24.
15. Buttar, 2020, p 417.
16. Hinze, 2013, p 82.
17. Carell, 1994, p 339.
18. Glantz, 2002, p 36.
19. Tieke, 2015, p 26.
20. Tieke and Rebstock, 2000, p 22.
21. Buttar, 2020, p 417.
22. Forbes, 2006, p 68.
23. Buttar, 2020, p 414.
24. Tieke and Rebstock, 2000, p 24.
25. Buttar, 2020, p 416.
26. Buttar, 2020, p 417.
27. Hinze, 2013, p 96 - 97.
28. Buttar, 2020, p 414.
29. Buttar, 2020, p 417.
30. Erickson, 1983, pp 243 - 244.
31. Hinze, 2013, p 113.
32. Erickson, 1983, pp 241, 243.
33. Buttar, 2020, p 417.
34. Erickson, 1983, p 243.
35. Michaelis, 1996, p 241.
36. Tieke, 1977, p 217.
37. Hinze, 2013, p 98.
38. Tieke, 1977, pp 217 - 218.
39. Forbes, 2006, p 68.
40. Hinze, 2013, pp 98 - 99.
41. Michaelis, 1996, p 241.
42. Gładysiak, 2021, pp 26 - 27.
43. Forbes, 2006, p 63.
44. Morville, 1993, p 4.
45. Forbes, 2006, pp 69 - 70.
46. Morville, 1993, p 7.
47. Forbes, 2006, p 70.
48. Tieke, 2015, p 42.
49. Senger-Ettelin, 2004, p 257.

50. Hinze, 2013, pp 106 – 107.
51. Mehner, 1985, p 419.
52. Tieke and Rebstock, 2000, p 31.
53. Michaelis, 1996, p 241.
54. Forbes, 2010, p 70.
55. Tieke, 1977, pp 223 - 224.
56. Tieke, 2015, p 47.
57. Forbes, 2010, pp 70 - 71.
58. Maclean, 1999, pp 28, 119.
59. Pohl, 2020, p 191.
60. Maclean, 1999, pp 28, 119.
61. Forbes, 2010, p 70 - 71.
62. Michaelis, 1996, p 241.
63. Morville, 1993, p 6.
64. Forbes, 2010, pp 72 - 75.
65. Morville, 1993, p 8.
66. Michaelis, 1996, p 241.
67. Morville, 1993, p 8.
68. Mehner, 1985, p 440.
69. Tieke, 2015, p 54.
70. Bayle, 1992, pp 99 - 103.
71. Forbes, 2010, p 78.
72. Morville, 1993, p 11.
73. Forbes, 2010, p 79.
74. Forbes, 2010, p 79.
75. Morville, 1993, p 8.
76. Michaelis, 1996, p 241.
77. Michaelis, 1996, p 241.
78. Rebentisch, 2009, pp 387 - 389.
79. Hinze, 2013, pp 120 - 121.
80. Hinze, 2013, pp 120 - 123.
81. Michaelis, 1996, p 241
82. Tieke, 2015, p 55.
83. Michaelis, 1996, p 241.
84. Hinze, 2013, p 124.
85. Michaelis, 1996, p 241 Tieke, 2015, p 57.
86. Tieke and Rebstock, 2000, p 41.
87. Forbes, 2010, p 82.
88. Hinze, 2013, p 127.
89. Forbes, 2010, p 84.
90. Mehner, 1985, p 458.
91. Tieke, 2015, p 60.

92. Forbes 2010, p 84.
93. Mabire, 1973, p 335.
94. Forbes, 2010, p 85; Tieke, 2015, p 60.
95. Mehner, 1985, p 458.
96. Tieke, 2015, pp 59 - 61.
97. Forbes, 2010, p 86.
98. Tieke and Rebstock, 2000, p 43.
99. Forbes, 2010, pp 86 -87.
100. Hinze, 2013, p 128.
101. Forbes, 2010, pp 87 - 88.
102. Forbes, 2010, p 91.
103. Mehner, 1985, p 461.
104. Tieke, 2015, p 62.
105. Tieke and Rebstock, 2000, pp 44 - 45.
106. Mabire , 1973, pp 388 - 389.
107. Tieke, 2015, pp 62 - 63.
108. Forbes, 2010, p 92.
109. Hinze, 2013, p 124.
110. Tieke, 2015, pp 63 - 64.
111. Forbes, 2010, p 97 - 99.
112. Hinze, 2013, p 124.
113. Forbes, 2010, p 100.
114. Mabire, 1973, p 380.
115. Mehner, 1985 p 465.
116. Hinze, 2013, p 128.
117. Tieke, 2015, p 66.
118. Senger-Ettelin, 2004, p 258.
119. Tieke, 2015, pp 67.
120. Tieke, 2015, pp 68 - 70.

5 Slovakia

1. Krátký and Šnejdárek, 1976, p 2157.
2. Mitcham, 2007, p 211.
3. Krátký and Šnejdárek, 1976, p 2157.
4. Krátký and Šnejdárek, 1976, p 2158.
5. Mitcham, 2007, p 212.
6. Krátký and Šnejdárek, 1976, p 2157.
7. Mitcham, 2007, p 212.
8. Krátký and Šnejdárek, 1976, pp 2157 - 2158.
9. Axworthy, 2002, p 259.
10. Mitcham 2007, p 212.

11. Axworthy, 2002, p 259.
12. Krátký and Šnejdárek, 1976, pp 2157 - 2158.
13. Axworthy, 2002, pp 266 - 267.
14. Judge, 2014, p 20.
15. Krátký and Šnejdárek, 1976, p 2158.
16. Venohr, 1969, p 179.
17. Axworthy, 2002, p 267.
18. Tieke, 2015, pp 74 - 75.
19. Tieke and Rebstock, 2000, p 53; Axworthy, 2002, p 269.
20. Judge, 2014, p 27.
21. Krátký and Šnejdárek, 1976, p 2160.
22. Mitcham 2007, p 212.
23. Axworthy, 2002, p 273.
24. Judge, 2014, pp 27, 33.
25. Krátký and Šnejdárek, 1976, p 2158.
26. Tieke, 2015, p 79.
27. Nafziger, 1999, p 190, Axworthy, 2002, p 261.
28. Venohr, 1969, p 181.
29. Axworthy, 2002, p 269.
30. Tieke, 2015, p 80.
31. Tieke, 2015, pp 80 - 82.
32. Venohr, 1969, p 186.
33. Krátký and Šnejdárek, 1976, pp 2159 - 2160.
34. Venohr, 1996, pp 196 - 198.
35. Axworthy, 2002, p 274.
36. Venohr, 1969, p 200.
37. Tieke and Rebstock, 2000, p 58.
38. Venohr, 1969, p 187.
39. Axworthy, 2002, p 272.
40. Tieke and Rebstock, 2000, p 58
41. Axworthy, 2002, p 276.
42. Venohr, 1969, pp 199 - 200.
43. Krátký and Šnejdárek, 1976, p 2161.
44. Krátký and Šnejdárek, 1976, p 2161.
45. Judge, 2014, p 24.
46. Mitcham, 2007, p 214.
47. Axworthy, 2002, p 288.
48. Venohr, 1969, pp 219, 226.
49. Pontolillo, 2009, p 137.
50. Tieke, 2015, pp 92 - 93.
51. Venohr, 1969, p 240.

52. Mitcham, 2007, p 214.
53. Venohr, 1969, p 253.
54. Krátký and Šnejdárek, 1976, pp 2161 - 2162.
55. Tieke, 2000, p 66.
56. Venohr, 1969, p 254.
57. Axworthy, 2002, p 293.
58. Venohr, 1969, p 254.
59. Venohr, 1969, p 255.
60. Judge, 2014, p 31.
61. Krátký and Šnejdárek, 1976, p 2167.
62. Tieke, 2015, pp 100 - 101.
63. Axworthy, 2002, p 298.
64. Venohr, 1969, p 262.
65. Axworthy, 2002, p 299 - 300.
66. Venohr, 1969, p 260.
67. Axworthy, 2002, pp 299 - 300.
68. Tieke, 2015, p 103.
69. Tieke, 2015, p 106.
70. Axworthy, 2002, p 301.
71. Krátký and Šnejdárek, 1976, p 2162.
72. Michaelis, 1997. pp 247 – 248.
73. Melnyk, 2002, p 201.
74. Axworthy, 2002, p 301.

6 Hungary

1. Glantz, 1986, p 115.
2. Glantz, 1986, pp 115-120.
3. Glantz, 1986, p 136.
4. Ungváry, 2003, p 12.
5. Tieke, 2015, p 121.
6. Husemann, 1973, pp 434-435.
7. Scherzer, 2009, p 549.
8. Tieke and Rebstock, 2000, p 82.
9. Tieke, 2015, pp 124 - 125.
10. Ungváry, 2003, pp 12-13.
11. Ungváry, 2003, p 37.
12. Glantz, 1986, p 136.
13. Pencz, 2002, p 76.
14. Husemann, 1973 p 436.
15. Tieke and Rebstock, 2000, p 84.
16. Husemann, 1973 p 437.

17. Husemann, 1973 p 437.
18. Husemann, 1973 p 437.
19. Tieke and Rebstock, 2000, p 84.
20. Glantz, 1986, p 141.
21. Rohrs, 2012, p 84.
22. Michaelis, 1997. pp 248 - 249.
23. Husemann, 2009, p 374.
24. Rebentisch, 2009, pp 416 - 419.
25. Husemann, 2009, p 375.
26. Ungváry, 2003, p 7.
27. Röhrs, 2012, p 85.
28. Tieke and Rebstock, 2000, p 87.
29. Thomas and Wegmann, 1991, p 18.
30. Husemann, 2009, p 375.
31. Rebentisch, 2009, p 419.
32. Tieke and Rebstock, 2000, p 87.
33. Hinze, 2018, p 285.
34. Rosen, 2018, p 311.
35. Tieke and Rebstock, 2000, p 91.
36. Rebentisch, 2009, p 419.
37. Tieke and Rebstock, 2000, p 87.
38. Scherzer, 2009, p 550.
39. Glantz, 1986, P.148.
40. Glantz, 1986, P.155.
41. Husemann, 2009, p 380.
42. Tieke and Rebstock, 2000, p 91.
43. Tieke, 2015, p 140.
44. Glantz, 1986, P.155.
45. Rebentisch, 2009, p 420.
46. Scherzer, 2009, pp 552 - 553.
47. Rebentisch, 2009, p 420.
48. Sánchez, 1996, pp 82 - 83.
49. Bender and Odegard, 1980, p 65.
50. Husemann, 2009, pp 386 - 87.
51. Glantz 1986, P.170.
52. Tieke, 2015, p 145.
53. Tieke, 2015, p 142.
54. Glantz, 1986, pp 160 - 170.
55. Husemann, 1973, p 451.
56. Tieke, 2015, pp 145 -146.
57. Husemann, 1973, pp 455 - 456.

58. Glantz, 1986, p 175.
59. Scherzer, 2009, pp 553 - 554.
60. Tieke and Rebstock, 2000, p 96.
61. Husemann, 1973, p 455.
62. Tieke and Rebstock, 2000, p 96.
63. Husemann, 1973, p 455.
64. Loza, 1967, p 616.
65. Tieke, 2015, pp 147 - 148.
66. Loza, 1967, p 616.
67. Tieke and Rebstock, 2000, p 97.
68. Stöber, 1984, p 317.
69. Doeberitz, 1986, pp 223 - 224.
70. Loza, 1967, p 617.
71. Thomas and Wegmann, 1998, p 261.
72. Számvéber, 2013, p 16.
73. Számvéber, 2013, pp 18 - 20.
74. Loza, 1967, p 618.
75. Thomas and Wegmann, 1998, p 261.
76. Számvéber, 2013, p 29.
77. Thomas and Wegmann, 1998, pp 261 - 262.
78. Számvéber, 2013, p 26.
79. Loza, 1967, pp 618 - 619.
80. Tieke, 2015, pp 150 - 152.
81. Husemann, 2009, p 395.
82. Husemann, 2009, p 396.
83. Tieke and Rebstock, pp 97 - 99.
84. Michaelis, 1996, p 253.
85. Tieke and Rebstock, 2000, p 103.
86. Hinze, 2012, p 331.
87. Stöber, 1984, p 317; Tieke, 2015, pp 160 - 161.
88. Mehner, 1984, p 334.
89. Michaelis, 2010, p 170.
90. Tieke, 2015, p 162.
91. Fischer, 1999, p 166.
92. Fischer, 1999, p 212.
93. Fischer, 1999, p 226.
94. Tieke, 2015, p 157.
95. Fischer, 1999, p 226.
96. Fischer, 1999, pp 184, 226.
97. Yerger, 1997, p 85.
98. Nafziger, 2001, pp 50 - 51.
99. Yerger, 1997, p 85.

100. Williamson, 2005, 52 - 53.
101. Michaelis, 1996, p 253.

7 Silesia

1. Ziemke, 1968, pp 419 – 425.
2. Kaps, 1953, pp 110 – 111.
3. Ahlfen, 1961, pp 142 - 143.
4. Kaps, 1953, p 111.
5. Ahlfen, 1961, p 144.
6. Hinze, 2005, p 141.
7. Hinze, 2005, p 147.
8. Gunter, 2002, p 176.
9. Hinze, 2005, pp 139 - 140.
10. Tieke and Rebstock, 2000, p 109.
11. Tieke, 2015, p 167 - 171.
12. Tieke and Rebstock, 2000, p 109.
13. Gunter, 2002, p 182.
14. Tieke and Rebstock, 2000, pp 107 - 114.
15. Ahlfen, 1961, p 147.
16. Ahlfen, p 147 - 148.
17. Hinze, 2005, p 140.
18. Tieke, 2015, pp 179, 199.
19. Gunter, 2002, p 169.
20. Tieke, 2015, p 184.
21. Michaelis, 2010, p 170.
22. Tieke and Rebstock, 2000, p 120.
23. Tieke 2015, p 185.
24. Röhrs, 2012, pp 220 - 226.
25. Harrison Ed., 2016, p 444.
26. Gunter, 2002, p 178.
27. Tieke, 2015, pp 193 - 194.
28. Tieke, 2015, p 195.
29. Gunter, 2002, p 179.
30. Tieke, 2015, p 196
31. Tieke, 2015, p 196
32. Gunter, 2002, p 178
33. Tieke and Rebstock, 2000, pp 125 - 126.
34. Ahlfen, 1961, p 147.
35. Gunter, 2002, p 180.
36. Harrison Ed. 2016, p 444.
37. Harrison Ed. 2016, p 467.
38. Harrison Ed. 2016, p 467.

39. Kaps, 1953, p 119.
40. Tieke and Rebstock, 2000, p 128.
41. Gunter, 2002, pp 201 - 202.
42. Tieke, 2015, pp 200 - 203.
43. Gunter, 2002, p 203.
44. Harrison Ed. 2016, 462.
45. Pencz, 2002, Page 169; Harrison Ed. 2016, pp 502 - 503.
46. Harrison Ed. 2016, 503.
47. Harrison Ed. 2016, Page 503.
48. Tieke and Rebstock, 2000, Page 131.
49. Gunter, 2002, pp 226.
50. Gunter, 2002, pp 226 - 228.
51. Gunter, 2002, Page 222.
52. Tieke, 2015, Page 207.
53. Gunter, 2002, Page 227.
54. Harrison Ed. 2016, pp 466, 503.
55. Gunter, 2002, Page 229.
56. Ahlfen, 1961, Page 195.
57. Gunter, 2002, Page 229.
58. Tieke, 2015, Page 210.
59. Gunter, 2002, Page 230.
60. Tieke and Rebstock, 2000, pp 134 - 135.
61. Gunter, 2002, Page 230.
62. Gunter, 2002, Page 230 - 231.
63. Tieke, 2015, Page 211.
64. Gunter, 2002, Page 231.
65. Pencz, 2002, p 169.
66. Harrison Ed. 2016, pp 466, 514.
67. Gunter, 2002, p 233.
68. Tieke, 2015, pp 215 - 216.
69. Harrison Ed., 2016, p 502.
70. Tieke, 2015, pp 218 - 219.
71. Tieke and Rebstock, 2000, p 244.
72. Harrison Ed. 2016, p 523.
73. Gunter, 2002, p 251.
74. Tieke and Rebstock, 2000, p 244.
75. Tieke, 2015, p 221.
76. Harrison Ed. 2016, p 523.
77. Tieke and Rebstock, 2000, pp 141, 143.
78. Gunter, 2002, p 252.
79. Gunter, 2002, p 267.
80. Gunter, 2000, p 270.

81. Tieke, 215, pp 224 - 230.
82. Kaps, 1953, p 221.
83. Michaelis, 1996, p 259.
84. Tieke, 2015, pp 234.
85. Michaelis, 1996, p 259.
86. Tieke and Rebstock, 2015, pp 234 - 239.
87. Michaelis, 1996, p 259.
88. Pencz, 2002, p 168.
89. Pencz, 2002, p 185.
90. Tieke, 2015, p 239.
91. Pencz, 2002, p 185.
92. Moniushko, 2002, p 195 - 197.
93. Pencz, 2002, p 186.
94. Moniushko, 2002, p 198.
95. Moniushko, 2002, p 199.
96. Hoffschmitt and Tantum IV Eds., 1969, p 145.
97. Moniushko, 2002, p 199.
98. Tieke, 2015, p 240
99. Tieke and Rebstock, 2000, p 152.
100. Michaelis, 1996, p 259.
101. Tieke and Rebstock, 2000, p 157.
102. Tieke, 2015, p 259.
103. Tieke, 2015, p 258.

Conclusion

1. Mitcham, 2007, p 74.
2. Mitcham, 2007, p 73.
3. Thomas and Wegmann, 1992, p 22.
4. Tieke, 2015, p 345.
5. Klietmann, 1965, p 512.
6. Keegan, 1970, p 109.

BIBLIOGRAPHY

Ahlfen, Generalmajor Hans von, *Der Kampfe um Schliesen*, Munich, Gräfe und Unzer Verlag, 1961.

Axworthy, Mark, W. A. *Axis Slovakia: Hitler's Slavic Wedge 1938-1945*, New York, Axis Europa Books, 2002.

Baade, Fritz; Behrendt, Richard F; Blachstein, Peter; Daim, Wilfried; Dedijer, Vladimir; Fabian, Walter; Gottfurcht, Hans; Gulick, C. A. Heer, Friedrik; von Hofe, Harold; Junnila, Tuure; Kalnins, Bruno; Reisen, Hans; Klenner,Fritz; Knoll, August M; Rorakas, Manolis; Lazarsfeld, Paul; Leichter, Otto; de Madariaga, Salvador; Marcic, René; Marcuse, Ludwig; Massiczek, Albert; Minder, Robert; Nenning, Günther; Oprecht, Hans; Pogats, Erich; Pollak, Oscar; de Rougemont, Denis; Saternus, Artur; Schönwiese, Ernst; Senghofer, Franz; Silone, Ignazio; Slama, Viktor; Stammer, Otto; Sturmthal, Adolf; Takahashi, Masao; Tau, Max; Thirring, Hans; Winkler, Ernst; Wirlandner, Stefan; Wotruba, Fritz; (eds.), *Unsere Ehre Heisst Treue: Kriegstagebuch des Kommandostabes Reichsführer SS Tätigkeitsberichte der 1. und 2. SS-Inf.-Brigade, der 1. SS-Kav.-Brigade und von Sonder-kommandos der SS*, Wien, Europa Verlag, 1965.

Bayle, Andre, *De Marsaille à Novossibirsk*, Paris, Histoire et Tradition, 1992.

Bender, J. and Odegard, W. *Uniforms, Organisation and History of the Panzertruppe*, San José, California, James Bender Publishing, 1980.

Bjerregaard, Jens Pank and Larsen, Lars, *Danish Volunteers of the Waffen-SS: Freikorps Danmark 1941-43*, Solihull, Helion and Co. 2017.

Bremm, Klaus-Jürgen, *Die Waffen-SS: Hitler's überschätzte Prätorianer*, Darmstadt, wbg Theiss, 2018.

Büchler, Yehoshua. *Kommandostab Reichsführer-SS: Himmler's Personal Murder Brigades in 1941*, in Holocaust and Genocide Studies Vol. 1, No. 1, PP 11-25, Great Britain.

Buttar, Prit, *The Reckoning: The Defeat of Army Group South, 1944*, Oxford, Osprey Publishing, 2020.

Carradice, Phil, *Night of the Long Knives: Hitler's Excision of Rőhm's SA Brownshirts 30 June–2 July 1934*, Barnsley, UK, Pen and Sword, 2018.*

Carell, Paul, *Hitler's War on Russia: The Story of the German Defeat in the East*, London, Harrap Ltd, 1987.

Carell, Paul, *Scorched Earth: The Russian-German War 1943–1944*, London, Harrap and Co. Ltd. 1994.

Christensen, Claus; Bundgård, Poulsen; Niels Bo and Smith, Peter Scharff, *Germanic Volunteers from Northern Europe*, in Böhler, Jochen and Gerwarth, Robert (eds.) *The Waffen-SS: A European History*, Oxford University Press, 2017.

Dacre, Lord, of Glanton, Foreword in Klee, Ernst; Dressen, Willi and Riess, Volker, eds. *"The Good Old Days": The Holocaust as seen by its Perpetrators and Bystanders*, New York, The Free Press, 1991.

Dorondo, David, R. *Riders of the Apocalypse: German Cavalry and Modern Warfare, 1870-1945*, Annapolis MD. Naval Institute Press, 2012.

Eby, Cecil D. *Hungary at War: Civilians and Soldiers in World War II*, The Pennsylvania State University Press, 1998.

Estes, Kenneth, *A European Anabasis: Western European Volunteers in the German Army and SS, 1940-1945*, Solihull, UK, Helion and Company, 2015.

Fischer, Bernd, J. *Albania at War, 1939-1945*, London, Hurst and Company, 1999.

Forbes, Robert, *For Europe: The French Volunteers of the Waffen-SS*, Stackpole Books, Mechanicsburg, PA. 2006.

Forczyk, Robert, *Moscow 1941: Hitler's First Defeat*, Oxford, Osprey Publishing Ltd. 2006.

Forczyk, Robert, *Smolensk 1943: The Red Army's Relentless Advance*, Oxford, Osprey Publishing Ltd. 2019.

Forczyk, Robert, *Velikiye Luki 1942-43: The Doomed Fortress*, Oxford, Osprey Publishing Ltd. 2020.

Forty, Simon, *German Infantryman: The German Soldier 1939-1945 Operations Manual*, Yeovil, Haynes Publishing, 2018.

Gładysiak, Łukasz, *Fated to Defeat: 33rd Waffen-Grenadier Division der SS 'Charlemagne' in the Struggle for Pomerania 1945*, Warwick, UK, Helion and Company, 2021.

Glantz, David M. 'Overview of Operations in Hungary 26 October–31 December 1944', *1986 Art of War Symposium*, Carlisle, US Army War College, 1986.

Glantz, David M. and House Jonathan M. *When Titans Clashed: How the Red Army Stopped Hitler*, Lawrence, Kansas, University of Kansas Press, 2015.

Glantz, David M. and Orenstein, Harold S. (Eds), *The Battle for L'vov July 1944: The Soviet General Staff Study*, London and Portland, Frank Cass Publishers, 2002.

Goldsworthy, Terry, *The Waffen-SS in Allied Hands: Personal Accounts from Hitler's Elite Soldiers,* Cambridge Scholars Publishing, 2018.

Gunter, Georg, *Last Laurels: the German Defence of Upper Silesia January–May 1945*, Solihull, UK. Helion and Company, 2002.

Harrison, Richard W. (Ed.) *Prelude to Berlin: The Red Army's Offensive Operations in Poland and Eastern Germany, 1945,* Warwick, England, Helion and Company, 2016.

Heer, Hannes and Naumann, Klaus, *War of Extermination: The German Military in World War II, 1941–1944,* New York, Berghahn Books, 2000.

Hinze, Rolf, *To the Bitter End: The Final Battles of Army Groups North Ukraine, A, and Centre–Eastern Front, 1944-45*, Oxford, Casemate Publishing, 2005.

Hinze, Rolf, *With the Courage of Desperation: Germany's Defence of the Southern Sector of the Eastern Front 1944-45*, Warwick, UK, Helion Publishing, 2013.

Hoffschidt, E. J. and Tantum IV, W. H. *Tank Data 2*, Old Greenwich, Connecticut, 1969.

Höhne, Heinz, *The Order of the Death's Head: The Story of Hitler's SS*, London, Pan Books Ltd. 1981.

Husemann, Friedrich, *Die guten Glaubens waren: Geschichte der SS-Polizei Division Band II 1943–1945*, Osnabrück, Munin Verlag GmbH, 1986.

Husemann, Friedrich, *In Good Faith: The History of the 4.SS-Polizei-Panzer-Grenadier-Division, Volume 2: 1943- 1945*, Winnipeg, Canada J. J. Fedorowicz Publishing Inc., 2009.

Judge, Major Sean M. *Slovakia 1944: The Forgotten Uprising*, Auckland, New Zealand, Pickle Partners Publishing, 2014.

Kaps, Dr. Johannes, *Die Tragödie Schlesiens 1945/46*, München, Verlag Christ Unterwegs, 1953.

Keegan, John, *Waffen SS: The Asphalt Soldiers*, London, Macdonald and Co Ltd, 1970.

Klietmann, Dr. K. G. *Die Waffen-SS: eine Dokumentation*, Osnabrück, Verlag "Der Freiwillige", G.m.b.H. 1965.

Knebel-Doeberitz, Major Rudolf von, '24th Panzer Division Operations', in Glantz, David M. (ed.) *1986 Art of War Symposium*, Carlisle, US Army War College, 1986.

Koehl, Robert L. *The Black Corps: The Structure and Power Struggles of the Nazi SS*, The University of Wisconsin Press, 1983.

Krátký, Dr. Karel and Šnejdárek, Dr Antonin, 'The Slovak Rising: Czechoslovakia August / October 1944', in *Purnell's History of the Second World War, Number 78*, London, Phoebus Publishing Company, 1976.

Kurowski, Franz, *Deadlock before Moscow: Army Group Centre 1942/1943*, West Chester, PA, Schiffer Publishing Ltd, 1992.

Lepage, Jean-Denis, *Hitler's Stormtroopers: The SA, The Nazi Brownshirts, 1922-1945*, Barnsley, UK. Pen and Sword, 2016.*

Littlejohn, David, *Foreign Legions of the Third Reich, Volume 4*, San José, **California,** Bender Publishing, 1987.

Loza, Dimitry Fjodorovics, *A Sovjet Csapatok Felszabadító Harcai Nógrád Megyében, 1944 December* in *Hadtörténelmi Közlemények*, issue 1967/4.

Luck, Hans von, *Panzer Commander: The Memoirs of Colonel Hans von Luck*, London, Cassell and Co. 1989.

Lumans, Valdis O, *Himmler's Auxilleries: The Volksdeutsche Mittelstelle and the German National Minorities of Europe, 1933-1945*, Chapel Hill, The University of North Carolina Press, 1993.

McCroden, Willian T. and Nutter, Thomas E. *German Ground Forces of World War II: Complete Orders of Battle for Army Groups, Armies, Army Corps and other Combat Commands of the Wehrmacht and Waffen SS: September 1 1939 to May 8 1945*, El Dorado Hills, California, Savas Beatie, 2019.

Mabire, Jean, *La Brigade Frankreich*, Paris, Feyard, 1973.

MacLean, French, L. *The Field Men: The SS Officers Who Led the Einsatzkommandos – the Nazi Mobile Killing Units*, Atglen, PA. Schiffer Publishing Ltd, 1999.

Marini, Alberto, *Del Cáucaso a Leningrado*, Buenos Aires, Niseos, 2006.

Mehner, Kurt, *Die Geheimen Tagesberichte der Deutschen Wehmachtführung in Zweiten Weltkrieg 1939–1945: Band 10: 1, Band 11: 1, Band 12: 1*, Osnabrück, Biblio Verlag, 1984, 1985.

Melnyk, Michael James, *To Battle: The Formation and History of the 14th Galician Waffen-SS Division*, Solihull, Helion and Company, 2002.

Michaelis, Rolf, *Die Panzergrenadier-Divisionen der Waffen-SS*, Erlangen, Michaelis Verlag, 1997.

Michaelis, Rolf, *Esten in Der Waffen-SS: Die 20.Waffen-Grenadier-Division der SS (estnische Nr.1)*, Berlin, Michaelis Verlag, 2000.

Michaelis, Rolf, *Die Waffen-SS: Dokumentation über die personelle Zusammensetzung und den Einsatz der Waffen-SS*, Berlin, Michaelis–Verlag, 2006.

Michaelis, Rolf, *Panzergrenadier Divisions of the Waffen-SS*, Atglen, PA. Schiffer Publishing, 2010.

Mitcham, Samual W Jr. *The German Defeat in the East 1944-45*, Mechanicsburg, PA. Stackpole Books, 2007.

Moniushko, Evgenii, 'Memoirs of the Soviet-German War, Part 4, Red Army Service in Silesia and Czechoslovakia during 1945', in *The Journal of Slavic Military Studies, 15:3*, pp 146-202, 2002.

Mooney, Peter, *Waffen-SS Knights and their Battles: The Waffen-SS Knight's Cross Holders Volume 3: August–December 1943*, Atglen, PA. Schiffer and Company, 2012.

Morville, Bruno de, *Galicie 1944:* 'L'Assault des SS Français', in *39–45 Magazine No. 87*. Bayeux, Editions Heimdal, 1993.

Nafziger, George F. *The German Order of Battle: Waffen SS and Other Units in World War II*, Pennsylvania, Combined Publishing, 2001.

Nevenkin, Kamen, *Take Budapest: The Struggle for Hungary, Autumn 1944*, Stroud, Spellmount, 2012.

Niepold, Gerd, *Battle for White Russia: The Destruction of Army Group Centre June 1944*, London, Brassey's Defence Publishers, 1987.

Oven, Wilfred von, *Hitler's Storm Troopers: A History of the SA, The Memoirs of Wilfred von Oven*, Barnsley, UK, Pen and Sword Publishing, 2010.

Pallud, Jean Paul, 'Budapest', in *After the Battle #40,* Battle of Britain Prints, London, 1983.

Pencz, Rudolf, *For the Homeland: The History of the 31st Waffen-SS Volunteer Grenadier Division*, Solihull, England, Helion and Company, 2002.

Pohl, Heinz, *Mord am Haarstrang: tod eines Ortsgruppenleiters*, Norderstedt, Books on Demand, 2020.

Pontotillo, James, *Murderous Elite: The Waffen-SS and its Complete Record of War Crimes,* Hagersten, Sweden, Leandoer and Ekholm Förlag HB, 2009.

Rebentisch, Dr. Ernst, *The Combat History of the 23rd Panzer Division in World War II*, Mechanicsberg, PA. Stackpole Books, 2009.

Rode, SS-Brigadeführer Ernst, 'Himmler's Field Staff (1944-44)', in Goldsworthy, Terry, *The Waffen-SS in Allied Hands: Personal Accounts from Hitler's Elite Soldiers*, Cambridge Scholars Publishing, 2018.

Röhrs, H. D. *Mit Arztbesteck und Sturmgewehr*, Dresden, Winkelried–Verlag, 2012.

Rosen, Freiherr Richard von, *Panzer Ace: The Memoirs of an Iron Cross Panzer Commander from Barbarossa to Normandy*, Barnsley, UK, Greenhill Books, 2018.

Sánchez, Alfonso Escuadra, *Feldherrnhalle: Forgotten Elite*, Bradford, UK, Shelf Books, 1996.

Schäufler, Hans, *Panzer Warfare on the Eastern Front*, Mechanicsburg, Pennsylvania, Stackpole Books, 2012.

Schmitz, Peter, Thies, Klaus-Jürgen, Wegmann, Günter and Zweng, Christian, *Die deutschen Divisionen 1939-1945: Heer / Landgestüzte Kriegsmarine / Luftwaffe / Waffen-SS, Band 4 Die Divisionen 17–25*, Osnabrück, Biblio Verlag, 2000.

Senger-Ettelin Jr. Dr F M von, *Die 24. Panzer-Division 1939-1945*, Utting am Ammersee, Germany, Nebel Verlag GmbH, 2004.

Siemens, Daniel, *The Making of a Nazi Hero: The Murder and Myth of Horst Wessel*, New York, I.B. Taurus, 2013.

Siemens, Daniel, *Stormtroopers: A New History of Hitler's Brownshirts*, New Haven, Yale University Press, 2017.

Stein, George, H. *The Waffen-SS: Hitler's Elite Guard at War, 1939-1945*, Cornell University Press, 1984.

Stöber, Hans, *Die Flugabwehrverbände der Waffen-SS*, Preuss. Oldendorf, Verlag K. W. Schütz KG, 1984.

Stoves, Lieutenant Colonel R, '1st Panzer Division East of the Danube, October–1 December 1944', *1986 Art of War Symposium*, Carlisle, US Army War College, 1986.

Számvéber, Norbert, *Days of Battle – Armoured Operations North of the River Danube, Hungary 1944-45*, Solihull, England, Helion and Company, 2013.

Thomas, Franz and Wegmann, Günter, *Die Ritterkreuzträger der Deutschen Wehrmacht, 1939-1945: Tiel 5: Die Ritterkreuzträger der Flugabwehrtruppen Band 2: L-Z,* Osnabrück, Biblio Verlag, 1991.

Thomas, Franz and Wegmann, Günter, *Die Ritterkreuzträger der Infanterie Band 2: Bialetzki–Bottler,* Osnabrück, Biblio Verlag, 1992.

Thomas, Franz and Wegmann, Günter, *Die Ritterkreuzträger der Infanterie Band 4: Canders–Dowerk,* Osnabrück, Biblio Verlag, 1998.

Tieke, Wilhelm, *Ein ruheloser Marsch war unser Leben: Kriegsfreiwillig 1940–1945,* Osnabrück, Munin Verlag GmbH, 1977.

Tieke, Wilhelm, *Horst Wessel: The Combat History of the 18.SS-Panzer-Grenadier-Division,* Winnipeg, Canada, J.J. Fedorowicz Publishing, Inc. 2015.

Tieke, Wilhelm and Rebstock, Friedrich, *Im Letzten Aufgebot: Die 18. SS-Freiwilligen-Panzergrenadier-Division HORST WESSEL*, Coburg, Nation Europa Verlags GmbH, 2000.

Trang, Charles, *La Division "Florian Geyer"*, Bayeux, Heimdal, 2000.

Ungváry, Krisztián, *Battle for Budapest: 100 Days in World War II*, New York, I.B. Taurus, 2003.

Venohr, Wolfgang, *Aufstand für die Tschechoslowakei: Der slowakische Freiheitskampf von 1944,* Hamburg, Christian Wegner Verlag, 1969.

Viet, Scherzer, 46. *Infanterie Division*, Jena, Scherzers Militaer Verlag, 2009.

Weale, Adrian, *The SS: A New History*, London, abacus, 2010.

Weale, Adrian, *Army of Evil: A History of the SS*, New York, Penguin, 2013.

Whiting, Charles, *Skorzeny: The Most Dangerous Man in Europe*, London, Leo Cooper, 1998.

Williamson, Gordon, *Knight's Cross, Oak-Leaves and Swords Recipients 1941–45*, Oxford, Osprey Publishing 2005.

Williamson, Gordon, *Loyalty is my Honour: Personal Accounts from the Waffen-SS*, London, Brown Books, 1995.

Yerger, Mark C. *Waffen-SS Commanders: Army, Corps and Divisional Leaders of a Legend, Augsberger–Kreutz*, Atglen, PA. Schiffer Publishing Ltd, 1997.

Yerger, Mark C. *Waffen-SS Commanders: Army, Corps and Divisional Leaders of a Legend, Krüger – Zimmermann*, Atglen, PA. Schiffer Publishing Ltd, 1999.

Zakić, Mirna, 'The Price of Belonging to the Volk: Volksdeutsche, Land Distribution and Aryanization in the Serbian Banat, 1941-4', in *Journal of Contemporary History Vol.49 (2) pp* 320–340, Sage Publishing, 2014.

Zaloga, Steven, J. and Grandsen, James, *The Eastern Front: Armour, Camouflage and Markings, 1941 to 1945*, London, Arms and Armour Press, 1983.

Ziemke, Earl, F. *Stalingrad to Berlin: The German Defeat in the East*, Washington DC, Dorset Press, 1968.

*These titles were digital copies of the original texts obtained from www.scribd.com.

INDEX

People

Units and organisations